W9-BSM-868

DANGER!

AN OUTDOOR LIFE BOOK

DANGER!

Explosive True Adventures
of the Great Outdoors

Ben East

Illustrated by
Tom Beecham

OUTDOOR LIFE · E. P. DUTTON & CO.
NEW YORK

Copyright © 1970 by Outdoor Life

Brief quotations may be used in critical articles or reviews. For any other reproduction of the book, however, including electronic, mechanical, photocopying, recording or other means, written permission must be obtained from the publisher.

Library of Congress Catalog Card Number: 73-132983

Designed by Jeff Fitschen

Manufactured in the United States of America
SBN 0-525-08855-5

This book is dedicated
to the men and women
whose adventures it recounts.

Contents

Death Waited in White	5
This Grizzly Climbed	19
Africa's Black Furies	31
A Live Rattler—Once Too Often	45
Too Much Bear	59
Cougar in the Barn	73
Killer Bear at Six Feet	85
Handgunner's Last Hunt	97
The Guide a Grizzly Scalped	115
Death Wore a Lion Skin	125
A Hell of a Way to Move	141
White Fury on the Barrens	159
The Silent Hunter	171
Death Came Running	187
Terror in the North	201
Winter of Starvation	217
Nightmare Spring	231
She Had to Have Moose	245
The Wolves Were the Worst	259
In the Jaws of a Bear	271
Old Shuguli	285
Bear That Broke a Jinx	301
How It Feels to Die	315

Introduction

THESE things happened.

I think that is the most important thing to be said about the 23 stories that make up this book.

Many people have said of my earlier book, *Survival*, published by Outdoor Life Books in 1967, that they find it hard to believe men and women could undergo such ordeals and survive. I think that will very likely be the case with this collection as well.

On that score, however, I can give complete reassurance. These may sound like tall tales, but they are true.

Each of them appeared originally in *Outdoor Life* magazine, for which I have worked as a field editor the last twenty-five years. I did editorial work of one kind or another on all of them.

Some I wrote from lengthy interviews, others from a diary, from letters, newspaper accounts and police blotters, hospital records and the accounts of friends who knew well the persons involved. Still others I rewrote or edited from manuscripts submitted to the magazine.

That is how I came to know about these happenings, and how this book came into being. It is also the reason I can say with absolute assurance that every story is true and un-exaggerated, told as the events took place. Not until *Outdoor Life* and I had satisfied ourselves on that score beyond a shadow of doubt did any of them see the light of day in print. There is high adventure here and narrow escape, but there is no make-believe.

Danger comes infrequently to the outdoorsman unless he courts it. Hunting, fishing, camping and boating are re-garded as safe sports, and rightly so. But when danger does threaten, it wears many guises.

It may be the deadly strike of a coiled diamondback, the rush of an enraged bear, the cold of a bitter night in the open without shelter or fire, the leap of an unseen cougar, the frothing rapids of a wild river, or the mis-step of a saddle horse on a narrow trail.

And just as danger may threaten in many forms, so does courage show many faces. I believe the stories in this book prove that to a degree that makes it needless for me to elaborate. Great courage, of one brand or another, shines through each of them. I have often asked myself if I would do as well, and I think that same question will be likely to occur to you who read them.

I have hunted with gun and camera, fished, traveled wilderness trails, ridden white-water rivers and camped in far-off places, for more than fifty years. I can count on my fingers the times when I have felt the chill of fright run up my back.

My closest call came in an encounter with a polar bear, on a bleak island in Hudson Bay more than thirty years ago. That deadly businesslike charge, and the shot that stopped it, are as clear in my mind as if it had happened last week. I carry no scars from it—the bear didn't get that close—but the memory will be with me as long as I live.

I have included the story here, its first appearance between book covers, by way of showing that I know at first hand something of the feelings of the people I am writing about, that danger and I are not total strangers.

I have a few acknowledgments to make. My thanks go, first of all, to the people whose stories these are, for their permission to tell them here. But for them, what befell them and what they did about it, no such book could have been written.

I know no better place than this to acknowledge my debt to Bill Rae, Editor-in-Chief of *Outdoor Life* and a valued friend. It was under his skilled editorial guidance that I wrote these stories originally—along with more than 500 other pieces I have done for the magazine in the last twenty years. If these are good tales, and I believe they are, it is due in no small part to the fact that he will have no other kind.

My thanks are due also to Kathleen Gunnells, the patient and painstaking typist who since 1950 has converted every manuscript I have written into clean and flawless form. I have been fortunate to have her help.

Finally, my deepest thanks to my wife Helen for her encouragement and her understanding of a writer's ways.

Ben East.
Holly, Michigan

Death Waited
in White

Five men walked out on the Lake Michigan ice that cold winter morning.

They had little reason to think the day would be any different from the many others like it when they had fished there for lake trout. Nothing was farther from their minds than the possibility that death was waiting out on those empty ice fields, or that one of them was crossing the beach for the last time on two good feet.

The winter fishing grounds were five or six miles out from Bay Shore, a hamlet on Little Traverse Bay midway between Petoskey and Charlevoix, at the northwest corner of Michigan's mitten-shaped Lower Peninsula. All five men lived at Charlevoix.

The date was February 8, 1936, a Saturday. The depression of the 1930's had about hit rock bottom then, and they were not fishing for fun. There was no winter work to be had and they fished for a living. If they caught trout they kept what they needed and sold the rest. If the catch failed there was no money, even for groceries.

There were 10 or 15 men at Charlevoix who fished every day when the weather did not prevent, going out right after daylight and staying until an hour before dark. On a good day they took five or six trout piece, weighing around five pounds. It was cold work but they liked it, and their families ate.

The best fishing was on reefs in 100 to 150 feet of water. They used linen lines, tarring them and taking the stretch out until they were almost as hard as wire. The bait was cut herring, and the lines were so stiff that a trout bumping the lure could be felt at 150 feet. And because there was no stretch in the linen the hook could also be set at that depth with one sharp yank.

Then the fisherman would wheel around, throw the line over one shoulder and go sprinting across the ice until the trout was flopping beside the hole behind him. That was the quickest and surest way of landing the fish.

The men had one small cause for worry that morning. The wind was out of the southeast, offshore, and the sky had the ugly look of storm. If the wind blew hard from that quarter the ice might break off and be blown out into the open lake.

The five talked it over before they left home and agreed to take no chances. They would move to safer grounds. Two blunt points, Big Rock and South, jutted into Lake Michigan north and south of Charlevoix. If the ice broke there it usually let go along a line between those points, about a mile offshore. The fishermen called that line the Crack. They'd fish there, where they could get back to land at the first hint of trouble.

When they were going out to their regular grounds they hauled a boat along. It was a 16-footer, clinker built. Loaded on an old Indian sled, it could be pulled by one big dog, with a little help in the rough places. But because they were going only a mile out they saw no need for the boat that day, and so left it and the dog behind.

They left the beach shortly after breakfast, dragging their outfits on small hand sleds. The equipment was light— ice spuds, lines weighted with the four ounces of lead needed to get the hooks down to bottom, a box of herring for bait. A net set beneath the ice near shore kept that supplied.

In addition, each man carried three poles and a blanket or strip of canvas six or eight feet long, for a windbreak. When they were ready to fish they spudded holes, set the poles in the ice to form a triangle, and hung the blanket or tarp on the two windward sides for shelter.

The ice was two to four feet thick, swept clean of all but a few inches of snow by the wind. When they got to the Crack they found an irregular line running across, where the field had broken away earlier only to be blown back and refrozen. One of the five, Clayton Brown, stopped there. His four partners went on a short distance. If trouble developed he would signal them and they could all be back on safe ice before the crack had time to widen.

The fishing within a mile of the beach was not as good as it was on the grounds farther out, but about an hour after Brown got his line in the water he caught a 6-pound trout. Nothing happened for another hour.

Then disaster struck with no warning. All of a sudden he was aware that his line was no longer hanging straight down in the hole. Instead, it was standing off under the ice toward shore. There was no current, and the meaning of that dragging line went through him like an electric shock.

Somewhere between the five men and the beach the ice had broken off. Now it was moving lakeward, driven by the rising wind.

Brown shouted a warning, and they grabbed up their gear and raced for shore, but they were not in time. Just off the beach 150 yards of black water separated them from safety. They were adrift on an ice field a mile or more across.

Brown was young and strong, and a powerful swimmer. If it had been 20 yards he might have risked trying to swim, he told me long afterward. But that open lead was too wide, the February water too numbingly cold. He knew better.

The men were not really alarmed. Although this had never happened to any of them before, it happened to someone almost every winter and there had never been a man lost. Always within an hour or two somebody would go out in a boat and take the stranded fishermen off. They were sure that would happen this time. They had nothing to fear.

Two thing worried them a little, however. First, the weather was turning worse. The wind was blowing a gale now and the temperature was dropping very fast. Second, the oldest member of the party, Gene Berst, was 72. How much cold could a man of that age take? As things turned out, Berst would survive the ordeal that was coming, only to die in an accident at a railroad bridge in Charlevoix the following summer.

The rest were younger. All were experienced outdoorsmen, warmly dressed and in good physical condition. Brown, a construction worker in summer when there was work to be had, was 25, stood six feet one, weighed 176 pounds, and prided himself on being able to pick up a 100-pound weight in each hand and walk off with ease. His father-in-law, Claude Beardsley, was 51; Cleo Lapeer was 50, his son Lloyd a boy of 17 or 18.

Right then, however, youth and strength were of little avail. The five could only stand helpless and watch the open water between them and the shore widen steadily and inexorably, as the wind drove the ice field toward the lake. They started to wave their windbreakers as a distress signal. That was all they could do.

They never learned who sounded the alarm on shore, but after an hour or two they saw people on the beach, and a while later a boat was brought down on a sleigh and launched. Things were turning out as they had expected.

The boat was from the Coast Guard station at Charlevoix, but it was a 16-foot flat-bottom skiff with only one set of oars, hardly adequate for the job. At that time of year, with navigation closed on Lake Michigan, the station's power surf boats were torn down for repairs, and nothing better was available.

By then the drifting men were a mile offshore and the wind was blowing harder than ever. But the Coast Guardsman at the oars was rowing with the gale and he reached them with no difficulty. Berst and the two Lapeers climbed in with him and they started back.

There was no heroism involved in Beardsley and Brown staying behind on the ice. The boat couldn't carry all five. It would take the three ashore and come back for them, and that would end the affair. Or so they all thought.

Almost at once, however, Beardsley and Brown realized it wasn't going to be that simple. With one man at the oars the skiff could barely make headway against the raging wind. It was 4 o'clock in the afternoon before the four men reached the beach. By that time the ice field had been carried three or four miles out, and was beginning to break up as heavy seas rolled under it.

It had not yet begun to snow. The two waiting men saw the boat, a distant speck across the churning water, start back toward them. Again the oarsman had the wind behind him, and he pulled up at the edge of the ice in about half an hour.

He was Earl Cunningham, from the Charlevoix station. "Let's get ashore," he urged.

Beardsley and Brown tumbled into the skiff and they shoved off. Just then the first snow squall swept across the broken ice, milk thick, shutting out all sight of land.

The first thing Brown noticed about Cunningham was that he was not dressed for the savage cold of that day. He was wearing a Coast Guard pea jacket over a light uniform, thin mittens, and overshoes. Brown never learned what was under them. As long as he worked at the oars Cunningham would be warm enough, but in that outfit he could not tolerate the bitter wind for long without exercising.

By contrast Brown's own clothing, based on long experience on the open ice, consisted of heavy wool underwear and shirt, two pairs of wool pants, a vest, leather jacket and sheepskin coat. He had a warm cap that he could pull down, heavy wood-chopper mittens, and his feet were protected by two pairs of thick wool socks inside warm carpet slippers, with fleece-lined overshoes outside. When fishermen left shore at that time of year they dressed for anything that might come along.

Cunningham rowed for a while, then Beardsley and Brown took turns. It was getting dark, and the air was so thick with snow that the three could see nothing but the black water around them, littered with bobbing blocks of broken ice. But it was plain that they were hardly holding their own against the wind.

They rowed for hours, the men not at the oars chilled and shivering. The skiff began to ice up, and they went to work with a single-bitted ax that Cunningham had brought out, one man in the bow and one in the stern, chipping away ice as hard as flint, while the skiff pitched and tossed on the smoking seas.

The men with the ax could not keep up. Slowly the load of ice grew heavier and the boat settled lower in the water.

As often as there was a lull in the driving snow they could see the distant lights at the top of the water tower in Charlevoix. Those lights seemed both to beckon and mock. By the fact that they drew farther and farther away the men knew they were losing their battle with the wind.

It was around midnight when they gave up. By then they had less than four inches of freeboard left and the boat was so heavy and sluggish with ice that they were barely moving through the water. Unless they got out of the wind-driven spray they could not hope to stay afloat much longer. They turned with the wind, rowing back toward the ice field, and conditions became a little easier.

The temperature fell below zero that night. Only those who have been out on Lake Michigan in such a storm can realize the treachery and savagery of those winter gales.

The three men overtook the ice as a wild dawn was breaking over the lake. They didn't know it then, but they were off Good Hart, some 15 miles north of the place where they had gone adrift, and Brown was to learn later that they were 12 miles out in the lake, too.

They could not get to solid ice. There was a belt of slush a foot or two thick all along the edge of the field. They forced the skiff into that slush, out of reach of the freezing spray. Fog and snow blanketed the lake and they could see no land at all. They no longer even knew which way they were drifting. But if their course was still northwest, Beaver Island lay in their path, 18 miles offshore. The best they could hope for was to fetch up on the beach there and somehow be able to get ashore.

Shortly after daylight they heard an aircraft go over, flying low, and knew that a search was under way. Planes flew over two or three more times in the next hour, but they could not see them and there was no hope they could be seen.

About 8 o'clock that morning Brown realized that Cunningham had lost consciousness. He had done what little he could for the Coast Guardsman, even trading mittens, but the cold was just too much. He shook and slapped and pummeled the unconscious man for half an hour, trying desperately to rouse him, but there was no response and at last Brown realized he was dealing with a dead man.

After the Coast Guardsman died Beardsley sat hunched in the stern of the skiff for more than an hour, not speaking. He was terribly cold, and it was plain that he had about given up hope. At last he made a startling announcement. "I'm going to get out of this boat and try to walk to shore," he mumbled.

"You're crazy," Brown told him sharply.

"I can't take this any more, I've got to do something," Beardsley insisted.

The slush around the skiff was frozen hard enough now

to bear a man's weight. Slim as their chances would be, Brown couldn't let his father-in-law go alone. The two climbed out and plodded off into the storm.

They had not walked 150 feet when the older man broke through the crust of slush and went into the icy water up to his armpits. He struggled for a minute, then lay inert with his arms resting on the ice. He did not speak after he dropped into the water, and Brown believes the shock killed him.

"Getting him out without breaking through myself was one of the hardest things I ever did," Brown said later. When it was finally accomplished he did not dare to try to drag the dead man across the frozen slush to the boat. He went back for a canvas windbreak, wrapped Beardsley in it and left him on the ice. Then Brown returned to the skiff to wait out his own fate. He could see little chance that it would prove to be any better than Earl Cunningham's and Claude Beardsley's.

It was now around noon on Sunday. Brown had been adrift more than 24 hours. The wind was dropping and the lake beginning to flatten out, but the temperature seemed to be dropping even lower.

the older man broke through the crust of slush and went into the icy water up to his armpits

He tore the seats out of the boat, broke them up with the ax, and tried to start a fire on the ice. But they were too water-soaked to burn and he used the last of his matches without getting a flicker of blaze.

He had had nothing to eat since breakfast on Saturday, and was getting weak from hunger. He used his ice spud to chop bite-size chunks off the frozen trout he had caught the day before, and to his surprise they tasted pretty good.

An old trapper he had met in Oregon years before had told him of a survival trick, and he still thinks he owes his life to it.

"Take your coat off," the trapper had said, "pull your cap down, put the coat over it and button it up, and fold your arms inside. With a little fire at your feet you can keep warm all night."

"I didn't have the little fire at my feet, but the rest worked fine," Brown recalls. The windbreak he had taken out on the ice was an old wool blanket. He wrapped it over the coat, and the cold did not seem too bad. But by now his feet had lost all feeling. He had gotten them wet in pulling Beardsley out of the water, and knew they were freezing.

The skiff was frozen solid in the slush, but the crust was not safe enough that he dared risk getting out to walk for exercise, so he just sat there in the boat with Cunningham's body.

He heard planes every little while all that day, but could not see them and knew there was no hope of rescue until the weather cleared, no matter how intensive the search.

It was just before sundown when the fog finally lifted and the sky cleared. For the first time Brown could see land and get some idea of where he was. The sun sank, yellow and cold, over the empty ice in the southwest, and he resigned himself to the fact that it was the last sunset he would ever see.

He heard no aircraft that evening, and decided that search had been abandoned. He didn't blame the searchers.

By this time they'd be looking for three bodies on the snow-swept ice, assuming the men had not been swamped and drowned, and the chance of making a find of that kind would be slim indeed. It wouldn't be worthwhile to keep on looking for dead men.

Brown didn't know it then, but he had one friend who never gave him up for lost. That was a doctor at Boyne City, a hunting and fishing partner of his. "Brown will come ashore," the doctor told the searchers. "It may be across the lake in Wisconsin, but he'll come in somewhere and he'll be alive."

Clayton Brown was asked many times afterward what he thought about during that long night while he waited, a prisoner of the lake, in an ice-sheathed boat with a dead man, and the body of his father-in-law lying frozen 50 yards away.

He thought about very little, other than to wonder if he could possibly live till morning and ever get back to shore. He does not believe a man does a lot of thinking in such an extremity as that. The animal instinct for survival takes over and crowds everything else out of the mind, he says.

Actually the marooned fisherman slept most of that night, exhausted from the cold and the long ordeal. Before dark he chopped off a little more of his frozen trout and ate it. Then he wrapped in his coat and blanket again, and lay down in the bottom of the skiff.

When he awoke Monday morning and raised his head to look around, the sun was up and the mainland shore was standing high and blue across miles of new ice. Lake Michigan had refrozen in the windless cold of the night.

He stood erect but found he couldn't walk. His feet were completely without feeling and his outer pants were sheathed in ice too thick to break. He got out his knife and cut them off, whacking away a piece at a time, the job made harder by the fact that three fingers on his right hand were frozen and useless.

He knew the Lake Michigan shore well enough to decide, from the high bluffs, that he was somewhere off Good Hart or Cross Village, well to the north of Charlevoix. To him it looked as if no more than five miles of new ice lay between him and the beach. It proved to be 12 instead.

Brown decided very quickly what he was going to do. Live or die, he was convinced he was on his own now. If he didn't get ashore before night came again, he'd never make it.

When he stepped out of the boat the frozen slush felt safe under him, and when he walked to the edge of it the new ice was strong enough. He ate a little more raw fish and trudged away. He told himself he'd be on the beach by noon.

He took nothing, not even his windbreak. This was an all or nothing gamble, and he was too weak to carry an ounce of needless weight. He would walk ashore or die trying. Either way he wouldn't need any equipment.

He was two miles from the boat when a lone aircraft went over, high up. He whipped off his coat and waved it, but the plane droned on out of sight. That was the last one he saw.

That was a bad walk. The ice was very rough, with ridges and hummocks where floating floes had frozen in the new matrix. He couldn't seem to lift his feet over those obstacles, and he fell so many times that he lost all count.

The new ice was so thin in spots that when he got thirsty he could kick a hole with his heel and get a drink. He crawled across the worst places on his belly. A few times he came to open cracks that had to be jumped. That was a hairy business, on feet that had no more feeling than two wooden stumps.

The day stayed clear and cold. By afternoon the man was moving so slowly across the endless ice that he didn't think he would make it. There was no choice but to keep on, however, unless he wanted to lie down and die where he was, and he wasn't ready for that.

Much of the Lake Michigan shore from Harbor Springs

north around Sturgeon Bay was unpeopled then, with only two villages, Cross Village and Good Hart. If he walked ashore at a place where he could not get help, he would be in bad trouble, for there was deep snow on the ground. But while he was still a couple of miles out, he recognized the spire of St. Ignatius Church, an Indian mission at Middle Village a mile or two south of Good Hart, rising above the timbered dunes. There'd be a few Indian families living there. He headed for it.

Some of the families got their drinking water from the lake. Out on the ice Brown hit their well packed trail, and just at sundown that Monday night he stumbled across the beach and took a path that led for 100 yards through the woods to the mission and the houses.

The first person he saw was on old Indian woman. He learned later that she was a member of the George Andrews family. She was busy on the woodpile in front of the nearest house.

"Can I come in and get warm?" he asked her.

She turned away without answering and started for the back door. Brown did not realize that she spoke no English and was going for someone who could, and for the first time in those three terrible days, he cracked. He picked up a stick of stovewood and padded after her.

"If you try to shut me out here in the cold you'll stay with me," he muttered. He meant it, too. In that crazed instant he'd have brained her without compunction.

She didn't hear him, or look around. She opened the door and called, and her grandson, a boy of about 16, came out.

"My name is Brown," the castaway told him. "I've been out on the ice."

There was no need to say more. The Indian family had heard the story on an old battery radio, but they had supposed that all three men were dead by now, and for a second the boy and the old woman stared as if Brown were something that had come out of a grave. They were close to right, too. Then they hustled him inside. The warmth of a fire had never felt so good.

He got his boots off, and one look confirmed what he already knew. His feet were lifeless white lumps. Apart from that he didn't feel too bad and the feet didn't hurt, either then or later. The Andrews family rustled up hot food, meat, potatoes and raisin pudding, and he wolfed it down. That was a mistake. It came up just as fast.

The boy left for Good Hart as soon as they got Brown in the house, hiking a narrow trail through the deep snow. A storekeeper there phoned the Coast Guard at Charlevoix with word that one of the lost men had walked in from the ice. Nobody would believe it at first, but not too long after dark a rescue party arrived. It consisted of county snow plows, a big crew of men with shovels, and two doctors. They didn't wait to open the road. They gave Brown a shot of brandy—maybe you think that didn't bite—put him on a stretcher, and carried him up the bluff to the plowed highway where an ambulance was waiting. By midnight he was under warm blankets in the Charlevoix Hospital.

Walking parties with sleds teamed up with an air search the next day in an attempt to bring in the bodies of Beardsley and Cunningham, but couldn't find them. On Wednesday the search succeeded, however, and they were brought ashore. It was none too soon. The day after that the ice broke free again and was blown into the open lake.

For Clayton Brown, although the aftermath wasn't exactly happy, it could have been worse. His frozen fingers recovered, but he remained in the hospital for weeks while doctors battled to save his feet. In the end it proved a losing fight. Gangrene developed, and in May both legs had to be amputated seven inches below the knees.

He had a couple of pretty bad years before he adjusted to that loss and was fitted with artificial feet and ready to use them. In that time he did accomplish one unusual thing, however. He learned to walk on his hands, actually on the knuckles of his clenched fists, in a sitting position, with his arms down at his sides and his stubs of legs held out horizontally in front. He got good at it, too.

"I could roll across a room about as fast as a man on two feet," he boasts.

Once he got used to the artificials, things went much better, even if the medics had shortened him by $4\frac{1}{2}$ inches when they fitted the legs. They thought he could keep his balance better that way.

He went back to hunting and fishing, which he had always enjoyed. More than one day in the years since, he has walked 15 miles in the deer woods on those cleverly designed wooden feet. In World War II he even got himself accepted for the Quartermaster's Corps and served three years as a heavy equipment inspector, chiefly in refrigeration.

Only once, however, has he ever found wooden feet better than the real thing. That was when he went hunting rattlesnakes in the Arizona desert some years back. He wore leather chaps down below his knees, and didn't give a thought to getting struck on the feet or ankles.

Living now at Harbor Springs with his wife Imogene, with three children married and away from home, he still does a lot of fishing, for stream trout, bass, coho salmon, steelheads, anything that will take a lure. And in spite of the fact that he broke a leg in a hard fall three years ago, he enjoys duck and deer hunting as much as he ever did.

If anybody had told him, before he went out on the ice that February morning, how close he would come to dying he'd have laughed at the forecast. And had there been someone with him the night when he lay in the skiff with two dead men, to predict that he would live to get ashore, he wouldn't have believed that either.

Today he'll tell you he figures he does not have a thing in the world to complain about.

He may be $4\frac{1}{2}$ inches shorter than he was in his early years, but when it comes to courage Clayton Brown stands as tall in my opinion as any man I have ever known.

This Grizzly
Climbed

THERE'S something about a bear track.

The young botanist who had found this one put his boot down beside it. The paw marks were almost as long as his own footprints and a lot wider, and the mark of 4-inch claws was plain and clear in the wet sand.

All of a sudden Napier Shelton felt small and alone. His wish to meet a grizzly face to face, a wish that he had nurtured for years, was evaporating right then like a patch of snow on a hot tin roof.

Shelton was by himself, walking over the wide gravel bars of the Toklat River in Mt. McKinley National Park, on a June evening in 1961. Low-hanging clouds and a light rain gave a somber, brooding aspect to the dark mountains enclosing the valley. Mist veiled the form of things. He was sure the maker of this track could not be far away, and in the twilight of that wet evening every shadow seemed to have the humped shoulders and dished face of a grizzly.

Shelton turned back, walking faster than usual. This was not the time or place to meet such a bear, he told himself.

19

He was 29 at the time, unmarried, a graduate student at Duke University at Durham, North Carolina, working on his master's degree in botany, and he was in McKinley Park to do research on plant life. He and his wife Elizabeth and their two little daughters now live at Ann Arbor, Michigan, where he teaches at the University.

He had hoped to join a scientific expedition that summer, but had not been able to find an opening, and so he and Jack van Wyk, a fellow student at Duke whose home was in South Africa, loaded Napier's small camping van and headed for the Alaska Highway on a 4,900-mile drive.

They removed the rear seat, rigged a table that could double as a bed, stocked the van with canned stuff, and camped on the way. They pulled off the road wherever night overtook them, heated up a can of something, and made themselves comfortable until morning. It was a good trip.

For Shelton the summer in Alaska represented the fulfillment of a dream. That part of the world had fascinated him as far back as he could remember. He would be studying vegetation, but it was the wild animals he was most interested in, above all the bears. As a kid growing up in Washington, D.C., he had read Ernest Thompson Seton's *Biography of a Grizzly,* and ever since he had longed to encounter this awesome brute and get to know it first hand. It had never occurred to him that the meeting might prove more than he bargained for.

He and Jack reached McKinley early in June. The night they arrived Napier went for a walk along the Toklat, and there he saw that first grizzly track. While that didn't really put a damper on his enthusiasm, it did give him a few second thoughts.

The two partners went on to the park campgrounds at Igloo Creek and put up their tent. Jack had no part in the research project. He had made the trip only because he wanted to see the country, and thought it would take him about as far from his home in South Africa as he'd ever get.

He planned to stay with Napier for two weeks, then fly back to Duke, where he had studies of his own to work on.

Because they were in a national park, it would not have been legal for them to carry firearms. Anyway, the idea of taking a gun along had not even occurred to Shelton. He saw no reason for it, for he did not believe that wild animals, even bears, would bother people unless they were given some good reason, and that he did not intend to do. He'd meet any bear he encountered on a friendly footing, and he was sure they'd reciprocate.

"Maybe I was overly influenced by things I had read in Seton's book," he told me afterward. "Seton had said flatly that the grizzly never attacks man, except when provoked."

Jack did not altogether share Napier's relaxed attitude. He had had a few experiences at home that had convinced him that wild creatures of many kinds can be dangerous, sometimes without cause. A cobra had spit venom into his eyes and blinded him temporarily, and another time he had shot the head off a deadly mamba that was upreared almost face high, and ready to strike. His father had killed a leopard with an ax as it leaped at him, and on a hunt Jack and his companions had come on a group of bushmen in a tree, with the half devoured body of a woman lying on the ground below. A lion had killed and fed on her just before the whites came along.

These encounters had made Jack cautious where all animals were concerned, and he carried a hatchet wherever he went. It wasn't much of a weapon, and it would have been worthless against a grizzly, but he felt safer with it along.

After Jack left for North Carolina, Napier was entirely by himself, but that didn't bother him. In the next few weeks he began to see enough grizzlies that they became a familiar part of the landscape. They seldom showed up near the campground, but up at the head of Igloo Creek and farther to the west it was not unusual to see half a dozen or more in a day, often from the gravel road that ran part way through the park. Many were sows with cubs, others were males traveling alone. In color they ranged all the way from dark chocolate brown to a startling palomino blond.

Every bear Napier had encountered so far was at a comfortable distance, and he was enjoying them hugely. They had fascinating facets of personality. He watched with deep interest the placidity of a mother nursing her young, the playfulness and devilment of the cubs, her savage ferocity if she suspected anything threatened them.

Gradually, however, the idea was being borne in on him that the grizzly is king of the tundra, and everything about him shows it. He walks over his windswept domain with a haughty and powerful arrogance, his gait a slow, bow-legged swagger. Shelton was coming to realize that this bear would retreat only from man, and then grudgingly.

As the summer wore on he heard stories of grizzly encounters that made him wonder whether his theories about peaceable bears were sound, too. There was the one grizzly that took a swipe at Hank Pallage on his own back porch, for no reason at all, for example. And another that gave Napier's neighbor, Joe Hankins, a good scare.

Joe worked for a big logging outfit on the west coast, but every summer for nine years he had been quitting his job and coming to Alaska for a lengthy vacation. His hobbies were hiking and taking pictures, and he had seen a lot of grizzlies. He was camped near Napier, sleeping in the back of his car, and they talked often about the bears. Finally Joe got too close to one and it came for him without warning. But it chased him only a short distance, then quit.

Shelton heard other stories, too, the usual run, of hunters, guides and prospectors who had blundered into a sow with cubs at close quarters, or had shot a bear and failed to kill it, and were no longer around. But he still doubted that the bears attacked unless they were provoked into it, he still wasn't afraid of them, and he still wanted to meet one face to face. He did take the precaution, however, of filling a

beer can half full of pebbles for a noise maker, and carrying
it with him wherever he went.

As the blueberries ripened in July the bears moved down
from the higher country and were seen more and more often
on the berry-covered slopes where he was doing his plant
studies. There were places where willow and arctic birch
grew so thick that the bear trails were actually tunnels, and
the only way a man could get through those tangles was to
follow the paths the grizzlies had made.

Shelton walked out of such a place one morning to con-
front a big, blond bear that was raking in blueberries only a
few yards down the mountain from him. Luckily, the wind
was blowing uphill and it was so busy with berrying that it
didn't see him. Otherwise, in all likelihood he'd have had
trouble right then.

He stared at the bear just long enough to discover that a
grizzly at close range imparts an overwhelming sense of
power and danger. For the first time that summer, he really
understood that there was risk involved in meeting these
bears. He was above timber line, with no trees nearby, so he
backed carefully out of sight, retreated quietly for 50 yards,
and then made all the racket his beer can was capable of.

It worked. The bear disappeared at a gallop, without
even looking back. But it took a few minutes for Napier's
hair to lie flat again.

About that time he was warned that people had seen a
sow grizzly with two cubs, new arrivals, on Igloo Mountain,
where he was working. After that, he was very careful to
keep his eyes open. He had seen enough by now to know
that if they should meet he wanted to give her plenty of
room to run without losing face.

A couple of days of rain came at the start of August,
and Napier kept to his tent. But the morning of the 4th
dawned sunny and warm, and after lunch he parked the
Volkswagen on the road above the campground, walked
across Igloo Creek on a fallen log, and pushed up into the

spruce. He was after sample borings from trees all the way from the creek up to timber line, a distance of 300 yards, to determine their age.

It was a bright, still day, with only a light wind in the treetops, and he was enjoying the peacefulness of the forest. By midafternoon he had worked up to the edge of the timber and was poking through a very thick under-story of brush. He found a 4-inch tree, and another that measured 8 inches, making a wind-buffeted stand on the mountainside. He took borings from them, and then noticed a larger spruce, at least a foot in diameter, with dense willows around it. It was the largest tree in sight, but only about 20 feet high, and the branches were twisted and scraggly.

Shelton left his pack on the ground about 10 yards from it, pushed through the brush, sat down and went to work with the boring tool.

He had no warning, no breaking of brush, no sound of movement at all. All of a sudden, a few steps below him, down the slope where his pack lay, the stillness was shattered by a loud, vicious "Warf!"

It was a sound of surprise and rage, half bark and half snarl. The man knew what it was without looking and he acted without thinking. His hands and feet reached instinctively for the nearest branches, which grew almost to the ground, and he went up that shaggy spruce with the speed and agility of a red squirrel.

But even as he climbed in desperate haste, the thought flashed through his mind that he was safe. Grizzlies, he had read and been told more times than he could remember, can't climb trees once they are past the age of cubhood. If he could get high enough before this one grabbed him, he had nothing to worry about.

He was 8 or 10 feet up the tree when he looked down for the first time. A big, snarling grizzly was scrambling awkwardly up after him. The branches, growing out horizontally almost like the rungs of a ladder, seemed to be helping the bear. However it was managing, it was coming fast.

Shelton reached for a branch above his head, but even while he pulled himself higher he felt the bear grab the calf of his left leg. He learned later that its teeth tore out instantly, ripping loose a big flap of skin and muscle, but at the time he felt no pain from the bite.

Again he tried to pull himself out of reach, but then the bear's teeth caught a firm grip in the heel of his rubber-bottom pac, and he felt a heavy weight loosening his hold and pulling him down. Branches broke in his hands and under his free foot, and he had a horrible sensation like falling into an abyss. The words "This is it!" flashed through his mind as if he had shouted them aloud. Then the pull on his foot was suddenly ended and he heard a crash and a thud as the grizzly tumbled down through the branches to the ground.

He started climbing frantically higher, but almost instantly he felt the whole tree shake and knew the bear was coming up once more. He reached a height of about 15 feet this time, and had only a couple more branches left above his head, when he paused to look down.

The bear was just below his feet, the most horrifying thing he had ever seen. The coarse blond hair on its head and shoulders was all standing the wrong way, its yellow teeth were bared in a savage snarl, its small eyes were blazing; and as it climbed it kept up a continuous low growling, like the sound two dogs make in fighting. Shelton could see that it was straining every muscle to reach him, too.

He smashed his boot down on its head, but that had no more effect than kicking a brick wall. For a moment Napier had a strange feeling of outrage. This bear had no fear of him as a human. It was trying to kill him as it would kill any animal it had treed or cornered. It had no business behaving that way, he thought. Then his feeling changed to one of disbelief, as if his mind could not accept the fact of the attack.

Teeth slashed into him again, high in his right thigh, but again he felt no pain. The animal bit down hard, then lost its

own grip in the branches, let go of his leg, and went tumbling
to the ground for the second time.

It did not try to climb again. For long agonizing minutes
it prowled around the tree, snorting and growling like a dog
worrying a squirrel, insane with fury and frustration. At
last it moved slowly into the willows, still snarling, watching
the treed man over its shoulder with a look that said as plain
as words, "I'm not through with you yet!"

Until now Shelton had felt none of his hurts, and had
done very little coherent thinking. The whole attack had
been so sudden and furious that it seemed to have over-
whelmed him. Although he had been sure the bear would
pull him down and kill him, he was not much aware of
being afraid after it grabbed him the first time.

But now he realized that his legs were hurting and he
was shaking very hard. He was in the top of a scrawny
spruce, with none too secure a hold, and he was sure the
grizzly was still in the brush nearby, waiting for him. When

teeth slashed into him again

he looked down at his legs, his trousers were hanging in bloody rags and he could see a row of tooth holes in his right thigh and a torn chunk of flesh hanging from his left calf.

He didn't dare to climb down, but at the same time he realized that he was close to the limit of endurance and couldn't stay in the tree much longer, no matter what happened.

Down at the foot of the slope he could see his car parked on the road. Those 300 yards of forest separated him from safety. One of the few thoughts that penetrated his stunned brain then was the full realization that he had no immunity to wild-animal attack simply because he was a human being, as he had always believed. He knew better now.

While he watched a car drove past on the road. He yelled at the top of his voice, but the distance was too great for him to be heard.

He waited 20 minutes, and decided he could not endure any more. He climbed down, step by step, filled with dread and terror every inch of the way. He put one foot on the ground, looked around at the brush that hemmed him in on every side, and lost his nerve. He labored up again, as high as he could go.

He waited a few more minutes, trying to peer into the thickets for some hint of the bear. At intervals he yelled and rattled his can of pebbles. A second car passed, down on the road, and he shouted for help again, but it went on. He soon realized that he could not stay any longer in the tree, whether or not the bear attacked again. He was growing very weak. Better to go down while he could still climb, rather than risk adding a fall to his other troubles.

He descended slowly, watching, listening, hardly breathing. Nothing happened. At the base of the spruce he grabbed his hat and hobbled for the road as fast as his wounds would allow, yelling, breaking brush, making all the commotion he could. Every second he expected to see a shaggy, palomino-colored brute come roaring at him.

It seemed to take him a lifetime to get to Igloo Creek. He slid down the bank, splashed across, and climbed to the road. He still had 200 yards to go to reach his car. He tried to run, but couldn't, and the specter of the grizzly haunted him every painful step. When he finally climbed into the car and slammed the door behind him, a hoarse "Thank God!" welled up out of his throat time after time.

From there on Shelton had plenty of help. The first person he saw was Dr. Adolph Murie, a Park Service biologist and eminent scientist, who had been studying grizzly bears for years. He was coming up the road in his green jeep, and as they met Napier shouted out the window of his car, "One of your friends bit me!"

He heard Murie yell back, "Well, I'll be—" and then the biologist spun his jeep around and followed the injured man to the Murie cabin, just across the road from the campground where Napier's tent was pitched.

Murie and his wife Louise gave Shelton first aid, and then drove him the 30 miles to the park hotel. A nurse in the infirmary there bandaged his wounds and gave him a tetanus shot. Then she looked through the hotel guest list, found an M.D. and summoned him. He walked in, very professional looking, took a hurried look at Napier's torn legs and walked right out again. Shelton learned later that he was a psychiatrist, and seemingly he figured that what had happened wasn't exactly in his line.

The park people phoned for a bush plane from Fairbanks to pick Shelton up, and Sam King, the park superintendent, loaned him a pair of pants for the flight. There wasn't much left of his own.

The plane flew him to St. Joseph's hospital in Fairbanks, and there Dr. Paul Haggland, a surgeon and hunter who had repaired many injured outdoorsmen, stitched him up, telling stories of his own encounters with bears while he worked.

Shelton's injuries were not as bad as they appeared. The calf of his left leg was severely torn, and the bear's teeth had left deep puncture wounds in his right thigh. But his heel was not hurt, just a hole punched through the pac, and there was no bone damage anywhere. He did have a small cut on his rear end that he didn't even know about until Dr. Haggland found it. A tooth had clipped him there. Luckily the bear had not used its claws, maybe because it needed them to hang on with.

When Dr. Haggland finished, he summed things up in three simple words. "You were lucky," he said with quiet emphasis.

Shelton left the hospital at the end of five days and went back to the park hotel. By August 24, 20 days after the encounter, he was able to drive, and left for his home in Washington, D.C. One of the park rangers who wanted to go to Philadelphia went along, and the two men had a pleasant, leisurely trip.

Nobody will ever know what accounted for the murderous attack. Murie told Shelton that he was the second person to be attacked, and the first to be injured, by a grizzly in McKinley Park. The bear was a pale blond, exactly the color of the female that had been seen on Igloo Mountain several times in the preceding week or two. But there were many bears of that color in the area, and no way to tell whether this was the same sow. Shelton saw no cubs, and to this day does not know the sex of the grizzly that mauled him. But the sow-with-cubs theory seems the most logical. Some of the park rangers were inclined to believe, however, that the bear simply walked out of the brush where he had dropped his pack, was startled by the smell of it, located the man instantly and flew into insane rage. Others suggested it might have been drawn in when it mistook the squeaking of Napier's boring tool for some small animal in distress.

What happened to the bear remains a mystery, too. It was not hunted down and destroyed. In fact, so far as Shelton knows nobody ever laid eyes on it again.

The day after the attack, rangers went up after Napier's pack. They saw no bear. After he got back to the hotel, the

Muries and two other companions went back to the scene with him, to retrieve two or three items of equipment he had dropped. He went with his heart in his mouth, imagining a grizzly behind every bush, but his fears proved groundless.

One thing they could not find, his boring tool. He has no idea what became of it, and he still does not know the age of that scraggly spruce that saved his life. But there was bear hair clinging to the branches 14 feet above the ground, and big limbs broken off where the grizzly had fought its way up and fallen out twice. Shelton had proof now of what he had known all along. The bear had climbed, not just stood on its hind feet and reached up.

"Just the other day," Napier said long afterward, "re-reading Seton's *Lives of North American Game Animals,* I came across the following: 'This bear never climbs. The hunter who succeeds in getting up a tree is as safe from a grizzly as from a bull.' All I can say is, I wish Seton—and anybody else who believes that—could have been along that day in McKinley Park."

The story had a little sequel. In 1965 Elizabeth and Napier went on a canoe trip in Ontario's Algonquin Park. They camped the first night at a site other campers had used before them. They did not know it, but the earlier party had buried garbage, and a black bear had found it. Unwittingly, the Sheltons set their tent only a few feet away.

The bear came in shortly after dark. Napier had hung their packs on a tree limb as a precaution, and it tried first to pull them down, so close to the tent that Shelton could hear its heavy breathing. When he yelled and drove it away from the packs, it started digging up garbage and padding around the tent, grunting and grumbling. It kept that up the rest of the night, in spite of all Napier could do.

"I didn't sleep a wink until he left at daybreak," Shelton told me in recounting the affair.

"I don't think I've ever put in a worse night. I have news for anybody who's interested. I'll never trust any bear again as long as I live."

Africa's
Black Furies

THE buffalo was a solitary bull, the native said, and very bad.

The man had flagged the hunters down at a small village on the Save River, to tell them his troubles. To begin with, his people were badly in need of meat. Second, this buffalo had been terrorizing the village, destroying garden patches and chasing anyone he encountered. He spent his days in thick reeds along the river, and they would find him there now. Would they kill him?

It wasn't an assignment either Fred Bear or Wally Johnson, his white hunter, was exactly eager to take on. True, Fred wanted a buffalo bad enough. He had made two previous hunts in Africa and had taken some good trophies, including an elephant, and there were only two animals he was really interested in this time, buffalo and lion. But if he took them he wanted to make the kills with a bow, since that was the only way he had hunted for more than 30 years. And he also hoped that Bob Halmi and Zoli Vidor, the two New York photographers who were along, would be able to make a motion picture record of the kills.

31

Fred realized he was setting his sights high. To the best of his knowledge, the total number of African buffaloes ever killed by a white man with an arrow could be counted on the fingers of one hand, and he was sure that getting pictures of such an encounter had not been done more than once or twice.

The buffalo that the native had told about didn't sound like the right sort of candidate for what he had in mind. The reeds along the river would almost certainly be too thick for either a bow kill or for the cameras. The men knew that at a village no more than three or four miles away a lone buffalo had killed five people in the last six months, and had not yet been hunted down. If they went into the reeds and pushed this cantankerous bull around, he might prove every bit as dangerous as that one.

Johnson cocked a quizzical eye in Fred's direction. "Want to have a look?" he asked.

"It won't hurt to look," Fred agreed cautiously.

Where the river bank dropped down onto wide flats covered with a dense tangle of bamboo-like reeds, they came on a makeshift camp, half a dozen reed sleeping mats spread on the ground. Natives were running a small home-brew operation there, making a potent variety of beer from the sap of palm tres. Wally asked them about the bad buffalo.

"He is there," one of the men declared, pointing to a spot about 60 yards out in the reeds.

"This bloke is probably full of palm beer," Wally muttered, "but we'll find out."

There's one bad feature about an undertaking of that kind. Once you start there's not likely to be much chance of backing out. Nevertheless, they scrambled down the bank and started into the reeds. They were 10 feet tall, with stems half an inch thick, and the hunters could see only a few steps in any direction.

Fred, who then headed the Bear Archery Company at Grayling, Michigan, was carrying a hunting bow of his own make, with a pull of 65 pounds, and four razorhead arrows, one on the string and three in a bow quiver. Rated one of the world's top bowhunters, he had killed grizzly bears, Alaska browns, a good Indian tiger (so far as he knew the first taken with a bow in the last 100 years), and even an elephant with that same kind of equipment. He had complete confidence in what it would do. But at the same time he knew it was poor buffalo medicine in such a place as they were in. There is almost no chance that any arrow, however well placed, is going to drop an animal as big and tough as a buffalo in its tracks, and that was what would be needed if this bull came for them. In the reeds the odds were against even getting a shot.

Johnson was carrying a Winchester Model 70 in .458 Magnum caliber. Fred had a Browning .375 Magnum along for emergencies. Wally handed Bear's rifle to one of his trackers. "He's a good steady boy, and handy with a gun in a pinch," he commented. In a place like that, and considering the close range necessary with a bow, it seemed wise to have two backup rifles.

Two of the natives from the beer-making party tagged along to show the hunters the buffalo. They said there were openings in the reeds where pictures could be made, but Fred didn't think it likely the bull would walk out in one of those places, and the only openings they found were buffalo trails crisscrossing in every direction.

They had walked only a short distance when they heard the bull jump and go lumbering off, no more than 20 yards ahead. They picked up his fresh track on a trail and followed it, moving very cautiously. Several times in the next half hour they heard him go thrashing through the reeds, never far away. "He's circling us," Wally warned.

Fred was feeling more and more like buffalo bait, and liking the situation less and less. Finally he and Wally held a whispered consultation and agreed the risk was too great. They turned back, walking single file, with the two local natives in the lead, the tracker next, then Wally just ahead of Bear. Halmi and Vidor were bringing up the rear, loaded down with camera gear.

The only warning the buffalo gave was a harsh, throaty grunt. That grunt came from a tangle no more than six or seven paces to the left of the trail the party was following, and it was enough to lift a man out of his shoes. In the same instant they heard a pounding of hooves and a great crashing of reeds, and the bull was coming hellbent.

Wally said afterward he had charged by sound and had headed for the men in the lead. They panicked. All three vanished in the reeds like so many groundhogs disappearing down a hole and Fred's rifle went with them. Then the buffalo came crashing into the trail 20 feet ahead. That was the first anyone had seen of him, and he spotted Johnson and Fred in the same split second they saw him. He swiveled around, with 20 feet to cover. Then Wally's .458 bellowed and he crumpled and skidded down in a black heap.

Johnson poured in a second shot to make sure. When the bull didn't so much as kick, Wally took three or four wary steps and bent over him. He had dropped just 10 feet away. Johnson had shot from the hip as the bull lowered his head for the toss, and had made an amazing hit. The 500-grain solid had gone in over the lowered head and broken the neck, and the bull had died as if lightning had struck him. They had killed their first buffalo on the first morning of the hunt, and had had about as close a call as Fred Bear could remember in all his years of hunting dangerous game. As a bowhunter he hadn't played much of a hand, but he was entirely satisfied with the outcome. Seeing that maddened bull sledged down with a single shot at 10 feet had been an experience so heart-stopping that he found himself wondering afterward whether he hadn't dreamed the whole thing. Had Wally's snap shot missed the spine one or more of the men would almost certainly have been trampled or gored to death. Fred made a mental vow that he'd do no more buffalo hunting in places of that kind.

They learned now one reason why this bull had been giving the native village a bad time. He had been caught by a hind foot in a poacher's snare and the wire had cut deep. The foot was swollen to twice its normal size and the walking surface was raw and bleeding. It must have hurt like blazes every step he took. No wonder he was on the prod.

Fred's party had left Beira in Mozambique for the camp on the Save on June 1, 1965, having flown by jet from Rome to Salisbury in Southern Rhodesia, and on to Beira by prop plane. They were going into an area that was regarded as among the best hunting country remaining in Africa, and the hunt got off to a very fast start. They killed the buffalo on June 2.

The party numbered eight: four bowhunters besides Fred, the two cameramen, and Jim Crowe, an outdoor writer from Detroit, who was along as a reporter but did not intend to hunt. The four bowmen, all hunting partners with whom Bear had made previous trips and all well known in archery circles, were Bill Wright of San Francisco, Dick Mauch from Nebraska, K. Knickerbocker from Virginia, and Bob Munger, a Michigan hardware and sporting goods dealer.

Although Zoli Vidor, around 45, was a professional movie photographer, he had had little experience in wildlife photography. However, he got a complete initiation before this hunt was over. Halmi, a few years younger, had been with Fred as cameraman on a tiger hunt in India in 1963 and an African safari in 1964.

The outfitter was Mozambique Safarilandia, directed by Werner von Alvensleben, formerly a Prussian baron. Bitterly anti-Nazi, he had fled one of Hitler's concentration camps, escaped to Mozambique, and started a career as a white hunter.

Fred had read and heard enough about Wally Johnson, who was to be his white hunter, to know that he was one of the best in the business. An old hand, around 50, he had been an ivory hunter in the old days, had held a professional hunter's license in Mozambique for many years, was a dead shot, cool and level-headed in any sort of pinch, and knew the ways of African game as well as any man.

To better their chances, and also because they were not all interested in the same trophies—Bill Wright wanted an elephant, for example—they agreed to disperse the party in separate camps. As a result Fred did not see much of his companions, with the exception of Halmi and Vidor. They trailed him faithfully with their cameras wherever he went.

A lot has been written and said about which of Africa's big five, elephant, rhino, buffalo, lion and leopard, is the most dangerous. Hunters with whom Bear had discussed it were not agreed, and Fred did not feel that he was qualified by experience to have any firm opinion. Given the right provocation and the right opportunity, he thought one will try to kill a man about as quickly as another. Certainly they are equally capable of doing it once they make up their minds.

"But I will venture one statement," Fred said afterward. "For pure meanness the buffalo takes first place, and everything about him tells you so. The elephant is a mountain of animal, I think perhaps the most awe-inspiring thing that walks the earth. The rhino is a low-slung tank on four legs and you get the feeling nothing can stop him. A lion close up is something to take your breath away, and the leopard is the sinister incarnation of power and fury held in leash. But in my book none of them can match the buffalo for malignant cussedness. You know the instant you lay eyes on him that he's ready for trouble.

"The sweep of his horns, their tremendous boss, the drooping ears, the burly neck, the cold, surly stare, his whole shape and attitude say unmistakably, 'Keep your distance. I hate you and all your kind, and if you tangle with me one of us is going to take a one-way walk.' To me he is Africa's black fury, and no other animal I have hunted flies the warning flag so defiantly."

For three or four days after Johnson killed the lame bull they had no luck, mostly because of Fred's determination to get movies of any hunting they did. They saw plenty of buffalo, including some good heads, and a few times watched herds of 50 to 100 go thundering off across the dry plains in a cloud of dust, but were never able to get close enough for a shot under the right conditions. Lugging camera equipment on such a hunt is a tough chore, and when you add sound gear, as they had, stalking becomes almost impossible, especially stalking to the close range necessary with a bow. They were putting themselves under a severe handicap, but there was no help for it.

The buffalo hunting was proving a rugged business, too. The country was rough and much of it was grown up with 6-foot brush. It was also broken by dongas, an African term for deep ravines and dry creek beds, that were heavily timbered and laced with thorn bush. By keeping to the open places they could go almost anywhere in the hunting cars, but buffaloes do not spend the day in the open and the actual hunting had to be done on foot. The Toyotas took an incredible beating and the men fared no better. There was rarely a day that failed to produce at least two flat tires from thorns or sharp pieces of wood piercing the casings. The thorns were equally rough on human skin, and many times they had to return to camp to repair damage to the cameras or themselves.

Wally relied chiefly on two ways of locating buffalo. One was to inquire of the local natives. They have to know the habits and whereabouts of every animal in their area in order to stay alive. The other was to watch for the brownish, sparrow-like tick birds that accompany buffalo herds from morning to night.

The buffalo grazes at night, waters early in the morning and leaves for his bedding ground about daylight. The daytime hours he spends in the shade, usually in thick cover. Morning after morning, while the hunters followed fresh tracks away from the river, they'd see flocks of tick birds searching for the herds. When the birds dropped down into the brush the men knew exactly where to go. When a herd stampeded and ran in the open the birds even followed them in the sky, waiting for a chance to light and go to picking ticks again.

When Fred's chance for a shot finally came the circumstances were totally unexpected and he had no time even to think about getting pictures. They were bumping across fairly open country in the hunting car when he caught a glimpse of a buffalo disappearing in a thicket. They circled the place and found the tracks of two coming out, headed toward a nearby donga.

"Both bulls," Wally decided. "One looks big. We'll send Luiz in on the track to follow them, and we'll drive around on the other side of the donga and be there when they come out."

Luiz was his head tracker, a steady and reliable native who had been with him for years and spoke some English. The two of them had been in more than one tight place together. Wally gave him instructions, he walked into the brush carrying Wally's spare gun, and the hunters rattled off.

They were no more than in position when the two bulls burst out of the bush, running straight for the car. Wally gunned it to get out of their path, but the bigger one wouldn't have it that way. He slued around and came for the Toyota in a headlong charge.

"What followed was as near to a mechanized bullfight as I ever hope to see, and I was both spectator and participant," Fred described it later.

That buffalo meant business. He made three or four determined passes, turning on a dime, tossing his head, kicking up boils of dust, grunting like an enraged farm bull. Wally twisted and dodged, shot the hunting car ahead, skidded it to a stop. The ground was rough and the men were sticking to their seats like a rider on an outlaw horse, hanging on with both hands. The buffalo missed a lunge by hardly three feet as Wally swerved away, and as he galloped beside them, close enough to touch, Bear found himself looking almost straight down on the burly black head and the curved tips of the wickedest looking pair of horns he had ever seen.

Then the bull connected. He slammed into the side of the Toyota near a hind wheel, hard enough to knock the car sideways three or four feet, skidded off and took the spare tire with him. One of the trackers, Juca, was hunkered in the back, holding a camera and rifle. The camera flew in one direction, the gun in another and Juca in a third. He landed flat on his back but the buffalo was circling around the rear of the car and didn't see him.

Wally brought the car to a screeching halt, but Juca didn't need rescuing. He was up and running without the bull even knowing he was there. Until it was all over Fred didn't even know the tracker had been thrown out.

By that time Fred had jumped out and had an arrow on the string. The buffalo must have thought he had won the

the bull slammed into the side of the Toyota, hard enough to knock the car sideways three or four feet

battle, or else his collision with the car had been more than
he bargained for. He made a circle around it and galloped
for the brushy donga, and as he pounded past, quartering
away at 35 yards, Fred let his arrow go. The razorhead
sliced into the rib cage and the shaft went in almost to the
feathers. Fred fully expected the bull to wheel and come
back, but he kept going. Maybe he realized he had hit something bigger and harder than he was.

He left a blood trail a blindfolded man could have followed and they found him dead 300 yards away, with
green paint from the Toyota ground into his horns. Those
tips Bear had looked down on were a little more than 40
inches apart, the horns spread 46 inches at their widest
sweep, and the boss was 12 inches across and very heavy.
He was a trophy to satisfy the most ambitious hunter.

"That was good shooting, and bloody good luck," Wally
said when the excitement quieted down. In his concern about
Juca he hadn't even known that Fred got an arrow off. Then
he added, "He didn't run far, either." He was plainly astonished that an arrow-shot buffalo should die so quickly.

Fred was an elated and happy bowman. He had taken
one of the two trophies he had come for and one that very
few bowhunters can claim, made a clean, quick kill with a
single arrow on an animal about as tough as they come. There
was one thing lacking, however. He had no film to show
for it. There hadn't been time even to think about the cameras until the action was all over. But his license entitled
him to a second buffalo. They'd try again and hope for a
better break on that score.

The next one they went after got help from a crippled
lion, however, and the combination proved too much. The
hunters stopped at a village early one morning, and a native
told them that buffaloes had been in his garden during the
night, as usual. He thought they'd find the herd now in tall
grass nearby or in the brushy hills beyond. There were very
many buffalo beds in the grass, he said.

It was too high and thick to hunt on foot, but Johnson

and Bear drove through it without finding anything. However, the hills paid off. They saw tick birds fly up from the thick cover of a creek bottom, scouted the place and found the tracks of two good bulls. Wally sent Luiz in with a rifle to push them out, while they went around to the far side. But the animals evaded the trap, crossed a stretch of flat country and took refuge in a big thicket.

The hunters circled the place on foot and got within 20 yards, close enough to hear the two bulls grunt and break brush, but again they slipped out unseen and went into another donga. Again Luiz followed them. Wally and Fred found a stand in an open place, where it seemed likely they'd come out, and Vidor and Halmi set up their cameras. The whole setup looked perfect at last.

But before long more angry grunts were heard, and next a series of snarls and deep growls that didn't sound much like buffalo. Then Luiz came flying out of the brush, yelling in his native Changaan, "A lion, baas! A she lion that is hurt. She came for me!"

He went on to explain that the lion had a crippled hind leg that looked as if it had been caught in a snare. Both she and the two bulls had charged him but he was up on a high bank that the buffaloes couldn't climb, and the lion had turned off. "Baas, I don't go back in there unless you go too!" Luiz finished.

Wally translated for Fred's benefit. "He sounds as if he means it," he added with a dry grin.

"I don't blame him," Fred retorted. "I'm not going in there either unless you go along—with a gun."

The buffaloes had gone out on the same side where they came in, the tracker said. So far as he knew the lioness was still in the thicket. The hunters inched cautiously in and found her tracks, but she had cleared out, and they gave up on the two bulls, since by that time they were out of sight and headed into country where the cameras could not be used.

Bear lost three days then because of bad weather and

light too poor for photography, but the party put in part of the time in very lively fashion, fishing for tigerfish in a deep pool on the Save near camp. The tigerfish ran up to 10 and 12 pounds, with the most wicked looking teeth seen in any freshwater fish. The rig was red-and-white spoons on spinning rods, and the fish struck savagely and fought hard. A small herd of hippos watched from the middle of the pool, keeping everybody's nerves on edge, and the fishermen carried rifles as well as rods, both for the hippos and for crocodiles. It was a strange setting indeed, and the fishing was exciting and unusual.

Fred spent two of those days alone in a blind at a waterhole with a long-lens camera, and made a record of the birds and animals he saw. It added up to an amazing score: 28 wildebeest, 72 impalas, 49 nyalas, 105 warthogs, 76 baboons, 28 monkeys, 7 zebras, 3 kudus, a mongoose, 3 saddlebill storks and 3 hornbills. He had never watched a more fascinating wildlife show.

A few days later, at another waterhole where he spent a night on a tree platform with Luiz, he chalked up a second high tally: 100 buffaloes, 12 kudus, 131 impalas, 32 warthogs, 132 baboons, 25 monkeys and 4 ostriches. The buffaloes were the only animals that barged straight in to the water with no show of caution. All the others approached warily, making frequent stops, but the buffaloes came as if they owned the place.

The most unusual thing Fred saw at either waterhole was a mock fight between two nyala bulls. The nyala is a medium sized, dark antelope, found only in that part of Africa, the bulls weighing up to 250 pounds. This pair never really got down to business, but circled each other with their tails held erect and their manes and the hair along their backs standing straight up, moving in slow motion. They threatened repeatedly to lock horns but always called it off in the nick of time. The graceful impala bulls also put on a noisy, flashy show, and they were more serious about it, crashing their horns together and butting heads with a resounding whack.

The weather turned good, and the hunters went after buffaloes again. They hunted hard for three fruitless days, and then early in the morning drove to the village of a native named Conjone, a local authority on buffaloes.

Conjone had recently taken a fancy to one of the wives of a chief and had been jailed for three months in consequence. The chief also had burned his crop of sugar cane. But if he was chastened his appearance certainly didn't indicate it. They found him wearing cowboy boots, khaki shorts, an ornately decorated jacket and a wide-brimmed hat pinned up on one side Australian style.

Whatever his weakness for women, however, he knew the local buffalo herds and their habits, and was glad to help, since the buffaloes were raiding crops and his people had not had meat for some time.

Right now, he said, several bulls were bedded down in tall grass just beyond a small patch of corn that would have been knee high if the buffaloes had not eaten it. He was right, too. Fred and Wally flushed two good bulls out of the grass without getting a shot.

Conjone then climbed on the back of the hunting car and directed them across country to a brushy area where he said they would find a large herd drowsing in the noon heat. They found one lone bull instead and drove him out of a brushy donga, but he got away.

Conjone insisted the herd was somewhere in the neighborhood. This solitary bull often hung around on its outskirts, he said, and he urged another look. His advice was taken, and his wisdom in buffalo ways was proved when the hunters came on a herd of at least 60 in the thick cover of that same creek bottom. The big beasts milled around, watching defiantly, reluctant to leave, and finally Bear and Johnson spotted what they had been looking for for two weeks, a good bull and cow by themselves, in an open place at the edge of the brush.

Fred had seen hundreds of buffaloes by that time and could have shot at least half a dozen, but never under the right circumstances for the pictures he coveted. Now at last here was an ideal situation, almost too good to be true.

There was plenty of cover for the stalk and he worked in to within 45 yards very easily. The bull was standing broadside, with ribs exposed. When Fred stepped into the open for the shot the buffalo saw him, threw up its head and gave him that sullen, truculent buffalo stare. But it made no move, either to charge or run off.

Halmi was in position behind Fred, with nothing in his way. Fred waited until he heard the camera start, then released his arrow. It drove almost out of sight between the bull's ribs. Both buffaloes wheeled and went crashing into the brush. But there was no doubt in Fred's mind that he had made a kill.

They circled the herd and gave them man scent, and the buffaloes cleared out. Bear and Johnson took the blood trail then, followed it 250 yards and found the bull lying dead in a thicket. He was not as good as the first one but was still a very satisfactory trophy, and at last they had the movie record of the buffalo hunt that Fred wanted so much.

That kill was the climax of 13 days of some of the hardest hunting he had ever done. The second buffalo had come fairly easy, but Fred figured by that time that he had earned him a dozen times over. Two of Africa's meanest had bowed to his bow, and he had had as exciting and thrilling a hunt as ever came his way.

A Live
Rattler
—Once Too Often

THE snake was lying stretched out full length on a big flat rock, and it was the biggest timber rattler that Dr. Charles Kuschel had ever seen.

Kuschel wasn't really snake hunting that Sunday afternoon. It was the third week in July, not the best time to find either rattlers or copperheads, and he had climbed the mountain above Lovelton, Pennsylvania, about 20 miles from his home, mostly to check on some small mountain ash trees he hoped to dig and transplant later. He knew he'd be in snake country, however, and was carrying a forked stick, snake hook and muslin bag, just in case.

He had sat out a very heavy thundershower in his car before starting up the old logging road that led to the ledge where the trees were, and although the sun had come out again it was still very humid and everything was soaking wet. All in all, he didn't expect to encounter any snakes, and he dropped his guard and did something he was usually careful not to do.

In a snake area, if you are wise you don't walk around gazing all over the countryside. Instead you concentrate on

a small semicircular space in front of you and to the left and
right of where you're walking. That way, although it's not
unusual to get close to a rattler before you spot him, you're
ready for him and there's not much chance he'll take you by
surprise.

Kuschel wasn't doing that. He was wandering along,
looking around, and was just two short steps from the snake
before he saw it. He was not afraid of snakes, but that one
gave him a real start, and the sight of it there in the open,
thick-bodied and sinister, was something he would remember
as long as he lived. Timber rattlers in the Pennsylvania
mountains come in two color phases, black and yellow, not
related to the sex of the snake. This was a black one, with
blotches faintly outlined in pale yellow, a beautiful but
deadly looking animal.

It had not rattled or made a sound, and without moving
from his tracks the doctor reached over and pinned it behind
the head with his forked stick. Hell broke loose instantly
and in a big way. The snake rattled angrily, threw its body
into violent thrashing, and sprayed a considerable amount
of the musk or scent that rattlesnakes give off when enraged.

This musk is emitted from two scent glands, one on either
side of the vent, and if the tail is off the ground, as when
they are being handled or bagged, they can spray it a distance of three feet or more. It has been compared with the
smell of sliced cucumbers, freshly mowed thistles and various
other things.

"My own feeling is that it doesn't really smell like anything but rattler musk," Dr. Kuschel said afterward.

It's not unpleasant, but once you come in contact with it
you are not likely ever to forget the odor. Because of the
humidity the scent seemed to hang in the air that day, and he
would have known that he was very close to a rattlesnake
if he had been wearing ear plugs and a blindfold.

At that time Dr. Kuschel didn't take rattlers home alive,
a practice he later adopted, so when he encountered venom-
ous snakes he killed them on the spot, not wanting to leave

them in the woods as a threat to others. After looking this one over and speculating as to its length (a steel tape showed later that it was 51 inches long), he dispatched it as he usually did, by severing the backbone just behind the head quickly and cleanly with a penknife. Then he took time to look around.

There was a large flat rock beside him, and when his eyes followed the edge of it he spotted the head of a second rattler just barely showing, no more than five feet away. The rest of the snake was back under the rock and there was no way to get it out, so Kuschel left it alone and looked around some more.

To his surprise he spotted a third snake about 20 feet back on the ledge, stretched out full length as the first one had been. It was another fine big specimen, and like the other two had not rattled. The doctor walked cautiously over, pinned it and killed it as he had the first.

He dropped the two dead snakes in his bag with due caution. Even the freshly severed head of a rattler is capable of delivering a severe bite, and a snake just killed can bite about as hard as a live one by reflex action if it is handled while the head is still intact.

By now Dr. Kuschel was fully alert to the fact that he was in a prime snake area, and he kept his eyes glued where they belonged. He had gone no more than 75 yards when he came across a fourth rattler, also stretched on a rock. He killed that one, put it in the bag with the others, and decided he had had enough. When he measured them later, the snakes were 51, 47 and 45½ inches long. They made quite a load and the doctor had 3½ miles to hike back to his car, so he called it quits and started down the mountain.

He had not traveled a quarter mile when he spotted two more, one big, the other small, coiled at the edge of the logging road. They hadn't been there when he walked up an hour before.

That was in 1963 and Kuschel had not yet acquired either snake-proof boots or snake tongs. Catching this pair with no weapons but the forked stick and the hook posed a problem, but he managed it by pinning one, lifting the other out into the road with the hook, and then keeping it on the defensive while he hooked the first one out. There he pinned and killed them one at a time.

His total score that afternoon was six rattlers seen and five killed, including the largest he had ever encountered. Not bad for a trip that wasn't even intended as a snake hunt. There was one curious thing about those six snakes. Not one had rattled or shown any sign of alarm or hostility until the man put his forked stick on its neck, despite the fact that he was close when he first saw them and no more than a step or two away when he pinned them. That proves one thing that every snake hunter learns sooner or later. You can't count on a rattlesnake rattling. If you get near enough, the snake is quite likely to strike first, if it's going to, and rattle afterward if at all.

At the time he killed the five timber rattlers that Sunday afternoon, Dr. Kuschel was 43 years old, an optometrist at Pittston, Pennsylvania, a city of about 15,000 midway between Scranton and Wilkes-Barre. His friends and hunting partners commonly called him Doc. He grew up and had lived all his life in that area, except for 3½ years in the Army during World War II, and had fished and hunted since he was a kid.

He became interested in snake hunting in 1957, and in a few more years trout and bass fishing and crow and woodchuck and deer hunting, which had been his first-love pastimes all his life, had to take a back seat.

"I came down with a real hard case of it," he says. "So far as I am concerned, hunting rattlers and copperheads the way I and a few partners do it outranks any other outdoor sport available in our part of the country for thrills, excitement and danger. When you go snake hunting you know you're after something that can fight back, and you can't afford to forget that for a second."

His hunting started slowly. He had been interested in

snakes as far back as he could remember, but despite all the fishing and hunting he had done in rattlesnake country he had never encountered one in the wild until 1957. Returning from a fishing trip that June, just out of Towanda he saw a timber rattler lying in the road ahead. He stopped and got out to look it over. Somewhere he had read that you could kill a snake by hitting it sharply behind the head with a small switch. He tried it and it worked. He put the dead snake in his empty creel and took it home.

Two weeks later, coming back from another fishing trip, the same thing happened again, and he decided that if rattlers were that plentiful in his neck of the woods he could have fun hunting 'em.

It took him a while to learn the tricks. In the first five years, from that June through the summer of 1961, he tramped more miles than he could estimate, spent countless hours searching for snakes—and found a total of exactly five. The trouble, he learned later, was that he knew neither where nor when to look.

In 1962 things picked up. His score that year climbed to 25. He matched that figure in 1963, almost doubled it in 1964 with a kill of 48, and by 1965 was taking more than 60 snakes a year.

As the years went along, he picked up partners who shared his enthusiasm. One was Gerald Schaefer, a biology teacher who had been hunting snakes since he was in junior high school, and who taught Kuschel much of what he came to know about it. Another was Glenn Spencer, an employe of the Pennsylvania Game Commission who had hunted rattlers and copperheads for 25 years and also was able to offer some expert coaching. Barry Spencer, a relative of Glenn, and Harold Kuschel, a young nephew of Charles joined the team, too.

Most of their rattler hunting was done, and still is, in the vicinity of Noxen, Forkston or Loveltown, north of Pittston. That country has an abundance of snakes, and den sites are easy of access because of many game-land roads and old logging roads, closed to vehicles, that lead up to good ledges at the top of the mountains.

The best hunting is in ledge areas in the vicinity of winter dens. The ledges range in height from six to 30 feet. Some of them are several hundred feet long, broken by crevices and fissures, with loose rocks of all sizes lying below them and on top. Ferns, huckleberry bushes and small trees provide ample cover, and in winter the snakes hibernate in those ledges. But Dr. Kuschel and his partners have never found any single rock or crevice where large numbers return year after year.

In Pennsylvania, May and June are the most productive months for hunting rattlers and copperheads, shortly after the snakes emerge from hibernation.

"We start our hunting in May," Kuschel told me. "The earliest I have taken one was May 5. Success depends on the weather, location of the ledge, and getting out on the right day, taking temperature and humidity into account. Often a rainstorm seems to be the signal for them to come out. But hunting them is like hunting any game; sometimes you find none on what appears to be an ideal day.

"I've read that ledges facing south are best, but early in the season I find more rattlers in those facing west. The snakes mate shortly after coming out of winter quarters, and at that time are likely to be found in pairs. Later, though you may find several in a relatively small area, they won't be lying together, and as the weather warms they scatter out in all directions and move to their summer feeding grounds, traveling as far as two miles or more. They have three basic requirements, food, water and cover, and if conditions are right some can usually be found around the den areas all summer. Although rattlers do most of their hunting at night, especially in hot weather, they are also likely to prowl during the day."

In summer both timber rattlesnakes and copperheads are likely to be found almost anywhere—in berry patches, yards, fields, gardens and even around buildings. And since that is also the time when farmers, picnickers, hikers, fishermen and berry pickers are in the woods and fields, and children are at play, that is when most snakebite accidents occur.

Dr. Kuschel recalls a trip he made to Dark Hollow to hunt copperheads, for example. When he checked a spot that had almost unfailingly yielded one or two snakes in the past, he found that every rock of suitable size had been picked up and moved to build an outdoor fireplace.

"Why someone was not bitten on that cook-out, I'll never know," he says.

Although he has spent less time hunting copperheads than rattlers, he finds the former fascinating reptiles—but never to be trusted.

The copperhead seems to thrive near civilization better than the timber rattler, maybe because of its more secretive habits and marvelous camouflage, and also because it does not rattle and give itself way. It is far more difficult to detect than the rattlesnake, especially if coiled in dead leaves, moves more quickly, and is not as likely to attempt escape. Usually a copperhead strikes at anything that comes within range, even snake tongs or a hook.

"I have flipped a flat rock over to capture one underneath, and had it land alongside another hidden in dry leaves and grapevines without causing the second snake to move," Kuschel told me. "They are tricky, vicious and likely to stand their ground. The rattler, on the other hand, usually has a getaway route handy and uses it if given the chance."

Fortunately the copperhead bite is less dangerous than that of the rattlesnake. For one thing, the venom is less toxic. Too, an adult copperhead averages only about three feet long, a full grown rattler close to four. And since the length of the fangs and amount of venom ejected depends on the size of the snake (an adult timber rattler may have fangs a half inch long) the copperhead bite is less deep and severe.

Once he really got into snake hunting, all the reptiles that Doc and his partners caught were taken home alive. At a later date they were killed if there was no demand for live specimens. Kuschel did not collect the harmless kinds unless someone had put in a request for them.

He uses homemade tongs for lifting the snakes out into the open, and either a hook or forked stick for pinning them. He rates the forked stick safe enough if handled properly and carefully, but points out that a snake hook can be made by simply bending ¼-inch steel rod into an L and fitting it with a broken golf club for a handle.

His method of picking up a rattler or copperhead is to pin it by pressing the head firmly to the ground and putting his foot on the body a foot or so back to prevent thrashing. He now wears snakeproof boots on most of his hunts.

"You can get along without them if you are careful," he says, "but they give a nice feeling of security."

Next he puts his thumb on one side of the snake's neck, his middle finger on the other side, and presses down on the top of the head with his index finger. With that grip, the snake is less able to twist its head or free itself.

Dr. Kuschel's formula for the rest of the capture goes as follows:

"Once you have him hard and fast, remove the hook, grab his body with your other hand and pick him up. A snake lifted by the neck alone is likely to thrash hard enough to break either your grip or his own neck. One warning. If you have a foot on his body, expect him to use it for leverage and try to draw his head back when you first take hold of him, and a big one is surprisingly strong.

"It's best to grab a snake quickly once you have him pinned. The longer you hold his head down the more irritated and hard to handle he becomes. Many bites happen during the picking-up process, so use extreme caution."

Sacking the catch is simple. Kuschel uses muslin bags 39 inches deep and 12 to 14 in diameter. He gets the snake started into the bag tail first. Small ones can be dropped right in. A big one is apt to stand on its tail, so he waits until it relaxes before releasing his hold on its neck. Once the snake falls to the bottom, he twirls the bag and ties a knot well up on the twisted section.

"But when you walk away carry the bag so it doesn't bump your legs or body," he warns. "The snake can strike through it very easily."

Among the snake hunters I have known, few have been interested in eating their catch. Many of them express great aversion to the idea that a snake is edible. Dr. Kuschel is an exception. He rates rattler meat very tasty. White and clean, it reminds him of froglegs, both in texture and flavor, and friends to whom he has served it all support his opinion.

His recipe for preparing it is to skin and dress the snake, preferably a large one for added meatiness, and cut it into lengths 3 or 4 inches long. (Some cooks prefer to cut the pieces shorter, in steaks about a half inch thick, because the dish looks less like snake that way.) He cooks it by frying in butter or bacon fat as you would fry fish.

If a snake hunter picks up poisonous snakes often enough, he stands a very good chance of being bitten. One false move can lead to trouble, and it happens sooner or later to just about everybody who handles these reptiles. Doc Kuschel knew that as well as anybody. Nevertheless, he picked up a live rattler once too often.

It happened on Memorial Day of 1963. He had passed up a chance to go to Canada on a fishing trip, for the reason that that is one of the best periods of the year for snake hunting, and his nephew Harold and he headed for a series of ledges at the top of South Mountain, about 15 miles from home.

They caught one medium size rattler, sacked it alive, found a big blacksnake and let it go after teasing it to hear it vibrate its tail in the dry leaves and put on a good imitation of a rattlesnake's buzzing. They ate lunch beside a clear mountain brook, left their snake and the knapsack and went on hunting along the Possum Brook road.

They had gone about a mile when they found another rattler in the grass at the roadside, lying in the round coil they assume when resting. It's not at all like the U-shaped loops of their fighting stance, although they can strike from it if they need to.

Harold Kuschel pinned the snake, and his uncle picked it up with his left hand. It was a 44-incher.

Doc liked to keep a small quantity of dried venom crystals on hand, to show to Boy Scout troops and other groups before which he often gave talks on snakes and snake hunting. He had extracted venom from the first rattler they caught that day, and wanted a little more.

Because he preferred to use his right hand for milking a snake, he dropped this one on the road, intending to change hands and pick it up again.

The snake made a bee line for the woods. Kuschel pinned it in a place covered with dead leaves and needles, using a forked stick—and made the cardinal mistake of not making sure the fork was tight up against its head. Next he reached down alongside the head instead of moving his hand up behind the stick.

That was all the rattler needed. It had a fraction of an inch of slack, enough to twist its head very slightly, and it bit like forked lightning.

One fang cut a quarter-inch slit in Kuschel's index finger between the knuckle and first joint. The strike was so fast that his nephew, standing just behind him, did not even see what happened.

"I've been bitten," the doctor said calmly.

He was asked many times afterward how he felt right then, and his truthful answer always was, "Stupid."

At first all he felt was a slight burning, and that alone did not necessarily indicate that any venom had been injected. Even a razor nick will burn. But after three or four minutes an area the size of a dime around the cut turned white and started to swell, and there was no longer any doubt. He was

next he reached down alongside the head instead of moving his hand up behind the stick

dealing with a genuine case of snakebite, how serious only the next hour or so would tell.

He was carrying a kit, as he always did on his rattler hunts, but the small suction cup would not stay in place, so he proceeded to suck out what poison and blood he could by mouth. While he was doing that Harold sterilized the small knife from the kit, and next Doc undertook to lengthen the fang cut and make another at right angles to it.

That may sound simple, but it proved otherwise. For some reason he expected his finger to be numb. It wasn't, and the knife hurt like blazes. He managed to grit his teeth and lengthen the fang cut, but that was all.

All this while they were standing with the snake still pinned. When his uncle needed two hands Harold took charge of the forked stick. But the doctor didn't want to try picking the snake up now, and his young nephew had never handled live rattlers, so before things got any worse he decided to kill the reptile in the usual way, by severing its backbone close to the head.

That proved a very painful chore, for by now the swelling had progressed to his thumb and across his hand to the wrist, and the pain and soreness were severe. He was also beginning to feel a strange, numb, tingling feeling in his lips and tongue. The two men held a very short conference and agreed their next move should be to make a start for the nearest hospital.

It was a good four miles back to where their car was parked. Kuschel realized now that the bite was more severe than he had thought at first. He wasn't at all panicky, but he knew that men had died from the bite of a timber rattler before they could walk that far.

They started down off the mountain at a slow walk. Whatever happened, the doctor knew better than to hurry or exert himself. When they got back to where they had left the first rattler in the bag he proceeded to kill it, and that was pure torture. He had to hold the snake in his left hand and use the penknife with the swollen and half helpless right, and it was almost more than he could manage.

It took an hour and a half to reach the car. By that time the swelling had reached to the elbow, but his general condition did not seem greatly worse and he could still walk. Harold and he had figured out that the Nesbitt Hospital in Kingston, across the Susquehanna from Wilkes-Barre, was the closest. Harold had no driver's license and the Memorial Day traffic was very heavy, so his uncle turned down the boy's offer to drive. By now the fingers on the bitten hand were so puffy that they could not be bent, and the palm was swollen to twice its normal size. Shifting gears was pure murder.

They parked in front of the hospital finally, and when

Dr. Kuschel tried to get out of the car he realized that his toes had that same numb feeling and his legs wouldn't do what he wanted. He took 10 or 12 staggering steps, regained some measure of control, and got to the nurse at the desk. "A rattlesnake bit me," he mumbled.

She hurried him into the dispensary and called for a doctor. Kuschel repeated his story, and the medic looked at the cut. There were no puncture marks. "You're sure it was a rattlesnake?" he asked.

"It's out in the car," Harold said quickly. "We've got two of 'em. I'll go bring them in." But the hopsital doctor turned that offer down in a hurry.

Kuschel was put to bed and treatment started at once. The hospital had Antivenin on hand, and luckily the skin test for horse-serum sensitivity proved negative. A 10cc vial was injected in five or six places in the swollen arm. The doctor also made a cross incision at the site of the bite, and the hand and forearm were then placed in an ice pack.

Kuschel experienced no nausea or dizziness, but the pain was severe and for the next 12 days he went through the typical snakebite victim's ordeal. A few days after he was bitten he developed what is known as serum sickness, a delayed reaction to the horse blood from which the Antivenin is prepared. That can happen even though the preliminary skin tests are negative.

His lymph glands became swollen and sore, his entire back broke out in blisters, and a series of them appeared on his arm from the wrist almost to the armpit. Next many small ones popped up on his tongue, and he had very severe pain in his arm and shoulder. Finally his fingers and toes became stiff and sore, as from arthritis.

These symptoms did not all occur at once, but each time he figured he could leave the hospital something else showed up. He still does not know how much of his suffering was due to the venom and how much to the serum sickness, but either way he was a very sick snake hunter for almost two weeks.

Released 12 days after being admitted, he had lost an average of a pound a day. He had a very sore hand for weeks afterward, and his index finger still gets numb and cold in weather much below 60 degrees. It even bothers him in hunting and fishing on cool days. And all this misery resulted from hardly more than a single drop of venom, if indeed it was that much, delivered by one fang, in a cut, not a puncture.

It was a dreadful experience, as snakebite almost always is, and when it was all over friends asked Doc whether he was ready to give up snake hunting. His answer was, "Not by any means." He is still at it, almost to the exclusion of other outdoor activities except when the snakes are not abroad, and he expects to do it the rest of his life.

"There's a peculiar excitement connected with it that's hard to describe," he told me afterward. "No matter how many fish you have caught or how many deer you have shot, the next hard strike you get or the next big buck you see still gives you a thrill. Every hunter and fisherman knows that, and it's far more true of hunting poisonous snakes, I suppose because of the element of danger. Almost every hunt has what the inexperienced would count a close call. It's a sport that costs next to nothing, yet for action and chills it's almost equivalent to a tiger hunt. I've had more than one spectator come close to a nervous breakdown just watching the proceedings. Quit snake hunting? I should say not!"

He'll never drop his guard again, however.

Too Much
Bear

THEY saw the bear's shadow before they made out the bear.

They were flying at 500 feet, following a lead in the arctic ice pack 180 miles off Kotzebue, Alaska, so far out at sea that the rugged Siberian coast was a low smudge on the horizon in the west. The lead, a big crack angling across the glaring white ice fields as far as the eye could see, was 30 to 40 feet wide and had frozen over with new ice in the bitter cold. It was probably two or three days old.

The hunters had followed it only a few miles when they spotted the dark shadow of the bear moving along at the foot of a ridge of snow-covered ice. He was following the lead too, looking for seals. On an overcast day they would probably have missed him, a white speck in that vast white landscape. Denny Thompson, the guide and pilot, nosed the Super Cub down for a closer look.

Although Thompson and his hunter, Art LaHa, had been in the air only three or four hours, they had seen six polar bears before this one. For the first forenoon of the hunt, that added up to exceptional luck, even though none of the bears was big enough to suit LaHa. When they circled over this one only 200 feet above the ice, however, he knew they had found what he had come to Alaska for. If he could put an arrow into this bear in the right place he would have a trophy to brag about.

The plane was probably the first the bear had ever seen. It seemed to anger him more than it scared him. He swung around to face it, bared his teeth in rage, and finally took off along the lead at a gallop. The hunters didn't follow. They were not interested in buzzing, hazing or driving him. All they wanted was one good look for size. Now that they had had that they went back upstairs to pick a spot where they could ambush him.

The fall before, in 1963, LaHa, a confirmed bowhunter, had gone to the Alaska Peninsula for a brown bear, with Thompson and his assistant, Cappy Capasella, as guides. He was lucky enough to down a good brownie with a broadhead. Now he really itched for a polar bear to add to his list of bowhunting trophies.

He had first seen Alaska 20 years earlier, as a young laborer on the Alcan Highway. Now 44, married and the father of two daughters, he owned and operated a supermarket in the little resort town of Winchester in northern Wisconsin, a few miles below the Michigan border south of Ironwood. Because business slacked off after Labor Day, each fall he operated a lodge and guided bowhunters, with whitetail deer as his specialty.

Art had killed a deer with a bow in Wisconsin every year since 1940, and each year since 1947 he had also filled a Michigan nonresident bowhunting license. He had taken five deer in Canada, a moose and a caribou in Newfoundland, and a mule deer in Nebraska, all that same way. And in Michigan, Wisconsin and Canada he had killed a total of 31 black bears with a bow.

"I realize that may sound like fantastic success," he told

me in commenting on his record, "but I doubt that any bow-hunter has put in more time at it than I have. Very few days of the hunting seasons go by when I am not in the woods, either with clients or hunting on my own."

It should be added that he is also an extraordinary woodsman and hunter.

As far back as he could remember he had regarded bears among the greatest trophies on this continent, and after he turned to a bow his zest for bear hunting grew. The big Alaska brown was the climax of a lifetime for him, but there remained one more trophy to take, the white ice bear that he rated king of all North American game. So he made arrangements with Thompson, an Anchorage guide and outfitter, for a hunt on the ice off Kotzebue in the spring of 1964.

It's not difficult to get face to face with a polar bear on the ice floes off the Alaska coast. For most hunters nowadays dog-team hunting, as the Eskimos used to do, is out. It's a method too uncertain and too hazardous. Instead they fly out over the ice in a light plane and look for big leads in the shifting pack. Seals use those huge cracks, to come up for air and to stretch out and take a nap. There are polar bears there, hunting the seals, and their everlasting search for food keeps them on the move and makes them easy to find.

"If a man had guts enough, I don't believe it would be difficult to lie down, mimic a seal, have a bear stalking you in short order, and decoy him in close enough for a bow kill," LaHa told me.

Many sportsmen frown on even the spotting of game from an aircraft, but in the case of polar bears, ranging the ice far offshore, it's about the only way to hunt them.

Although bear hunting on the ice may get under way as early as the middle of February, the outsider should think twice before heading for the ice fields at that time. The mercury is still scraping bottom, the Arctic blizzards are

savage and prolonged, and hunting is likely to be held up
for days at a time.

LaHa knew all that. Nevertheless, as the February days
ticked away his fever mounted uncontrollably and he grew
more and more impatient. He bugged Denny by long distance at his Anchorage headquarters repeatedly. Thompson
was keeping in touch by phone daily with Art Fields, a
famous Eskimo guide, at Art's waterfront restaurant in
Kotzebue. As soon as Denny got word that conditions were
right he'd let LaHa know. Art was to be his first client of
the year.

The long awaited call came toward the end of February.
The frigid weather along the northwest coast of Alaska was
easing, Denny reported, and polar bears were moving in
toward shore. The blizzards were slacking off and the
chances were good they could start hunting as soon as they
arrived.

LaHa left Chicago for Anchorage on a jet liner on
Sunday morning, March 1. Some of the flight was along the
route of the Alaska Highway where he had worked 20 years
before, and he even managed to pick out the site of the construction camp where it had been his job to keep black bears
out of the meat house. It was dark when the jet touched
down at the Anchorage airport. Denny and Cappy were
waiting, and the three had dinner together and went over
their plans. It was a fine reunion.

Art spent a couple of days around Anchorage taking
movies, and bought his nonresident hunting license. It cost
only $10, but if he filled it he'd have to fork over another
$150 for a polar bear tag.

They left shortly after breakfast on Wednesday with two
Super Cubs, Denny at the controls of one, Cappy the other,
and headed northwest through Rainy Pass, flying above
some of the most breathtaking mountain scenery in Alaska.

They would use the two planes as a team on the bear hunt.
That is close to standard practice in hunting over the ice
fields, for reasons of safety. If one aircraft is forced down

or damaged in landing, or if any other mishap occurs, the second, airborne in reserve, can do whatever is needed. Hunting the offshore ice with one plane by itself is foolhardy, as more than one party has learned the hard way.

They landed at McGrath and stayed a day, again to make movies, and finally touched down at Kotzebue around noon on Friday in a blizzard, with a bitter cold wind sweeping in off the ice and the air thick with snow.

The blizzard died away during the night and as the weather cleared the mercury plummeted. It stood at 50 below when the party took off the next morning, with Cappy and Fields in one plane, Denny and Art in the other.

They found big leads about every 10 miles and cruised along them, one after another. They were only a short distance out of Kotzebue when they spotted their first small bear, and they had no trouble finding five more, but none that they wanted.

The assignment LaHa had set himself, to be among the first handful of white men to kill an ice bear with a bow, was such a difficult one, both time-consuming and dangerous, that very few guides would take bowhunting clients. The Eskimos did it regularly in the old days, but nearly always with the help of a pack of dogs that kept the bear occupied while an arrow—or even a spear—was driven home. To make things more difficult, if Art was going to achieve his goal he wanted the bear to be a good one, well up in the trophy class. Short of that, he would settle for no bear at all.

They counted six bears that forenoon, and then sighted the big one. Denny coasted down and landed two or three miles ahead, on smooth ice near the lead. Cappy set his plane down alongside and the four held a brief council of war. They completed their plans in a hurry, both because they figured the bear wasn't going to give them much time and also because the noonday temperature was still hovering around 45 below.

Cappy would take off and circle overhead, far enough away not to disturb the bear, so he'd be airborne in case of any mishap. Fields and Denny and Art would find a hiding place along the edge of the lead and wait for the bear.

Cappy flew off, and Denny got out a big comforter and the thermo-heater for the engine of his Cub. He turned off the switch of the idling motor, set the heater in place and covered motor and heater as snugly as possible. At 45 below an engine cools very fast, and they knew that if theirs failed to start they would face a frigid wait while Cappy ferried them back to Kotzebue one at a time.

By the time Denny had the motor wrapped, Fields and LaHa had found a place where they thought they could waylay the bear, behind the upturned hummocks of a pressure ridge just a few yards from the lead. They didn't get into their blind any too soon. By the time Denny crept in and hunkered down with them they could see the bear half a mile away, coming at a swinging walk.

Art had turned his movie camera over to Denny. He'd try to make pictures of the kill. Fields was carrying a 12-gauge pumpgun loaded with buckshot. That's unusual medicine for a polar bear but Fields seemed convinced it would do the job at close range. He'd back LaHa if the bear gave trouble, and Denny had his .375 Magnum Winchester Model 70 handy, just in case.

A polar bear at bow range, wounded or just mad, is nothing to fool around with, and they all knew it. The white bear is big and powerful, vindictive, terrible in his rage, and has to be rated in the front rank of the world's dangerous game. Above all, however, LaHa was hoping the guns would not have to be used. No animal can be counted as a bow trophy if there's a bullet or pellet hole in the hide, and he didn't want his plans thwarted that way if it could be helped.

From their hiding place, if the bear went between them and the lead as they expected, Art would get a side shot at about 30 feet. His bow was a Cheetah model, made by the American Archery Company, with a pull of 75 pounds.

That's heavier than average, but LaHa was 5 feet 10 and weighed 195 pounds in hunting condition, and he had gradually accustomed himself to that 75-pounder for bears because it delivered peak performance in balance and power. For deer and other game he used a lighter bow.

His arrows were 30-inch shafts with 3-bladed broadheads. He had a length of clothesline wrapped around his waist, to prevent his bowstring from slapping against his loose parka and the bulky clothing underneath and deflecting his shot. String slap can cause an arrow to fly high, wide and not handsome.

He decided to let the bear walk past and try to put an arrow angling into its chest cavity from the rear. He did not expect to kill it in its tracks, but all three men were wearing white parkas and he was hoping the bear wouldn't locate them.

The first time he raised up for a look it was 100 yards away and still coming. He ducked down in a hurry. Fields and Denny sensed from his actions that whatever was going to happen would happen very soon. Denny lifted the camera and Art was ready with his pumpgun, but they both stayed down out of sight. They would depend on Art to do the looking.

The next time he peeked the bear was 30 yards off, looking directly at them, and it saw his face the instant he lifted above an ice hummock. It didn't even wait to take a second look. It let out a snort that sounded like a cough, and then it was coming at a rolling gallop, with its head swinging snakelike from side to side. LaHa straightened up from his crouch and brought his bow back to full draw.

"I don't know whether he charged because that's standard polar bear behavior, but I don't think so," Art said afterward. "I suspect he was still riled up from our plane circling over him, and when he spotted me he thought he saw something he could handle and let his temper go, like a man who's been doing a slow burn. Certainly he made a beeline without a second of hesitation. When I thought it over later I concluded we'd have been better off had we stayed entirely away from him with the plane and not stirred him up."

Denny and Fields did not realize the bear was charging. Bundled as they were from head to foot, they had not heard its angry snort. Out of the tail of one eye LaHa caught a glimpse of them, still crouched behind a big block of ice, and he was glad for that. At least they wouldn't dump the bear prematurely with their guns.

Art swung his arrow with the bear as it came, and when it was close enough for a sure thing he let the arrow go. The bear was just 12 feet away when the arrow sliced in, burying itself at the juncture of his neck and left shoulder. Afterward Art recalled thinking that at least it would turn him.

It did, but not far enough. The bear swerved and went past so close that LaHa could have jabbed him with the bow, and Art could see the feathers and about 10 inches of arrow standing out from the thick white fur, and blood streaming down the shoulder. Then the animal was on top of Art and Denny, still hunkered a few feet away at LaHa's left.

"There wasn't time to be scared, but under pressure like that it's amazing how many thoughts can flash through a man's mind in a fraction of a second," he recalled later. "I was hoping my two partners would roll out of his way, and I was hoping just as fervently that they'd notice the blood from the arrow wound and hold their gunfire as long as possible. From the location of my shot and the blood that was pouring out, I didn't think that bear had long to live."

Denny dropped the camera and grabbed for his .375 while Art was trying to get a second arrow out of his back quiver. Then the bear's left forefoot smashed down on the camera, driving it into the hard snow, and LaHa saw another big paw strike Denny's gun barrel and flip the rifle into the air. In the same instant Fields shoved the muzzle of his pumpgun almost against the bear's head—and Art heard a faint click as the gun misfired.

Fields dodged to the right with a spinning roll and the bear leaped entirely over him. He slammed a second shell into the chamber and the 12-guage bellered. The shot had no effect, but the bear did not turn back to finish what it had started. Instead it kept going, walking away, fighting the arrow, biting savagely at its shoulder.

Fields dodged to the right in a spinning roll and the bear leaped entirely over him

"Don't shoot again!" Art yelled. "I got an arrow into him good."

The bear disappeared around a bend in the lead, and the three hunters drew a deep breath all around and took inventory. It was now 2:30, the warmest time of the day, but LaHa's mittenless right hand was stiff from the cold, and when they tested the camera they found it wouldn't run properly and the film had been broken. They had missed the hunting picture of a lifetime.

Next they test-fired the shell that had failed to go off in Fields' pumpgun and it fired on the second or third try. Apparently there was nothing wrong with it, but the firing pin had turned very sluggish because of the extreme cold.

The big question was whether LaHa had killed the bear. He was sure he had, and Denny and Fields were inclined to agree. "At least he didn't kill us," Denny said a little grimly.

In a few minutes Cappy set his plane down nearby. He reported the bear had gone into an area of broken pressure ridges and was still traveling, not fast but too fast for a man to overtake.

"He's bleeding a lot and he looks wobbly," Cappy said. From the air he had seen that the animal's left foreleg was soaked with blood, and Arctic foxes had picked up the trail and were licking at the blood in the tracks.

They could not catch up on foot, and could not land near the bear because of rough ice, and both planes were low on gas. A few miles back, on the way out, they had found a smooth level area and Denny had landed and unloaded seven 5-gallon cans, leaving a green sleeping bag as a marker. Little as they liked to leave the bear at that point, they had no choice now but to fly back there and refill the tanks.

The wind had blown the sleeping bag away and it took longer to locate the cache than they expected, but they finally found it, set both planes down, refueled, and went back to look for the bear.

He had disappeared without trace, somewhere in the

rough ice. Earlier his blood trail had been clearly visible to Cappy from the air, but now there was no sign of it. Either the foxes had disposed of it or he was no longer bleeding. And to make matters worse, only a little daylight was left.

They searched as long as they dared. LaHa wanted to make camp on the ice by himself with their emergency tent and rations, and let the guides come back in the morning and pick him up, but they refused flatly. The Civil Air Patrol was still looking for the bodies of two hunters who had stayed on the ice overnight under similar circumstances, they told him.

When they finally gave up the search there was no longer time to fly back to Kotzebue before dark, so they headed for Point Hope, the nearest land, 150 miles up the coast to the northwest. It was dusk when they landed there and taxied up to the door of a restaurant on the waterfront. Denny and Cappy had mildly frostbitten faces and looked as if they were wearing white masks. Maybe because he was on the portly side, LaHa had come through without damage, and vigorous rubbing soon fixed the two guides up.

They perched on stools at the restaurant counter and gulped down hot coffee.

"I don't think I've ever been more downhearted in my life," LaHa said long afterward. "I was sure my arrow would kill the bear, and so far as we had been able to tell Fields' shot had missed him outright. In all likelihood he was lying in some cave in an ice ridge now, dead or dying, the trophy I coveted more than any other I'd ever take, and there seemed almost no chance that we could find him. Denny and Cappy and Fields were almost as downcast as I was, too."

A dinner of caribou hamburgers and home-made Eskimo bread left everybody feeling better, but Art still wasn't very cheerful.

When they turned on the radio after dinner they heard Civil Air Patrol pilots talking among themselves. They were conducting a search for the trio. Denny had radioed

Kotzebue as soon as they landed at Point Hope but the message had not gotten through, as sometimes happens in the Arctic, and once a plane is overdue, other flyers lose no time looking for it.

The radio message had reached an amateur operator in the Fairbanks area, however, and very shortly he got through to Kotzebue and the three hunters heard a general broadcast to the search planes, calling them back. By the time that was all straightened out the loss of the bear didn't loom quite so tragic. Art began to be thankful that they were ashore and warm and safe.

Point Hope had a comfortable hotel, and the Eskimo hospitality left nothing to be desired. Most of the plumbing was frozen, but there was plenty of ice melting on the stoves to furnish water for washing and drinking. The plywood walls groaned in the creeping cold that night, and nails popped with reports like rifle shots, but the party slept in clean beds under good wool blankets.

Just before Art dozed off Denny called to him, "Did you ever have it better back home?" and he had to answer no. A tired and anxious bear hunter could not have asked for more.

They talked the next morning with a group of Point Hope Eskimos about the chances of finding the bear. None of them thought it possible, but everybody agreed that the only thing to do was go out and look. So the two planes flew back over the ice and started to search the area where Cappy had last seen the bear, and all of a sudden Fields' voice blurted over the radio, "There he is, right below us!"

The bear was walking slowly across broken ice, and now they saw something that sent LaHa's spirits tumbling once more. Its left shoulder and foreleg were caked with frozen blood—and on the right side of the head, around the ear, there was a second patch of blood bigger than a man's two hands. That meant that Fields had hit the animal with his shotgun after all, and it was disqualified as a bow trophy.

It turned out that his hit was close to a freak. The charge

of buckshot, fired when the bear was hardly more than six or seven feet from the end of his gun, had grazed the fur on the neck, all but one pellet. That had gone into the flesh just back of the ear and was embedded in neck muscle. How that single pellet, fired at such close range, had happened to connect when the rest missed, LaHa never figured out. It had done no real injury to the bear, but that one round hole in the pelt was enough to ruin things for Art's purposes.

They still had the job of finishing the bear off. Denny found a place ahead where they could land, and he and Art walked back and tried to get up to it behind ice hummocks. They got within 100 yards, and Denny handed Art his .375. "Kill him," he said. "You can't claim him anyway."

It took four shots in the lungs to do the job, and Art was afraid poor shooting was to blame. Denny's Winchester was short, with iron sights, and didn't fit him. On top of that, he had shot a rifle very rarely in many years. But when he said something to the guide to the effect that he hadn't turned in a very good performance, Thompson didn't agree.

"It wasn't your fault," he said. "You were dealing with a tough customer. You hit him in the right place, but a big polar bear can carry a lot of lead. More than one has taken that much medicine from the most expert rifleman."

LaHa's license was filled, his hunt ended. He was going home without a bow trophy, as more than one bowhunter had done before him. The fact that they had killed a big polar, well up in the trophy class, with a beautiful thick pelt, didn't make it any easier. The bear squared 10½ feet, and Lee Miller, an Alaska game biologist from Anchorage, stationed at Kotzebue for the bear season, estimated he'd have weighed 1,200 pounds. Art's broadhead had gone into the left lung, but not deeply enough to kill him as a well placed arrow should.

In spite of the outcome, however, LaHa told me he didn't feel like complaining. The bear had given them a close shave, but they had come through unhurt, and it had been the most exciting hunt he had ever made.

Cougar
in the
Barn

ONE day in late May, hiking up the trail that runs along the Atnarko River from Lonesome Lake to his home place, Jack Turner came across a big buck lying a couple of yards off to one side, freshly killed by a cougar. At that time of year its antlers were only velvet-covered stubs, just starting to grow, but Turner judged that by fall it would have been at least a good 4-pointer.

The cat had waylaid it in the trail. Blood and tufts of hair showed where the deer had gone down. The cougar had then dragged its kill aside, fed, and covered the carcass with sticks and litter. That meant that in all likelihood it would be back.

Where the Turners live, on an isolated homestead in the mountains of British Columbia 25 miles from the nearest road—and that's not paved for 50 miles one way and 250 the other—pork is hard to come by. They almost never get any, and because cougar and lynx taste more like pork than any other meat they know about, Jack kills them every chance he gets and they eat all he kills.

He does not get many cougars, for although they are by
no means rare in the mountains around the Turner place
they are shy and furtive in the extreme, seldom seen and
then no more than a glimpse. This one, hanging around its
kill less than a mile from the house, was an opportunity too
good to pass up. Jack did not think he'd have much trouble
killing it, and he made up his mind that he'd keep after it
until he got a shot.

Most people would consider the Turner family's life an
extremely lonely one, but it suits them to a T. They have
160 acres on the Atnarko two miles above Lonesome Lake.
Jack's wife Trudy homesteaded the place before they were
married in 1957. About 30 acres of it are down on the river
flats, the rest up on the timbered mountainsides.

Lonesome Lake is about as remote and isolated a spot as
you can find, but they think it and the Atnarko valley are
also as beautiful as any place in the Coast Range, and of the
few people who have seen it not many have disagreed.

To get to it, you leave paved highway No. 97 (which runs
north from the Trans-Canada Highway at Cache Creek,
through Prince George, and links up with the Alaska Highway at Dawson Creek) at Williams Lake and drive west
toward the coastal town of Bella Coola on a rough and
dusty gravel road. Two hundred miles out on that road—if
you make 200 miles in six or seven hours you're doing well—
at Nimpo Lake, about halfway between Kleena Kleene and
Anahim Lake, you can charter an aircraft and fly 25 miles
in to Lonesome, which lies at the bottom of a steep-walled
slot between snow-capped mountains. Nobody who makes
that flight will ever forget the beauty of the place.

That's not the way the Turners get in, however. From
their place a foot and horse trail leads out, by way of Lonesome and Stillwater Lakes, to a point on the gravel road
50 miles east of Bella Coola. Lonesome Lake is seven miles
long, Stillwater is three. They keep boats and outboards on
both, and in summer that cuts 10 miles off the hike. In
winter it's a 25-mile hike, on snowshoes if the snow is deep

enough. Some winters it isn't. Jack goes out about once a month to get mail. That is almost their only contact with the outside world. When he and Trudy and their 11-year-old daughter Susan go to town, which isn't often, they make the 25 miles to the road on foot and by boat and then hitch a ride to Bella Coola.

The first few years of Susan's life, Trudy carried her in a small homemade chair lashed to a packboard, but when she was 8 she could hike 25 miles with her parents in a day and carry a small pack of her own.

Trudy's father, Ralph Edwards, homesteaded a place at the head of Lonesome Lake in 1912 and he and his wife lived there for more than 55 years. Trudy and her brother John were born there. However, when it came time for Susan to arrive, in January 1959, the Search and Rescue Branch of the RCAF flew Trudy to Vancouver.

The Turners and Edwards were the only two families in the Atnarko valley and their nearest neighbor, a widowed Indian woman living by herself three miles from the road, was more than 20 miles away. That is a situation that calls for a real love of wilderness, as well as a shot of self-reliance, but the Turners prize the elbow room they have.

Jack has spent a fair share of his adult life in the woods, much of it by himself. He was born in Vancouver in 1931, lived there until 1940, on Vancouver Island the next four years, and in the West Kootenay area for two years after that. He started making frequent one-day trips into the forest and onto the ocean, all alone, from 1940 on, and after 1945 those trips became longer and more elaborate.

For 10 years before he came to Lonesome Lake in 1957 he roamed and worked all over British Columbia, sometimes by himself, sometimes with other men, surveying and doing forest engineering work. A lot of the jobs involved bush living alone. So naturally the life at the Atnarko homestead does not seem lonely to him. And that valley has been home to Trudy since she can remember.

They keep four horses and two cows and a bull, cutting

hay on 20 acres of cleared meadow land around the house, and growing their own beef. They also have a few hens and a fine garden. They can get all the trout they want in the Atnarko, and it's no trick to knock over a deer or moose in hunting season. You may find it hard to believe, but their food costs are only $100 a year.

The house, barn and outbuildings are of log, and most of their furniture is home-made. Since everything they get from outside has to be brought in by packhorse and raft from the road (they even packed in their stove, a hayrake, and the shakes for the roofs) they do without all but the essentials. For example, they make their own harness from untanned, dried cowhide. It's strong enough that Jack can hitch a team to a 40-foot log and skid it out of the lake without any trouble. That same material covers the floors, too, and it's as durable as the best linoleum.

The garden and hay land are enclosed with rail-type fence, built of logs and eight feet high, to keep moose and deer out. The fence is also intended to discourage bears, but doesn't always succeed. Over the years they have had more bear encounters than you could shake a stick at, not a few of them literally in the door-yard.

For instance, in the fall of 1961 they killed a beef and disposed of the entrails by burying them, as usual. But a couple of nights later a young black bear, a quarrelsome little runt that wouldn't have weighed much more than 100 pounds, found the leavings and dug them up. Jack knew the bear would be a nuisance, hanging around the buildings, so he took his rifle and went out to chase it off up the mountain. It didn't chase very well. It growled and grumbled and refused to run, but finally walked away, carrying a chunk of the refuse and eating as it went.

It was only 30 feet ahead of Turner, in open brush, when it finished its snack. It swapped ends instantly, ripped out a louder and nastier growl, and came for the man like a hornet. Jack does not like to kill any animal unless there is a reason for it, but he had no choice that time. The bear meant business, and Jack floored him on about the third jump.

Then there were the two big grizzlies that wandered into the yard one day and started to chase the hens, no more than 25 feet from the house. They weren't threatening the family and it was an entertaining show, but the Turners couldn't put up with it. Hens are fragile and, where they live, hard to replace, and bears play rough. In fact Jack wasn't even sure these two were playing. It was a situation that had to be taken care of, so he grabbed his rifle, ran out and shot both of them, without moving more than 10 steps from the porch.

Jobs that pay wages are few and far between in places as isolated as Lonesome Lake, but the Turners have an unusual and interesting one. They earn most of their cash from the Canadian Wildlife Service at Ottawa, feeding a flock of trumpeter swans that come down from nesting grounds farther north every fall to winter on Lonesome Lake.

The swan-feeding operation goes back almost 35 years. The lake has been a traditional wintering ground for trumpeters for as long as anyone knows, probably because the upper end is shallow and the Atnarko, flowing through it, keeps it open. If thin ice forms in a cold night, as sometimes happens, the swans quickly break it by lighting on it (they weigh up to 35 pounds) and the current sweeps it away.

In 1936 Lake Creek, dropping into the lake at the lower end over a 1,300-foot waterfall, carried down so much rock and debris that it dammed the outlet and raised the level of Lonesome several feet. The swans, bottom feeders that feed by tipping rather than diving, were no longer able to reach their natural food supply, and many of them died of starvation that winter.

Among the hunters Ralph Edwards guided the next fall

was John P. Holman, a sportsman and conservationist from the United States, and a prominent member of the National Audubon Society. At that time the trumpeter swans, biggest and most majestic waterfowl on the continent, were a vanishing race, headed for what appeared to be inevitable extinction. The total population in the United States was only a few more than 100, about a fourth of the number that now winters on Lonesome Lake each year, and the Canadian population was down to an estimated 500, scattered through the remote wilds of northern British Columbia.

Holman interested himself in the plight of the Lonesome Lake flock, which then numbered only 30-odd. He persuaded the Canadian government to undertake a feeding program to save this remnant. Wheat was horse-packed in, and Edwards took on the daily job of scattering it for the swans. When she was old enough Trudy took over. From 1948 to 1958 the grain was flown in, instead. In 1958, a year after Trudy and Jack were married and came to their present place, they under-bid the airlines and got the contract to bring the grain in by packhorse and raft.

The swan flock has built up to a point where it numbered 420 in the winter of 1969–70, and the birds eat between six and seven tons of wheat each winter. It is trucked from Bella Coola to the foot of Turner's trail, and getting it from there to the feeding area is a job that takes from four to six weeks in September and October, working from daylight to dark every day. The packing has to be finished before freezeup in early November.

There's a wagon track for three miles from the road. The grain is freighted that far by wagon. From there the Turners pack it to the lower end of Stillwater Lake on their four horses. Next they raft it to the head of the lake, load it on the horses once more and pack it another three miles to the foot of Lonesome. The last leg, the seven miles from there to the feeding ground, is also made by raft.

While they are at it, they take in everything they need

for a year, too, food, tools and whatever else is necessary, but their part of the load never amounts to more than a ton.

From the time the swan flock arrives in late October until the birds leave, usually not later than February or early March, either Trudy or Jack makes the five-mile hike down to the feeding area and back and puts out the daily ration of grain. They walk 150 miles a month, an average of about 500 a year, a total of close to 7,000 for the 13 years they have been doing it. Some of the walking is on snowshoes, but most of the time they are not needed, since the trail is kept well packed by walking it every day. However, it's work the Turners like, and they get a lot of satisfaction out of watching the steady growth of the trumpeter flock.

Getting back to the cougar Jack wanted for meat, he walked down the trail before daybreak and again in late afternoon, for three days, and waited around a couple of hours each time, hoping to ambush the cat at its kill. It was feeding regularly, but apparently only between darkness and first light, for he failed to get a glimpse of it.

One thing puzzled him. To judge by the way the deer carcass was disappearing the cougar was eating heavily, but each time it fed it moved the carcass to a new location, something he had not known one to do before. Every morning he found what was left of the deer dragged back a little farther into an area of windfall and down timber, and carefully covered with sticks and litter.

He pussyfooted in just at daylight the fourth morning as usual, stopping behind a clump of trees 30 or 40 yards from the carcass. It had been moved again, dragged to within three or four steps of a log that lay on the ground in a little open place—and the cougar was sitting beside the log. She—it turned out to be a young female—hadn't seen or heard the man, but the brush was too thick for a shot so he waited.

For a few minutes nothing happened. Then the cat sprang out, grabbed the deer and dragged it a couple of feet closer to the fallen tree, keeping low and moving fast, giving

Turner no chance for shooting. Next she bounded across
the log and flattened down, so that all he could see were her
round ears over the top of the log. But from the way they
moved he could tell that she was turning her head first one
way and then another, keeping a very sharp watch in all
directions.

Jack was carrying a .30-30 Winchester Model 94 with a
Lyman peep sight, an old and somewhat battered but still
very reliable gun that he takes with him just about everywhere he goes, for reasons of safety. He has had to use it in
self-defense quite a few times, when he ran across grizzlies
that were looking for trouble, something that's not uncommon along the Atnarko, and the old rifle goes with him on
all his hikes, slung over his shoulder by a length of nylon
cord.

Without a scope, he wanted to be sure of his shot before
he cut loose at the cougar, and at no time did she stand up
on all fours and expose herself in the open. She watched for
a long while, then suddenly leaped across the log a second
time and wrestled the deer a couple of feet nearer her
hiding place.

In the next hour and a half she repeated that performance
three times in all, until the carcass was wedged right against
the log. Each time, after she moved the kill, she leaped back
into hiding and Jack could see, from watching her ears and
the top of her head, that she was still keeping an eye peeled
as if she were lying in wait for something that might show
up from any direction at any minute.

He knew the cat was not aware of his presence, and her
actions were as puzzling as anything he had ever watched.
After she moved the deer carcass the third time she came
back over the log, settled down, with most of her still hidden
from his sight, and ate a little venison. But she still acted
restless and wary. She left off feeding very soon and leaped
back behind the upturned roots of the tree once more,
where she could be on her kill again in one short jump, and
Turner could still see her head swing this way and that. He

finally made up his mind that she had deliberately laid a trap for an intruder of some kind, but what it might turn out to be he couldn't even guess.

He got the break he was waiting for at last. A raven flopped down in the alders 20 feet behind her, making quite a clatter as it alighted. She leaped to her feet and wheeled that way as if stung. For the first time in almost two hours she was up on her feet and in clear view. Jack didn't lose a second. He was using factory-loaded 170-grain softpoint cartridges in the .30-30. His shot smashed in behind her shoulder, and she fell dead in her tracks.

She was in good condition, weighing around 100 pounds, just right for what he wanted. When he dressed her he opened the stomach, and was more puzzled than ever. He found only a few pounds of deer meat, and that didn't square at all with the heavy feeding he had observed on the carcass.

Trudy and he agreed they had a minor mystery on their hands, but they were busy with the usual spring work and didn't have time to think much about it. Certainly they had no inkling of the hair-raising sequel that was coming.

About two weeks later Susan went out to the chicken house one afternoon to get the eggs. It's a small log building, standing a short distance from the barn. She was gone only a few minutes when her father heard her call, in a tone that had to mean trouble.

He ran out on the porch. The hen house door was closed to a narrow crack, and Susan was yelling through that crack. Standing on the ground in front of her, less than three steps away, was a gaunt, hard-looking cougar. It was holding one of Turner's white hens in its mouth, but didn't seem to be paying much attention to the hen. It was staring fixedly in the direction of the child, and if her screaming had scared the big gaunt cat there was no sign of it. Susan had started to step outside, seen the cougar waiting for her, and ducked back in. It acted now as if it knew she was a prisoner and it could afford to wait.

*standing on the ground in front of her, less than three steps
away, was a gaunt, hard-looking cougar*

Jack shouted to her to stay inside and keep the door shut. At the sound of his voice the cat turned, sauntered unconcernedly through the open door of the barn 20 feet away, and disappeared inside.

Turner hurried back into the house for his rifle, ran down to the barn, closed the door and fastened it on the outside. He figured then that he had Mr. Cougar exactly where he wanted him.

Next he got a ladder, put it against the outside of the barn and climbed into the hayloft. Then he crossed the loft and went down another ladder into the stable, where the cat had vanished.

With the barn door shut the light was very poor, but after a minute Jack saw something white moving in a calf manger. He watched until he could see that it was the hen, being mouthed as the cougar fed, and then he made out a pair of greenish eyes watching him above that patch of white.

He put the sights of the .30-30 between them and touched off. His 170-grain softpoint went exactly where he wanted it to and the cat never knew what hit it. Jack climbed back outside and took Susan to the house.

The cougar proved to be a male, the most gaunt and hungry looking animal Turner had ever seen. It appeared to be about the same age as the female he had killed two weeks earlier, and they may well have been litter mates, but this one wouldn't have weighed more than 60 pounds. It was nothing but skin and bones.

One look told the reason. The cougar's throat, face and mouth were full of porcupine quills, many of them festered, and there were others in the stomach, too. At some time in the past the cat had also suffered a severe break in a hind leg. It had healed now, but had probably contributed to the animal's poor condition, since he couldn't hunt much while it was healing. That broken leg might even have gotten him started on porcupines.

The whole thing had been the strangest cougar encounter

in Jack Turner's experience, but when he and Trudy thought it over they came up with what seemed an entirely logical explanation. They knew now what the female had tried to ambush the morning Jack shot her at the deer carcass, or at least they thought they did.

It was Trudy's theory, and Jack concurred, that the disabled male had been following the female and feeding on her kills. That would account for the fact that although a lot of the deer had been eaten, her stomach held only a little of it. She must have got fed up with his pilfering finally, and dragged what was left of the buck in beside the log in a careful attempt to bait a trap for him. It was well laid, too. The two hours Jack watched her, she was waiting for him to come in, scanning the timber on all sides so she'd be ready, and moving the bait exactly where she wanted it, within one short leap of her hiding place behind the log. If the male had shown up she'd have been on him in a flash. And considering the condition he was in, she'd have given him a very hard trouncing and probably killed him.

The Turners never had any proof, of course, but that's the way they accounted for all that happened. When Jack killed the female he deprived the male of the livelihood he was relying on, since he was no longer in shape to make kills on his own. Two weeks later, driven by hunger, he invaded their yard and took the hen. And under those conditions, it seems very likely he would have attacked Susan as well had he had the chance.

As it was he had given her a bad scare, and Jack admitted that for a few seconds, when he saw the cat standing there in front of the chicken house door as if waiting for her to come out, a chill went up his back, too. As Trudy commented later, the Turners don't have many neighbors, but every now and then one comes along that they could do without. But at least Jack got a couple of cougar skins out of the deal and the family had some first-rate substitute for pork from the fat young female. The starving male wasn't fit for food.

Killer Grizzly
at Six Feet

I<small>N</small> the summer of 1957, the year Jack Turner and his wife Trudy moved to their new home on the Atnarko River above Lonesome Lake, Trudy went down to the garden one morning to get vegetables for lunch and came back mad as a hornet, and worried too.

She had surprised a sow grizzly with two young cubs, tearing the garden apart. Their prized rows of peas, beans, beets, squash and other vegetables had been half dug up and reduced to a shambles. The bears left voluntarily when Trudy showed up, which was somewhat unusual in the case of a sow-and-cub combination, but a lot of damage had already been done and it was a sure bet there was more to come. The old grizzly would be back. The Turners were dependent on that garden for a big share of their winter's food supply and they knew they would have to take strong measures to save what was left.

They are people who kill nothing needlessly. Trudy and Jack both have strong feelings on that score. But they don't hesitate to hunt for meat or to protect their property, either.

In this case they especially disliked the idea of doing away with a whole bear family, but there was no choice. Once the mother was killed they would have to shoot the little ones to save them from death by slow starvation.

Trudy's parents were the only neighbors for more than 20 miles. Her father, Ralph Edwards, who had lived on Lonesome Lake since 1912, came up with a bit of advice. If they killed one of the cubs, he thought the sow would be very likely to take the other one and leave the country. That would be much better than killing all three. They decided to try it.

They started sleeping in the open at the garden, with Jack's .30-30 Winchester Model 94 carbine, ready for the bears. For three nights nothing happened. But the fourth morning just at daylight they heard the grizzlies tearing things up again. When Jack grabbed the rifle and rolled out of his sack, however, the old lady saw him and hightailed for the woods with the cubs at her heels. She was out of sight in the timber before he could get a shot.

He followed and overtook the family in very thick brush. He could hear them moving off ahead, and after a minute or two he caught a glimpse of one of the youngsters and clobbered it then and there, killing it in its tracks.

He had no desire to pick a fight with the sow by walking in on her right then, so he backed cautiously out into the clearing, keeping his eyes peeled, and Trudy and he went back to the house for breakfast. He'd give the old bear ample time to clear out if she was going to.

He went back in a couple of hours to check on things. When he got to the place where he had killed the cub, walking slow and careful, it was gone, but he soon found a faint drag trail leading off into the brush. He followed it 30 feet, walking even more slow and careful, and it ended in a small pile of leaves and litter. The sow had buried her dead cub.

There was no sign of her or the live one, so Jack started

to do a little looking around and got the surprise of his life. He found a second blood-marked drag trail, starting near the first one, and after a minute or so he figured out what had happened. The two cubs had been running broadside to him, side by side and both in line with his shot, with the old bear following them. He had not seen the second cub in the thick cover, but his one shot had killed the two of them and the mother had dragged them both off. She wasn't going to be in a very good frame of mind.

Turner followed the second blood trail about 200 feet, until it ended as the first one had, in a raked-up mound of sticks and duff. And in that same instant he saw the old grizzly, standing in a thick windfall 100 feet away.

She wasn't growling or blustering. In fact she hadn't made a sound. But her little piglike eyes were blazing, she had them riveted on the man, and she looked mad all over.

They stared at each other for maybe 30 seconds, although it seemed much longer than that to Jack, neither of them moving an eyelash. Then she came for him in a fast rush, businesslike and deadly. Forty feet away she stopped and stood erect, growling and raging, sore to the roots of her tail.

"I couldn't blame her," Jack said afterward. "I had given her more than reason enough."

In a situation of that kind you have to decide at some point whether the animal can be bluffed out or whether it has to be killed. There wasn't much question this time, and when she dropped down and started for him again, moving at the hair-raising speed with which a bear attacks at close range (experienced hunters say they can outrun the best horse for a short distance, even in good going) Turner decided she was close enough. He smashed a 170-grain softpoint into her heart at 35 feet and she was dead almost as soon as she hit the ground.

That was Turner's first grizzly encounter at the new home (he had had bear trouble earlier, in other areas of British

Columbia) but it was destined to be far from the last. The Atnarko, rising in the rugged mountains to the south and fed by the melt waters of year-around snow and ice fields, is a major salmon stream. The salmon runs move in in September, starting with sockeyes and humpbacks, followed by the coho run. When the salmon appear the grizzlies start coming down off the mountains to fish in the valley where the Turner homestead lies. Salmon make up the main part of the bears' diet the rest of the fall and into December, when the coho run ends, and they get pretty numerous around the place. Jack once counted 10 adult grizzlies and five cubs along a 7-mile stretch of the Atnarko, all in one day, and he figures that on the average there are 10 or a dozen adults hanging around in that immediate area all through the fall, within a 6-mile radius of his house, up the river and down. With that many around, you're likely to run into one any time and any place.

Toward the end of October in 1965, for example, when Turner finished the annual job of packing in grain for the trumpeter swan flock he and his wife feed each winter, he and Trudy and their daughter Susan, then 6, moved their four horses to what they call their upper pasture, 15 miles up the Atnarko valley, where they sometimes run stock.

On the way up they encountered a female grizzly with three cubs. She got a little too aggressive for comfort, but Jack put a shot into a tree and scared her off. On the way back they saw two more, one at a time, but those gave them no trouble. Then they got home, only to find a medium-sized one walking around the yard 100 feet from the house, and he refused to let them in. They tried to drive him off but couldn't and finally Jack had to kill him.

"With grizzlies you never know when one will decide to pick a fight," Turner told me. "So I rarely venture beyond the cleared fields around our house without hanging that battered old .30-30 over my shoulder."

That precaution has saved his skin or his family's on at least two occasions, too.

A few years after he killed the garden-raiding bear family, he was finishing the fall job of grain packing, with his family, and the three of them undertook the hike of a mile and a half up the Atnarko from Lonesome Lake to their place after dark. They knew that wasn't exactly a good idea, and it's something they don't do often. But they were tired from days of packing and rafting wheat in from the road, and they disliked the idea of camping out in the woods another night when they were so close to home. They have a good wagon road along that part of the river, and they decided to risk it.

It was late October, the salmon run was at its peak, and there were likely to be fish-hungry bears all over the valley, but Jack hoped they wouldn't encounter any of them.

He was walking ahead and Trudy was following, carrying Susan in a small chair lashed to a packboard. The child was only about three at the time. The night was pitch dark and Turner saw nothing of the two cub grizzlies in the trail ahead. The first inkling he had that they were there was when he heard something scamper off into the brush 20 or 30 feet in front of him, and then there was the sound of two small animals crashing through a windfall to his right. The next thing he heard was the unmistakable growl of an angry grizzly and a third animal scrmbling up the 5-foot bank of the Atnarko on the other side of him. He knew from the noise that this one was not small and it took only a split second to figure that it was the sow, leaving her fishing and barreling up from the river to come to the rescue of her cubs.

She hit the trail about 20 feet in front of Jack and if she knew where the cubs had gone she paid no attention. Instead she whirled and came for him like forked lightning.

Turner could see her only as a black shape in the darkness, almost in is lap. He had the rifle in his hands by then, ready for action, but the light was too poor for him to see the barrel, let alone the sights. Behind him Trudy dodged around a tree, hoping that would give her and Susan some protection. Jack pointed the gun at the bear and hammered three fast shots in her direction, when she was only 10 feet away. She didn't bawl or grunt. Just spun around and ran, and he didn't know whether he had hit her or not. Half a minute later they heard her or the cubs go clattering up the mountain, breaking brush as they went. The Turner family made it the rest of the way home without incident.

The next morning Jack went back to find out what had happened. One of his shots had connected but he never learned where or how much damage it did. He found a little splash of blood in the trail and a few scattered drops on the leaves in the direction the bear had run, but the sign petered out when she went into the windfall. He hunted for four hours, along the river and up the mountainside, but found no trace of her or the cubs and they never saw hide nor hair of any of the bear family again.

As events turned out, those two encounters with cantankerous grizzlies were probably a good thing. They alerted Jack Turner for the next one he met, and that time he really needed to be ready.

In May of 1965 he left the house before breakfast one morning, just at daylight, and started up the Atnarko to repair the log fence that kept their milch cow from straying 15 miles up the river to join the family's other cows and bull in the upper pasture. They have that same type of fence, eight feet high and built of logs laid up like rails, enclosing their garden and the hay land around the house, too, to keep moose and deer out.

Because of the fence job Jack was carrying an ax, and as usual he had the .30-30 Winchester slung across his back by a length of nylon cord. He was not expecting to see a grizzly, for they rarely come down that low except in the fall when the salmon are running. But where Turner lives there is always the likelihood of running across a black bear or catching a fleeting glimpse of a cougar. And anyway, he makes it a routine practice to carry the rifle on all his hikes, just in case. It goes almost everywhere he does.

He had two miles to walk, on a good horse and cattle trail leading to the upper pasture. Most of the way the trail is within sight or hearing of the river.

It was a fine spring morning. The Atnarko brawled along on his left, tumbling and frothing down its rock-strewn gravel bed, a little milky from snow melt, as beautiful a river as you could find anywhere. Bunchberry and a few other early flowers were blooming along the trail, birds were flitting in and out of the brush, and Jack was enjoying every minute of his walk.

He came to a place where the trail, winding through big cedars and cottonwoods, opens out into a little sunny glade no bigger than a house. He rounded a bend, and there in the center of that glade stood the biggest grizzly he had ever laid eyes on, and he had seen more than 200, in just about every part of British Columbia, in the previous 20 years. The bear was staring straight in his direction and it was just 40 feet away.

It barely gave him time to be startled. It had seen him first, probably had watched him approach for half a minute or so. He rounded the turn in the trail, their eyes met and locked—and the bear was on the way. One instant Jack saw it, a fraction of a second later it was coming for him in a savage rush, running like a dog closing on its prey. It gave him no warning, not so much as a growl or a single popping of its teeth.

Turner was asked afterward whether it snarled or bawled as it ran at him. He does not know. It all happened too fast for him to remember details of that kind, but to the best of his recollection the bear was drooling as it came and he heard a low growl rumbling in its throat.

Jack dropped his ax and whipped the Winchester off his back, all in one motion. He had two things to do before he could shoot and he did them very fast. For reasons of safety, he makes it a rule to carry the rifle loaded in the magazine but not in the chamber. So he had to lever home a shell. And the Lyman peep sight with which the gun was equipped was folded down. It had to be raised.

The bear was almost on him when he slammed his shot, and even in that brief flash of time he recalled thinking that he'd have time for only one. He was using 170-grain softpoint factory loads. He hit the grizzly dead center between the eyes, just over the bulge of the nose, and the softpoint blew its whole brain out through a hole in the back of the skull. It was still running full tilt when Jack shot, but its head went down between its forelegs and it fell almost straight down. It didn't seem to roll or skid when it hit the ground, and it was so dead it didn't even twitch. Jack backed off a few steps, held the rifle on it and waited until he was sure there wasn't a spark of life left.

The sooner a bear is skinned after it is killed the better, so far as the condition of the pelt is concerned. Jack wanted Trudy to help him skin this one, and he decided to put off fixing the fence, go home and eat breakfast, and come back with her and take care of it without any delay.

The family ate, and then she and Susan both went back with him. Even he was a little surprised at what they found. His ax lay in the trail just six feet from the bear's nose. That meant the grizzly had been only about three feet from the muzzle of the rifle when he shot. He hadn't realized it had gotten quite that close.

It was a buster, by far the biggest grizzly Turner had ever seen, and save for being a little thin on the sides the pelt was a handsome trophy, well furred on the shoulders and along the back, rich dark brown in color.

What accounted for that furious charge the instant the man came into view around the bend in the trail?

"I'll never know the answer to that," Jack told me.

The bear was a male and there was no question of cubs being involved, nor could he find any evidence that it had been feeding on a dead animal anywhere in the vicinity.

Grizzlies in that area hardly ever make a kill of their

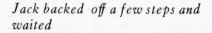

*Jack backed off a few steps and
waited*

own, unless they happen to get the odd chance at a sick or
helpless deer, mountain goat or cow. But they do feed on
any cougar or wolf kill they happen to find, as well as on
deer and moose that are wounded by hunters and left in the

woods to die. And once they take over such a carcass, they usually consider it theirs and run off all trespassers, too. But there was no sign of anything like that in the case of this bear.

Later that day, however, Turner did come across its bed, a 10-minute hike up the trail from where they had met. It had crossed the Atnarko and left the wet imprint of its body where it lay, apparently most of the night.

It must have started down the trail shortly after daylight, encountered the man and simply made up its mind that it was either going to run him off or teach him a lasting lesson. Probably the fact that he walked so close without knowing the bear was there had a lot to do with it. An animal as big and short tempered as a grizzly is very likely to resent any intruder at short range. They seem to think that if you weren't looking for trouble you wouldn't crowd them, and if trouble is what you want they are ready to oblige. That was likely the case this time.

Jack stretched this one's hide and they cleaned the skull and laid it aside. The more he looked at that skull and compared it with other grizzly skulls he had seen (he had several from kills of his own) the more it puzzled him. It was just too big to belong to an ordinary grizzly.

Finally he started to wonder whether he had killed a rare and unusual hybrid, the result of a chance mating between a grizzly and one of the big brownies from the coastal country of Southeastern Alaska, one that had strayed inland from its usual haunts and left a descendant behind. Turner had never heard of such a cross but the more he thought about it the more logical it seemed.

He finally wrote to I. McTaggart Cowan, a dean at the University of British Columbia at Vancouver, and a widely respected wildlife authority and an official measurer for the Boone and Crockett Club, and put the question to him. Cowan replied by suggesting that Jack ship the skull for examination.

He took that advice, and when Cowan's verdict came, in

May of 1966, he got another surprise. He had not killed a hybrid bear. The skull was that of a true grizzly. But apparently he had taken a new world's record for that species.

"According to my most careful measurements your skull measures 17 1/16 long and 9 12/16 wide, totalling 26 13/16," Cowan wrote. Turner had measured it before he sent it to Cowan and made it 27, and he knew that the world-record grizzly at that time, listed in the 1964 edition of the Boone and Crockett Club's "Records of North American Big Game," scored 26 10/16. That skull came from a bear killed at Rivers Inlet, B.C., in 1954.

"Barring the eventuality of another equally large skull having turned up within the last year, this certainly seems to me to be a new record," Cowan went on.

Jack had some misgivings as to whether his bear would finally go into the Boone and Crockett list as a new world's record. When he smashed his shot into the grizzly's head at two yards he had blown a good-sized chunk of bone out of the right side of the skull, toward the back, and he knew that the Boone and Crockett score-keepers follow very strict rules where damaged skulls are concerned.

On that score, however, Cowan had this to say: "I am sure that the remaining portion of the skull is yielding completely accurate measurements. If anything, the width would have been a little greater had the skull been intact."

In the end Turner did not quite take top place. He entered his bear in the 1966–67 Boone and Crockett Big-Game Competition, and came out with an official score of 26 10/16, which left it tied with the No. 1 grizzly killed in 1954.

But on the basis of what Cowan told him, Jack still believes that he shot the biggest grizzly ever taken anywhere, and everything considered, he was well satisfied with the outcome. The shot that dropped it, three feet from the muzzle of his rifle, almost certainly cost him the world-record grizzly crown. But when he fired that shot it was either him or the bear, and he knows it.

Handgunner's
Last Hunt

It was a cheerless, windy September day, with the tops of the mountains obscured by heavy clouds. But no rain was falling, and visibility down by the sea was good. It was no worse than fall days are likely to be along the bleak coast of the Alaska Peninsula, in fact better than many.

The red-trimmed, white Super Cub N1640A warmed its engine, turned for the takeoff across the choppy, lead-colored waters of Chignik Lagoon. The little plane came up on its floats, throwing twin rooster tails, lifted clear and headed east along the coast.

Two men watched it fade to a speck and go out of sight in the overcast sky. They were Capt. Alec Pedersen, 40-year-old owner and skipper of the salmon boat *Jeanette Sue,* and Leroy Hall, winter storekeeper at the Chignik Cannery. Pedersen had talked a few days before with the two men now leaving in the Cub, Hall had sold them gas and supplies only that morning. He believes he was the last to see them alive.

It occurred to him that although flying conditions were not bad at Chignik the men might encounter dirty weather if they continued east as far as Shelikof Strait and Kodiak Island. But neither he nor Pedersen suspected that they were watching N1640A take off on its last flight, that no one would ever lay eyes again on the pilot or his passenger, and that within a few days the Super Cub would be the object of one of the most intensive air searches ever mounted in Alaska.

One of the two men who disappeared from sight and from the earth that gray morning of September 27, 1965, was Al Goerg, a big-game hunter, handgun buff and freelance writer from Port Angeles, Washington, well known in outdoor circles across the country. The other was 30-year-old Darrell Pennington, known to his friends as Swede, of Forks, Washington, an experienced Alaskan bush pilot who was at the controls of the Cub.

Goerg, 53 years old, had operated a gun-shop business for a number of years at Port Angeles, where he and his wife Anne had lived through the 25 years of their marriage and where their two sons and daughter had grown up. He had sold the shop in 1964 to devote all his time to hunting and fishing, the field testing of outdoor equipment, and writing. He had hunted in South America, Hawaii and Alaska, as well as nearer home, and had published two books, *Pacific Northwest Hunting,* and *Pioneering Handgun Hunting.* The latter came out in June of 1965, only three months before he was lost, and won praise from sportsmen abroad as well as in this country.

"Al Goerg had helped to carry handgun hunting into a new era," Bob Cole, a friend and hunting partner said of him afterward. "He hunted with animal cunning, seemed to thrive on dangerous situations, and his methods were basic and effective. As a result of his writing people were losing the old gun-on-hip, offhand shooting ideas about handguns. He made many realize that a handgun with a scope is a fine hunting weapon, handier than a rifle and a little more challenging."

In "Mountain Goat with a Handgun," in *Outdoor Life* for June of 1957, Goerg had told of killing a good trophy goat in the Cascade Mountains of central Washington with an unscoped Colt .357 Magnum loaded with lead bullets he had hollow-pointed by hand. His was in all likelihood the first goat ever killed with such a firearm.

In "Should We Kill Bears This Way?" in the magazine in August, 1962, Goerg reported on the snaring of blacks on Washington's Olympic Peninsula, an all-out war waged by timber interests, and raised the question whether a game animal rated among the top trophies in the country did not deserve a better break.

And in January of 1965, less than a year before he went on his final hunt, *Outdoor Life* ran another exciting story of his, "Bears with a Handgun," in which he related how he and a hunting partner killed two good blacks on a spring hunt in the Olympic Mountains, using Smith & Wesson .22 Jets that fired 37-grain hollow points at almost 2,000 feet per second. Both revolvers were fitted with J-2.5 Weaver scopes.

A few months after that story appeared Al Goerg left for Alaska on the hunting and fishing trip that was to prove his last. He flew north from Port Angeles to Anchorage on September 7. There he rendezvoused with Pennington, who was to fly him on the hunt. From Anchorage, the following day, the two men headed west for the lakes, rivers and wild mountainous country of the Alaska Peninsula. For almost three weeks little was heard from them. To this day no one knows precisely where they went or all the details of the hunting and fishing they did.

Anne Goerg had two brief letters from her husband. One was written from Anchorage on September 8, the day he and Pennington left there. The second, from King Salmon on the Bristol Bay side of the Peninsula, was dated September

17. In it Al reported that he had had wonderful luck, had
gotten the fishing story and pictures he wanted, and said the
two men were headed west down the Peninsula for another
week or so of hunting.

That same day the Super Cub refueled at Port Heiden,
125 miles west of King Salmon. Then the hunters dropped
out of sight again. On September 24 they landed on Chignik
Lagoon, a big brackish inlet connected with the sea by a
narrow channel, the site of the isolated Chignik salmon
cannery, 150 miles west of Kodiak Island. The cannery
had closed for the season a few weeks earlier but Hall, the
winter storekeeper, was still there, as was Capt. Pedersen.

Goerg and Pennington bought gas and a few supplies
from the storekeeper. They told Pedersen they were camping
at a small research cabin on Black Lake, about 20 miles
inland from Chignik Lagoon, that their hunt was winding
up and they'd be leaving for home in a few more days.

They asked about a good place to make brown-bear pictures, and Pedersen, who worked as engineer aboard a crab
boat in winter and was a licensed guide and pilot, handling
bear hunters in spring and using a small float plane on his
hunts, recommended the Hook Bay area 20 miles to the east.

The two had brought caribou and moose meat to Chignik
and given it to the native families there, probably in com-
pliance with Alaska's wanton-waste law, which requires that
the flesh of all game except bears, wolves and wolverines be
salvaged for human use.

Then, on September 27, the Super Cub came into Chignik
again, refueled, and vanished in the cloudy sky in the direction of Kodiak Island and home.

Goerg and Pennington had been scheduled to return to
Anchorage by September 22, but their failure to arrive on
time caused no concern. It was not uncommon for Al to
overstay his time on a hunt, and for 25 years he had urged
Anne never to worry if he was overdue.

"A hunting trip doesn't end in a certain number of days,"

he had told her many times. "It ends when a man gets what he goes after. Don't worry about me. I'll write or call as soon as I get where I can."

She tried to follow that advice now. But as the days dragged on and no word came, fear mounted in her that something had gone wrong. She controlled it and waited until the end of the first week in October. By then her misgivings had grown to certainty and she sounded an alarm. On October 9 aircraft N1640A was reported to the Coast Guard Air Station at Kodiak as missing, and the search was launched. It was long and determined, even by Alaskan standards.

Pennington and Goerg had filed no flight plan before leaving Chignik. There were no facilities there for doing that. Capt. Pedersen believed, however, that from his conversation with them he knew what they intended to do. They had come from Anchorage by way of King Salmon, and he thought they meant to go home that same way, first crossing the Alaska Peninsula to the Bristol Bay side, rather than flying by way of Shelikof Strait between the mainland and Kodiak Island. He believed their first stop would have been at King Salmon, where they had been seen earlier, and that they intended to file their flight plan there.

In any case, because their route was not known the search area had to be a huge one. It was also as difficult a place as any on earth in which to locate a downed aircraft.

It extended east and west for 500 miles from Homer on the Kenai Peninsula to Pavlof Bay, 75 miles west of Chignik on the Alaska Peninsula, and in addition it took in all of Afognak and most of Kodiak Island. It included thousands of square miles of timbered mountains, countless bays and arms of the sea, the rock slides and snow fields of the rugged Aleutian Range, all of Katmai National Monument, the awesome Valley of 10,000 Smokes, and the barren, unpeopled wastes of the Alaska Peninsula.

Some of the country was open, but some of it was so

heavily forested that a wrecked plane, down in the spruce and alder and devil's club, might never be found. There were smoking volcanoes and lofty snow-crowned peaks, like Chiginagak, Veniaminof and Aniakchak, where an aircraft might crash, be covered by fresh snow and lie hidden to the end of time.

Somewhere in that vast tangle of wilderness N1640A was down, unless it had fallen into the sea instead, the two men probably hurt or dead. Although the search was concentrated along the beaches and on the big inland lakes where a float plane would be most likely to land in the event of trouble, it also combed that huge roadless block one square mile after another.

Coast Guard, Air Force and Civil Air Patrol planes flew a total of 45 sorties that added up to almost 200 hours in the air, carrying observers on every flight.

On October 20 Anne Goerg could no longer endure the agony of waiting at home for word that did not come. At 2:30 in the morning of a sleepless night she suddenly decided that she must go to Kodiak and take part in the search.

At Kodiak she joined Gail Denny, a Sitka school teacher who was engaged to Pennington. The two women chartered five private aircraft to help with the search, in addition to the massive efforts being made by official agencies, and they went out on some of the flights themselves as observers. Anne remembers flying so low she could see bear tracks in the sand of the beaches.

As the days went by hope faded that the missing men would be found alive. If the Cub had come down along the coast or on a lake the air search could hardly have failed to locate it. And if it had landed somewhere in the mountains and Goerg and Pennington were able to travel, they would have made their way out to the beach and been sighted. Both were competent and experienced outdoorsmen. They could be counted on to get themselves out of whatever difficulties they confronted, unless they were injured or already dead. Of course any severe injury meant death unless they were found soon.

The official search was abandoned toward the end of October, with snow covering most of the area and winter not far away. Anne Goerg went home, feeling that everything possible had been done and confident that any fresh leads would be carefully checked.

"In Alaska a search never ends," she had been told. "Every plane that goes up looks for the one that's missing. Even passengers are alerted to keep an eye on the ground."

She arranged for private aircraft to do more searching if weather permitted, and the last sortie was flown by Bob Leonard of Kodiak Airways on November 16, along the north shore of Shelikof Strait, with winter at hand. He found nothing.

There was good reason for the failure of the long search. A day or two before it began heavy snow had fallen on the mountains in the Chignik area. What the searchers had looked for all those weeks was a small white aircraft that, although they could not know it, lay now in a twisted mass of wreckage buried deep under the new snow, on a steep mountainside on Cape Kumlik, only 40 miles from Chignik Lagoon where the last flight had begun.

"At least three times I personally searched the exact area where the plane was found," Orin Seybert, head of Peninsula Airways at King Salmon and a bush pilot who had done a lot of flying over the Alaska Peninsula, told *Outdoor Life*. "But by that time the snow was down to sea level and the wreckage was covered."

Back in Port Angeles Anne Goerg clung for a time to a frail thread of hope, but as the savage gales of winter swept across the Alaska Peninsula and snow many feet deep locked it in, she resigned herself to the fact that the two men were dead.

She had been a teacher in Indiana before she and Al were married, and she went back to that, taking a job in the Port

Angeles school system, and also continuing to sell by mail order the items of outdoor equipment he had developed. By spring the only hope she kept alive was that some day the wreckage of the Super Cub would be found, ending her nagging wonder as to just what had occurred.

That was slow to happen. The snow-covered mountainside on Cape Kumlik kept its grim secret for 10 long months. In July of 1966, however, persistent rumors began to be heard around Chignik that an unidentified fishing boat had found the missing plane, but that those who made the discovery were keeping silent for reasons of their own.

Then, on the morning of July 23, definite word sputtered over the radio at the Coast Guard Rescue Co-ordination Center at Kodiak, from the Chignik Cannery. Aircraft wreckage had been sighted on a mountain on Cape Kumlik. The seine boat *Judy C,* owned and skippered by Rudolph Carlson, had seen a flash of sunlight reflected from metal, some 1,500 feet above the sea, and had made the find. That evening a second radio message reported that no evidence of human remains had been found but that there were a pair of pants on one of the aircraft seats. The mystery was deeper than ever.

Radio communication was poor at the time, and the Coast Guard did not learn who had gone ashore and found the pants. To this day the records do not clear up that point.

That same evening Carlson talked about the find to his friend Capt. Pedersen, the salmon boat skipper who had watched the Super Cub take off from Chignik Lagoon that cloudy day the previous September. Because he had met and talked with the two men, Pedersen felt a special interest in their fate.

For the next four days heavy fog blanketed the coast and hid the mountains. But on the morning of July 28 a strong west wind blew the fog away and he headed his 36-foot *Jeannette Sue* for Cape Kumlik to have a look.

The mountains on Kumlik rise abruptly from the sea, treeless and barren, with grassy tundra above the beach. The nearest timber, except for alder tangles along streams, is in the Katmai country 100 miles or more to the east, and the peaks are bare rocks.

Capt. Pedersen saw what he was looking for when he was 15 miles away, the wreckage of a small aircraft lying below the crest of a steep slope on the north side of Cape Kumlik, where his friend Carlson had told him it lay.

He, his son Morry, and Knud Olsen, a nephew, went ashore to walk up to the wreck. It was a 4-mile hike, uphill all the way and part of the time on very steep slopes. It took the three men two hours to reach the scene, some 500 feet from the top of the mountain.

There was nothing left of the Super Cub but the crumpled fuselage, frame, floats, engine and pieces of wing, all rolled into a tangle of wreckage or scattered over the slope. It was clear at once that no one could possibly have survived the crash that had demolished the plane. The men in it had died instantly.

The number of the aircraft, still intact, read N1640A. The fate of Al Goerg and Darrell Pennington was finally established beyond all doubt. "It was just a long sadness that had found an ending at last," Anne Goerg said of that sorry discovery.

There were questions still to be answered. To begin with, the wreckage lay on the north slope of the mountain. Flying from Chignik, the men would have come over Kumlik from the south. Just what had happened?

The Pedersen party climbed the steep rock slide to the crest of the mountain, and cleared that up. The Cub had approached from the south, probably turning inland to cross the Alaska Peninsula on the way to King Salmon, and had tried to fly through a saddle between two peaks. Either because the mountain tops were hidden in clouds that day or because a strong and turbulent downdraft had caught them unexpectedly, they had failed to clear the ridge and had slammed into the mountain a few feet below instead. So narrow was the margin by which the two men had met death that the plane, somersaulting from its terrific impact, had cleared the crest completely and smashed into the rocks 30 feet down on the other side. Another dozen feet of altitude would have spelled safety. And had they flown one more mile to the east they could have gone around Cape Kumlik at sea level.

Orin Seybert believed turbulence had been their undoing. "The way they went they needed about 2,500 feet to clear,"

they failed to clear the ridge

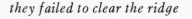

he said. "The wind was from the northwest that day, blowing off the mountains, which would mean strong up-and-down drafts, and it seems they were heavily loaded. It would be easy to get caught without enough altitude if they were cutting it close to start with."

The prop and float bumpers lay where N1640A had first hit. Apart from them, the only part of the aircraft that had stayed on the south side of the mountain was a chunk of wing that had slid or rolled 600 feet down the steep slope before it came to rest. Capt. Pedersen found it there. The rest of the Cub had rolled and tumbled 500 feet down the north slope, apparently starting a big rock slide with the force of its crash.

Alec Pedersen believes that slide holds the answer to the second question, why no bodies were found with the wreckage. Save for a few fragments of bone, apparently scattered by bears or wolverines, he found nothing of the remains of the two men who had been in the plane, and he thinks that most or all of their bodies may still be buried under that slide.

In a small ravine on the mountainside, a quarter mile below the wreckage, Morry Pedersen made the big find of the day, Al Goerg's sea bag, intact and in relatively good condition.

That bag held, among other things, Al's Model XP100 Remington Fireball, a bolt-action handgun with hand-made stock, fitted with a Redfield 2x scope. The stock was partially crushed and the leather holster covered with mould from close to a year of exposure, but the action and barrel were undamaged. Also in the bag were a pair of Bausch & Lomb 7x35 binoculars, two compasses, a pocket knife, some ammunition, a spoon and fork, spare camera lens and tripod, spinning reel, prayer book and small notebook, a few items of clothing and 26 rolls of film. The film proved the most revealing find of all.

Twelve rolls of it had not been exposed. Unprotected from weather, they were torn and mildewed. But 14 exposed rolls, some color, some black-and-white, had been carefully wrapped in double plastic bags, securely tied, and were in perfect condition. When Anne Goerg had them developed, weeks later, they provided a fascinating record of the hunting and fishing the two men had done.

Capt. Pedersen took back to Chignik with him everything he found, to be turned over to the proper authorities.

On August 1 a three-man official party flew to the site in a helicopter piloted by Lieut. Cmdr. George H. Garbe, Head of Operations at the Coast Guard Air Station at Kodiak. The other two men aboard were Elwess Dyer of the Anchorage office of the Civil Aeronautics Board and Trooper John Malone of the Alaska State Police.

They conducted an on-the-scene investigation of the crash. Garbe reported the findings as consisting of aircraft wreckage strewn over a wide area, human bones, teeth and hair, clothing, a shaving kit, a small vial of gold nuggets, and the converted handgun already recovered. The wreckage lay at an elevation of about 2,100 feet, higher than had been estimated earlier, below a saddle between two peaks overlooking Aniakchak Bay.

Trooper Malone sent *Outdoor Life* a summary of what he observed. "The investigation disclosed that the aircraft was under power, struck below the saddle and then slid down the north slope," he wrote. "The majority of the baggage was strewn on the side of the slope from the point of impact for 100 feet down. It is believed the wreckage was further scattered by spring snow slides. Above the cockpit area and immediately below the wreckage, unidentifiable human remains were found."

Mel J. Personett, Alaska's Commissioner of Public Safety, said in response to an inquiry, "Some details of an investigation such as this do not belong anywhere other than in a police report," but he did not elaborate.

All the personal effects recovered at the crash site by Capt. Pedersen and the official team were placed in the custody of U.S. District Judge John B. Mason at Kodiak, to be sent on to Anne Goerg. More than a year after Al was lost, she received the relics of the ill-fated flight, his hand-gun, the exposed films he had taken on the trip and the few cameras with him, a Rolleicord and a Ricoh, two pairs of other things that had been found.

One major puzzle remained unsolved. Al Goerg had two binoculars, and five guns in addition to the Remington Fire-ball. The guns were a Smith and Wesson .44 Magnum hand-gun with Weaver scope, a favorite that he usually wore when hunting; a Winslow Bushmaster Regent rifle in 7mm Remington Magnum caliber; an Ithaca Model 37 slide-action shotgun in 12 gauge; an Ithaca 12-gauge single-shot, scoped; and a Numrich muzzle-loading, black-powder rifle.

Of this equipment only one pair of binoculars and the Remington handgun were found and returned to his widow. Did that mean that the wreck had been discovered and looted of everything of value that could be found, weeks before the *Judy C* spotted it on July 23, as rumor had claimed? And did the looters then keep silence for understandable reasons?

The missing binoculars, cameras and guns hinted strongly that such was the case. Capt. Pedersen was convinced of it, and during the investigation Trooper Malone said he had reason to believe it had happened.

"There were boats in Aniakchak Bay continuously from about July 1," Orin Seybert pointed out. "I'm sure the wreckage was sighted within days of the time the snow re-ceded."

Anne Goerg was later asked to furnish the serial numbers of the guns to Alaska authorities, against the chance they might turn up someday, and she herself believed the plane had been found and looted.

Of the few personal effects that were recovered, only the 14 rolls of exposed film threw any light on where Goerg and Pennington had gone between their departure from An-chorage on September 8 and the time they left Chignik for home 19 days later, what hunting and fishing they had done and what their luck had been.

It had never been Al's custom to keep a diary and this trip was no exception. The small notebook found in his sea bag contained only a few notations on the cost of spring and fall hunts, air fares and the rates for aircraft charter, a list of Anchorage hotels and motels, and one terse reference, undated, that read, "Went to bear and moose lake by compass, due west. This lake is about 30 miles from Black Lake."

Neither Al Goerg nor Darrell Pennington left a log behind, but from the mute evidence of the pictures they had taken it was possible to piece together a story of a successful and exciting trip, in the remote and beautiful country between Katmai and Chignik. Those pictures constituted a remarkable diary from two men dead almost a year before the films were found in the mildewed sea bag on the mountainside above Aniakchak Bay.

Al and Swede had been in the Katai National Monument, for they had a shot of a trail sign marking the Brooks River Ranger Station there. They had made wonderful catches of salmon, steelheads and dolly vardens, and had caught grayling on at least one occasion. They had visited an unoccupied cabin, and climbed the wooden ladder to the cache to store their own supplies on poles beyond reach of bears.

They had encountered some bad weather, for a few of the pictures showed the Super Cub moored to the beach on a black and foggy day, with angry surf hammering at the pontoons. They had photographed waterfalls on unidentified rivers, and huge brown bear tracks along the muddy banks of salmon streams and in the sand of beaches. They had found the usual remains of salmon half eaten by bears.

The men had killed two caribou and a moose. Because they posed pictures of the scope-sighted Remington handgun with the moose rack, it seemed likely that Al had shot it with that gun. One of the caribou was posed the same way, and another shot showed him walking up to it carrying the Fireball. There was also a red fox that he probably killed with it. All in all, it seemed apparent that for him the trip had been primarily another handgun hunt, one of the many he had made.

On a treeless beach, the pictures showed, he had downed a good brown bear, but he was carrying the Bushmaster Magnum that day.

It had been a productive hunt, and finally the two men had succeeded in achieving one of the major objectives Al had had in mind from the time he planned the trip. He had made an agreement with the Wright & McGill Company of Denver, makers of Eagle Claw fishing tackle, that he would undertake to get them a highly unusual picture for use in their advertising, a shot of him in an Alaskan stream using their equipment, with a brown bear fishing in the same pool.

It was a hazardous undertaking and it took nerve, for the big browns dislike company at close range, especially on their fishing grounds, and their resentment is likely to be hair-triggered and violent. But Goerg and Pennington brought it off. In fact they came close to doing it twice, and the pictures proved it.

The first one, that almost filled the bill, showed Al standing in tall grass on the bank of a stream, holding a freshly caught fish, and near the far bank a burly bear busy with its own fishing. They were not quite in the pool together but they did not lack much of it.

The prize picture was made on a big river somewhere in the mountains, with timber along both banks. In it, Goerg was in midstream, fishing a stretch of fast water, and downstream a bear was standing near shore, staring fixedly in his direction.

If Al Goerg had lived he might well have been as proud of those two pictures as of any trophy he ever took with a gun. As one of his friends said, "What a damned shame that such a good trip had to end in a crackup on a cloud-hung mountain top!"

Outdoor Life ran the Al Goerg story in May of 1968, after many months of patient detective work in putting it together.

It was illustrated with more than a dozen of the pictures Goerg and Pennington had taken, and any reader identifying the location of the pictures was asked to write the magazine. A gratifying flood of mail resulted, and a great deal of the mystery was cleared up.

"The photograph of Goerg and the bear was taken at Dumpling Mountain on the Brooks River," wrote John Walatka of Northern Consolidated Airlines from King Salmon. "Before I wrote this letter, my wife and I went to the exact spot.

"The picture of the food cache and ladder was taken at the National Park Service campground at Brooks River. The tower in one of the pictures is the Kulik Camp Tower, a wind-charger that kept batteries charged. And that's Jim Marlatt's old cabin on the right in the same picture."

Another reader, Russell L. Todd of California, identified a picture that showed Swede wading a river just above a waterfalls as having been taken at the famous Brooks River Falls in Katmai National Monument.

Duane Phinney of Washington recognized a picture of the plane moored on a storm-swept beach, with part of a small cabin showing at one side. "The cabin is located on Black Lake and belongs to the Fisheries Research Institute of the University of Washington," he wrote. "I was in charge of a sockeye-salmon research project there in 1964, and spent many nights in it. It is left open in winter so it can be used by stranded hunters or flyers."

And more than 30 months after the story appeared, in January of 1970, David Bogart, who had been the ranger in charge at Katmai National Monument from 1962 to 1965 and who had met Al Goerg a couple of years before his death and talked Alaska with him, wrote to identify still another of the pictures.

"The bear tracks are on the Savonoski Delta, not in mud or sand but in volcanic ash," he said.

The most surprising development of all came in May of 1968, almost two years after the wrecked aircraft was found.

A year before that Jim Cloward, operator of a gun shop in Seattle, had received for reblueing and other repairs a rifle in rather poor condition.

It was a Winslow Bushmaster, Regent grade, in 7mm Remington Magnum caliber. That was the make, model and caliber of the rifle carried by Goerg, one of his five guns that Alaska State Police and the U.S. Coast Guard believed were taken from the wrecked Piper Cub by unknown persons, before its discovery on Cape Kumlik was made known.

Most revealing of all, Al Goerg's name was engraved in the Redfield 3x to 9x Variable scope on the rifle.

Knowing little or nothing of the Goerg tragedy, Cloward did not connect the rifle with it until a year later, when he read the *Outdoor Life* story.

He then reported the affair to Seattle police and also got in touch with Anne Goerg. At that point the final link in the chain of evidence was forged. The serial number of the gun Cloward had repaired was that of Goerg's Bushmaster.

Long before that, however, the gun had been claimed by the man who brought it in for repairs. Cloward was able to furnish his name, address and a description of him to Seattle police, and a detective learned that he had left Seattle the previous October "to go back to Alaska." The information was turned over to Mel J. Personett, Alaska Commissioner of Public Safety and head of the State Police.

At that point the case took an unexpected turn. About the time Jim Cloward was reading the story in *Outdoor Life* and putting Seattle police on the track, the man who had the gun also read it. He went at once to the Alaska State Police with the rifle and his story.

He and a companion, he said, had found the demolished

aircraft in July of 1966. They had searched the area, but finding no trace of bodies had concluded that the wreck was an old one, previously discovered and reported, and he had taken the rifle in the belief it was legitimate salvage.

The police accepted the story. Today the Bushmaster is back in Anne Goerg's hands, the riddle solved.

"The case is completed, and no prosecution is anticipated," Personett told me.

The Guide
a Grizzly
Scalped

Roy Hamilton came into the moose-hunting camp on Boss Mountain that cold October night with news that electrified everybody. He thought he and the hunters he was guiding had seen a grizzly that afternoon.

They had caught a glimpse of a bear running off through a thick growth of firs. When they walked up to the place they found what was left of the decayed carcass of a cow moose, most of it eaten, that the bear had been feeding on. They figured that a hunter had shot her early in the fall, out of season, and left her in the woods to rot.

"I didn't see enough to be sure," Roy said, "but I don't think that bear was a black!"

It was the fall of 1963. There were six hunters in the party, camped on Boss Creek, in rough, heavily timbered country a few miles west of Wells Gray Provincial Park, in British Columbia 200-odd miles north of the United States border.

Wells Gray has some of the finest snow-peak scenery in that part of British Columbia. It also has an abundance of mountain game. The park itself was closed to hunting, but the area around it was top country for moose, caribou, sheep and goats.

The outfitter was Bus Hamilton, Roy's father, in summer the operator of the Ten-ee-ah—which is Shuswap for moose—Fishing Camp on Spout Lake north of Lac la Hache. In the fall he outfitted and guided hunters in the mountains east of his place.

Among the guides working for him this time was Eddie Dixon, a 44-year-old Shuswap Indian from the Canim Lake Reservation east of Lac la Hache. Dixon had only one arm, and that was to play a major part in what was coming.

Eddie was guiding two hunters from Las Vegas. George Riddle was a steel-company contractor, Cleo Cripps headed a firm that made and installed air conditioning equipment. Riddle was 56, Cripps about 20 years younger.

The party was using a sleeping tent, but doing its cooking in the open. Although it was only late October, the weather in the high country was cold, and there were about eight inches of snow on the ground. Conditions were rough for hunting and, likely for that reason, nobody was having much luck with moose, the main thing they were after.

Then Roy Hamilton came in with his story about the bear he had seen, and Dixon's two clients lost all interest in moose hunting. "What are we wasting our time on them for, if there's a grizzly around?" Riddle asked. "I'd rather have one bear rug than a dozen moose."

Cripps agreed, and the three men started to lay their plans for the next day. Roy told Eddie exactly where to find the moose carcass. They would have a look at it the first thing in the morning, and if they failed to find the bear they would wait around for him. Sooner or later he was almost sure to come back to it.

About that time Bus Hamilton, who was in charge of

the party, sounded a warning. "Don't forget what you're after," he said. "Nobody ever knows what a grizzly will do, but if you shoot him and don't kill him you'll likely have a fight on your hands. Keep your guard up."

"I guess we didn't take him as seriously as we should have," Dixon admitted later.

He had lived in bear country all his life and had plenty of dealing with blacks, but had never hunted grizzlies, and neither had the two Las Vegas hunters. But they pointed out to Bus that there wasn't much danger of a bear getting close enough to three men with good guns to do any damage. Famous last words!

They rode away from camp at daybreak the next morning, in a light fall of snow, with a miserably cold wind sweeping through the timber. Riddle was carrying a .30-06 Winchester Model 70, Cripps the same rifle in .300 Magnum caliber. The guide's rifle was a 6.5mm Norwegian Krag, a converted military gun. They were well equipped for what they had in mind.

Between a quarter and a half mile from the place Roy Hamilton had described, they stopped and tied the horses and went ahead on foot. They were getting close to the spot when Dixon heard ravens squawking up ahead. "The bear is home," he told Cripps and Riddle in a low undertone.

"How do you know?"

"Hear those birds? He's keeping them away from their breakfast."

They were 90 feet from the grizzly, moving carefully through fairly open jackpine, before they saw him, and it was plain to the guide in the first instant that he knew they were there. He had heard or smelled them, and was standing beside the moose remains with his forefeet up on a log, broadside, swinging his head from side to side and sniffing to get a better noseful of secnt.

Hunters who have had wide experience with grizzlies say it's almost a sure bet that if one lets you get as close as 90 feet he intends to come for you. There is very little chance that a man can approach that close without the bear knowing it, and by that time he has made up his mind what he is going to do. If he decides to clear out, he's already gone. If he's still there, you can expect a rumble.

Eddie didn't know that at the time, but likely it would have made no difference. The hunters didn't lose a second. Dixon touched Cripps on the shoulder and pointed the instant the bear came into view, and Riddle barked, "Let him have it, Cleo."

The .300 Magnum bellowed, and the bear dropped off the log and spun in a series of cartwheels, like a big overgrown cat. Eddie saw a patch of red start to spread on his side, but too far back, and he had a hunch there was trouble coming.

The guide slammed a shot from his 6.5, but it had no effect.

"Keep firing," he yelled at the two hunters. "When that bear lands he's going to come for us."

It proved a good forecast. The grizzly started for them the instant he regained his feet, bawling and growling, smashing through a thick growth of small cedars. They could see only his back. Eddie shot again in the hope of stopping him, but missed, and then the bear broke into the open 50 feet away and all three men were shooting at once.

In all, they hit the grizzly six times as he was coming at them, without knocking him down. He was shot twice in the mouth, one on each side of the jaws; once in the throat; twice in the chest, again on each side; and once in a foot. Those six were in addition to Cleo's first hit just behind the ribs.

At some point somebody belted him back on his rear end. He slowed, skidded to a stop and went down on his haunches for a second. Then he was up and coming again as if nothing had happened.

The guide had had three shells in his Krag to start with. That meant only one was left after the bear came out of the thick brush. Eddie used it and was out of soap. In that same instant he heard Cleo yell, "My gun is empty!"

Dixon was one-armed, as I mentioned earlier. He had been working in a sawmill in 1959 when a small stick fell against the headsaw. He reached for it and his left hand went down between the saw and the table. He couldn't get hold of anything to yank himself free, and the saw, chewing into his sleeve, pulled him down three times. It was either his neck or his arm, so he let the arm go. It was severed below the elbow and since then a steel hook had replaced the left hand. He got along with it well enough, but found it awkward for some jobs. A one-armed rifleman can't reload as fast as a man with two hands, for instance, and Eddie knew now that he was going to have to go into a bear fight with an empty gun.

"Split up!" he yelled.

Cripps dodged 10 or 12 feet to his left, Riddle about the same distance to the right. For some reason the bear got its eye on George about that time and swerved straight for him. Dixon saw him poking fresh shells frantically into his Winchester, but the guide knew the grizzly wasn't going to allow enough time for that.

It all happened in a second or two. Eddie was a few years younger than Riddle and thought maybe he could move faster. Besides, he was the guide and it was his job to keep the bear off his hunter if he could. He took one quick step as the grizzly came around a small jackpine, and jabbed the stock of his rifle in its face to divert it.

The bear grabbed the stock, put his teeth clear through it, split it as if spikes had been driven in, and tore the butt plate away. In the same instant he slapped the rifle out of Eddie's hand with a forepaw and it went spinning into the brush 30 feet away. Then he walloped the Indian on the shoulder and knocked him flat.

Dixon shoved his steel hook into the bear's mouth to keep the enraged brute away from his face, but the bear

took care of that about the way it had the rifle. Eddie
didn't lose the hook, but the hard fiberglass cuff will carry
teeth marks as long as it lasts. The grizzly bit down once,
cuffed the steel hand aside and grabbed the guide's good
arm. Dixon felt him crunch down and thought that arm was
a goner, too. But luckily, although the teeth went all the
way through, they missed bone.

"I suppose it's only natural for a man to have strange
thoughts at a time like that," Eddie told me.

The thing he remembered most clearly afterward about
that savage attack was the bear's horribly foul breath in
his face. It had been feeding on moose carrion, probably
for two or three weeks, and the smell was as bad as if the
man were being rolled in the stuff, face down. It was almost
unbearable and he would never forget it.

The whole thing happened too fast for Dixon to know
when Cleo and George got fresh ammunition in their rifles.
The bear was standing over him, and for a second or two
they hesitated to shoot for fear of hitting him.

The grizzly let go of his arm and grabbed his head in
its jaws. If it could have gotten a little better hold it
would have crushed the skull like an eggshell. As it was,
its teeth slipped and all it succeeded in doing was peeling
away the man's scalp, all the way from his right ear up to
the top of his head. It even took the top part of the ear
along.

Fortunately, that was the last bite the bear got. Cripps
and Riddle fired almost together, from less than 10 feet
on either side, and the bear collapsed and rolled on top of
Eddie. Their presence of mind and quick shooting were all
that saved his life. In a few more seconds the grizzly certainly would have gotten him by the neck or head and
finished him with one crunch.

It had not stopped bawling and raging for an instant
from the time it started for them until it fell on him.

the grizzly let go of his arm and grabbed his head in its jaws

George and Cleo couldn't see much of the guide for bear blood, and for a minute they thought they had shot him as well as it. They said later that was the worst fright they got during the whole affair.

The grizzly was lying on top of Eddie, his good arm was useless, and he couldn't get up. They had to pull him out from beneath the bear and help him to his feet. When he looked around the grizzly was still moving and trying to raise its head. Dixon was half out of his senses by then but he still knew enough to be scared.

"Brain him," he begged, "before he gets up again."

George Riddle took care of it with a shot in the head, and then they turned their attention to the guide, wiping the worst of the blood off and giving him what first aid they could, including bandaging his torn scalp back in place.

They were in a bad fix, five miles from camp in rough country with heavy timber and deep canyons. Eddie was hurt so badly he wasn't sure he could stay in the saddle without help. His right arm was paralyzed, and a steel hook isn't worth a great deal on a horse.

But Cripps went back and brought the horses up. They boosted the guide onto his, and he hooked the reins over the horn and let the horse have its head, and they began the long tough ride back to camp. The injured man was bleeding badly but nothing could be done about that.

When they got close to camp George rode ahead to get the car started and warmed up. They had 35 miles to drive to 100 Mile House, over a rough gravel road, in addition to the horseback ride, but just four hours after the bear knocked him down Dixon was in the office of Dr. Peter Mudge and the doctor was starting to patch him up.

Eddie had spent 55 days in a hospital at Williams Lake at the time he lost his arm, and that was enough hospital to last him a lifetime. He didn't feel too bad this time, and Dr. Mudge agreed that he could make repairs about as well in the office.

It took him $2\frac{1}{2}$ hours to finish the job, scraping Eddie's skull, sewing his scalp back in place, fixing the torn ear, cleaning and closing the deep bite in his arm (he required 44 stitches in all) and loading him with antibiotics.

"The part I liked least was the skull scraping," Eddie said afterward. "The doc went right down to the bone, and that really hurt."

He was weak and groggy for a few days from the loss of blood, but he recovered very fast and in three weeks he was back guiding for Bus. He had better luck on that trip, too. He took two hunters out for moose and they both killed good bulls the same afternoon. It was too late in the day to get back to camp, so the three of them siwashed out in the snow that night.

The story of the bear attack was carried in newspapers over most of Canada and in many places in the United States. It even appeared in the New York *Times*. One paper headlined it, "Bear Scalps Indian."

The grizzly weighed around 400 pounds, but as the story circulated it grew heavier and Eddie grew older. The bear finally wound up at something over 800 pounds in newspaper accounts, and the guide got to be more than 50 years old.

The day after the grizzly was killed Roy Hamilton and another guide went back to skin him. They found him in bad shape, bloated from the carrion in his belly, with the pelt beginning to turn green in spite of the cold weather. Getting it off was a repulsive job, so bad they both vomited before they were through. But they got the skin and head back to camp, and Riddle and Cripps left for Las Vegas with the trophy rolled in a plastic bag to keep the smell in. Despite the condition of the skin, it turned out all right when a taxidermist finished with it, too.

Cleo and George said at the time that they were through hunting grizzlies for life.

"I don't know whether they have kept that resolution or not," Eddie told me. "But I do know one thing. If I ever have a run-in with another one I doubt it will be because I go looking for him. The next time I might not have partners along with the coolness and courage of those two. If they had lost their heads or run off I'd have been a dead Shuswap in about one more minute."

Death Wore
a Lion Skin

THE lion came in low and very fast, seemingly out of nowhere. Pete Barrett saw Henry Poolman knocked aside, and the next thing he remembered he was looking down at the top of the great cat's head, and it had his left forearm between its jaws and was crunching down on bone.

Barrett's rifle was in his right hand and he belted the lion hard with the barrel, a futile, instinctive blow that had no more effect than a slap with a hat. The cat's swift, savage rush carried Pete to the ground, and he fell on top of it with his wrist still in its mouth.

"If I live 100 years I'll never forget his huge black-maned head only inches from my face, his eyes blazing into mine like orbs of yellow fire," Barrett told me. "Although it takes time to tell it, it happened and was over with in seconds. But the details are branded indelibly in my mind."

They had not started out after a lion that morning. It was a buffalo they wanted. Poolman, Barrett's wife Jean, and he had left camp before daylight with two black trackers and gun bearers, Gatia and David.

125

They were camped at the foot of Mt. Kilimanjaro, in excellent game country midway between Tsavo National Park and the Masai Amboseli Game Reserve. They had been three weeks on a Kenya safari and this was the last day.

It had been an exciting hunt and they had taken some splendid animals, including a rogue elephant that came as an unexpected bonus; it carried almost 100 pounds of ivory on each side.

A 57-year-old retired manufacturing executive from Buffalo, New York, with a wife and three grown sons, Barrett had taken every opportunity to hunt during the last 20 years, mostly for ducks, upland birds, deer and elk.

It started when he moved to Boise, Idaho, with his family in 1949. There's great duck shooting around there and the bug bit him. From that he went on to big game. The Barretts lived at Boise for several years, and by the time they left, Pete had done well on deer and elk and had livened things up by killing a bear and a bobcat or two.

In the spring of 1966 an invitation came along that was more than the Barretts could resist. They were spending an evening with friends, Steve Spaulding and his wife Belle. Steve was in his late fifties, an executive with the Buffalo Aeronautical Corporation, and a year or so before he and Belle had had a very successful hunt in Kenya.

Out of the blue that night Steve said, "We're going back next winter. How would you two like to join us?"

It didn't take long for Pete and Jean to accept, and Steve started to make arrangements with the Nairobi safari firm of Ker, Downey and Selby. A hunt was booked to start March 1, 1967. The party was assigned four top-grade hunting blocks, and they got two of the best white hunters in the business, Henry Poolman and Terry Mathews.

Much as Pete enjoys hunting, he had never been greatly interested in trophies, and he did not want to start an African collection or go on the trip looking like a glory-seeking American sportsman. That problem was solved when the Buffalo Museum of Natural Sciences, where he had contacts, asked him to convert the hunt into a quasi-scientific project by bringing back bird and animal specimens for their East African collection. The museum would arrange the necessary permits for anything not covered by the regular licenses.

The four flew to Nairobi via Zurich the last week in February. They put in two or three days getting acquainted with their hunters, obtaining proper safari colthing, and visiting the Nairobi National Park for a look (for Jean and Pete the first) at Africa's rich and teeming variety of wild-life. They saw a great variety of game within 15 minutes of downtown.

They left Nairobi on the morning of March 1, heading north toward their first camp in dry hilly country near the south end of Lake Rudolph, in the Northern Frontier District. The group consisted of 30 in all. There were Steve and Belle, Jean and Pete, Poolman and Mathews. They had 24 safari hands, who would serve as skinners, trackers and gun bearers, and would staff the commissary department. The blacks were all natives of Kenya, mostly from the Kikuyu tribe.

The Spauldings had Terry as their white hunter and they rode north with him in his Land Rover. Jean and Pete would hunt with Henry, and they were in his Toyota Landcruiser. Both vehicles were 4-wheel-drive and would be used as hunting cars.

It was quickly apparent that the Barretts had drawn an ace hunter. Thirty-six years old, Poolman stood about 6 feet 2 and weighed 220 or better, without an ounce of fat. He knew African game as well as a man can, was tireless at following an animal, a crack rifle shot, cool and sure in a pinch. If he had a fault it was contempt for danger to himself. His right thigh was badly scarred from an encounter with a lion a few years before.

A Nairobi paper would call him, after his death, "a great

bull of a man," and the description fitted in its most compli-
mentary sense.

When he was not off on safari his home was on a fine farm
at Naro Moru, north of Nairobi, where he lived with his
wife and their daughter Adelaide, then 5 years old.

The second day the party reached the native town of
Baragoi, consisting of a mission school, a small store and a
cluster of mud huts. There they set up camp on the banks of
a dry wash just outside the 3-mile protected zone around
the town.

The area was good game country, especially for various
antelopes, and it teemed with birds. In the next few days
they took oryx, gerenuk and Grevey's zebra and got a head
start on their bird collection.

Terry Mathews was an authority on the birds of East
Africa. He had borrowed two excellent bird skinners from
the Nairobi National Museum to accompany the safari. The
variety and number of birds was amazing and the two
skinners were soon busy from sunup until after dark every
day, preparing study skins. Terry took care of the labeling
and helped with the skinning.

By the end of the safari they had collected more than 300
birds, representing 230 different species and ranging from
hummingbirds to vultures and marabou storks. Except for
the larger kinds they were shot with a .410-gauge shotgun
or .22 rifle, using No. 12 "dust" shot. Out of the 300 only
three were mutilated badly enough to be unusable.

Before they left Nairobi they had been told of a trouble-
hunting rhino that was bothering herdsmen on a ranch near
Rumuruti, about 150 miles south of Baragoi. When they
were offered a permit to kill it they jumped at the chance,
for rhinos are becoming scarce in Kenya and getting a permit
to take one is far from easy. If they shot this one, it would
provide a specimen of major importance for the Buffalo
museum.

They drove south to the Milner ranch at Rumuruti and
set up tents in the front yard. They were given the use of

the guest-house bathroom facilities, a real luxury on safari, and for the next few days they lived like kings, invited to hunt on neighboring ranches and enjoying new-found friends.

Steve and Pete caught up with the renegade rhino the first morning. They came on it at 30 yards, as it was browsing in shoulder-high bush. Barrett was carrying a .458 Magnum Winchester Model 70, Steve a .470 Holland and Holland double. Both were loaded with 500-grain full-metal-case bullets.

The rhino whirled to face them but changed its mind, swung broadside and pounded across in front, hidden by thick brush. When it broke into the open they fired together, and the huge ungainly brute actually turned a somersault. Its head dropped, its horn dug into the ground and the massive body flipped heels over applecart.

One bullet had gone through the heart, the other had entered the neck, passed through the brain and come out the forehead, nicking the back horn. It had been an easy kill, but after all a rhino is a rhino, and they were able to send the skin back to the museum for a full body mount.

They took impala, gazelle, water buck and more birds at that camp. Lions were bothering a herd of prize Santa Gertrudis cattle on a neighboring ranch and they put out baits, but attracted no takers.

They left at the end of five days, stopped in Nairobi to drop off their trophies and replenish their supply of film. Then they drove south 200 miles to two hunting blocks at the foot of Kilimanjaro.

They camped on a small creek about 30 miles north of Rombo, a Masai manyetta, the usual collection of mud-and-cowdung huts. But because the Masai are herdsmen this village was in the form of a kraal, enclosed by a boma of thornbush inside which the goats were kept and the cattle driven at night for protection from lions, leopards and hyenas.

Here the hunters hoped to take buffalo, fringe-eared

oryx, reedbuck, eland and lesser kudu. They were due for a bonus, too. On their first trip past Rombo they were stopped by a native game warden. He spoke no English but Henry was fluent in Swahili, and talk flew back and forth between them. Finally Henry turned to Pete with a broad grin.

"Bloody elephant is tearing up their corn patches and storage huts," he explained. "The blighter has to be shot, and he's offering us the chance. What do you say?"

Pete said yes in a hurry. A chance at an elephant was something he had not even thought about.

Early the next morning the game warden and his assistant led Poolman and Barrett out to a waterhole and showed them the dishpan-size tracks of the renegade bull. The hunt turned out to be a long hard walk. The country was dust-dry, and as the sun climbed the day got very hot. They followed the tracks for seven hours. When they finally overtook the elephant he was standing in an open place at the edge of a clump of trees 200 yards ahead.

The stalk was easy. Brush hid the men the first 150 yards. At the edge of cover, hardly more than 40 yards away, Henry spoke a short sharp order: "Take him now. He's seen us."

Pete was carrying the .458 Winchester with solid bullets. Henry had emphasized that the fatal shot on an elephant is in the "earhole," a spot on the side of the head just in front of the ear, marked by a fold of skin. A bullet there goes into the brain and kills instantly.

Barrett thought he knew what to look for, but the massive gray brute was backlighted by the sun, with the side of its head in shadow. Pete made out a dark patch that he took for the earhole and put his 500-grain solid into it. The elephant didn't flinch. He tried again in the same place and it whirled and ran.

Pete got another chance and shot for the spine, but didn't quite connect. The bull was getting away, wounded, and Henry did what a white hunter is supposed to do. He fired his .470 and broke a hind leg.

Barrett learned something then. An elephant can't travel on three legs. This one pitched forward so hard he drove his tusks into the ground and lay helpless on his huge belly. Pete ran in to about 10 feet, and that time he found the earhole. The bull died without a struggle.

He was a very good elephant. One tusk weighed 99 pounds, the other 96.

"But I'll never kill another," Pete told me. "This one had to be destroyed, and if we had not done it the game warden would have. But that huge majestic animal was too awesome in death for me to want to do it again. And when I learned that the Masai will not eat elephant meat, and that the great carcass must go to the hyenas and vultures, I felt even worse."

Steve was taking some good animals, including a buffalo that made the record book. And a couple of days after Pete shot the elephant he had the luck to come on a big bull eland. He went after it, got two quick shots as it ran off and hit it both times. The first shot broke a shoulder and should have put the animal down, but they had to follow him a mile before they got close enough to finish him off. He had 29¾-inch horns, good enough to put him on the official Rowland Ward record list.

They came finally to the morning of March 21, the last day of the hunt, and Barrett was still without a buffalo. He and Jean and Henry got up at 3:30, and at daybreak they were 55 miles from camp, in an area where they had seen buffalo but no shootable bulls.

They had made a small change in arrangements that day, a change that was to have unbelievable consequences.

Ethia, one of the two old and experienced trackers and gun bearers who regularly went with Henry—the other was named Gatia—had eaten too much meat from Steve's buffalo the night before and was too sick to hunt that morning.

Henry replaced him with David, a young native in his

20's, who was just getting started as a gun bearer. He was mission-educated and spoke some English, but had had very little experience, and what was coming was to prove tragically too much for him.

They parked the hunting car at the foot of a hill that offered a lookout, and Henry and Pete started to climb it. Henry reached the crest while Pete was only halfway up. He took one quick look, wheeled and came back with a wide grin on his face.

"How would you like a lion?" he asked. "There's a bloody good one over there. Black mane and all. You're in luck, maybe."

They hurried back to the Toyota and drove around the hill to the foot of a low ridge where they'd have scattered clumps of brush to cover the stalk. They left Jean there in the car.

Pete took the .458, Henry carried his .470 double. He gave Gatia a 7mm bolt-action Brno belonging to Pete, and handed Pete's Browning over-and-under 12-gauge shotgun, with buckshot in both barrels, to David. The bearers would carry these as backup guns only. Poolman did not intend that the two blacks would use either the rifle or the shotgun, but the extra guns would be there in case trouble developed at close quarters.

They got within 125 yards with no difficulty. From there the ridge was open, grown over with short yellow grass and strewn with boulders. There was no cover even to crawl through, and the lion saw them coming. He was standing broadside, an arrogant, magnificent looking cat, and Pete didn't need to be told not to wait any longer. But just as he was ready to shoot the lion started to run.

Pete had had buck fever many times in his life and had it hard, but it had not bothered him once on that African hunt. He concluded afterward, however, that it hit him then. Certainly he didn't make as good a shot as he could have. The lion was behind a bush before he could fire. When it came into sight again it hesitated, and he got its shoulder in the sights and touched off.

"High," Henry barked, and with that the lion really ran.

Pete sent two more fast shots after it before it went over the ridge, but they showed no effect and he was sure he had missed. Then Gatia and David, higher on the slope, started to yell in Swahili.

"He's down," Henry translated. "You clobbered him! Come on."

They climbed and crossed the ridge quietly. The lion was lying on his belly with his back toward them, not more than 20 yards away. Pete had a strong feeling he was not dead. His position was wrong.

A year later, when Pete finally got a look at the skull, he learned all that will ever be known about what his shots had done. One of them had broken the cat's lower right jaw.

It seems unlikely that that alone would have stopped the lion, and if he lay down to ambush his pursuers he picked a poor spot. Barrett will always believe that another of his shots had gone into the body, possibly into the lungs, and prevented Simba from running off. But he'll never be sure, for in the end hyenas tore the cat apart before he could be skinned.

Pete and Henry crept halfway down to him and Pete stopped and started to bring his rifle up for another shot. Just then Poolman said, over his shoulder, "Congratulations!" and in the same instant Pete saw the great maned head turn. The lion looked back at them and rolled as if to regain its feet. Then Poolman sprang in front of Pete to put himself between his client and danger, and blotted the cat out.

It all happened in a fraction of a second, and Barrett will never be clear on one point. He seems to recall that he fired from the hip as the cat rolled and before Henry leaped between them but he can't be sure. Gatia unloaded all the guns at the end, before he put them in the hunting car, but when Pete asked him later whether his had had an empty case in the chamber the native could not remember.

Henry had been at Pete's right and a step or two ahead. He and the two gun bearers were nearer to the lion than Pete was, and it could have gotten to them easier. But for some reason it singled him out for the attack.

"Because I was the one who had hurt him in the first place?" Pete asked himself when it was all over. He'll never know.

In any case, the cat had its sights set on Barrett and what it did was typical lion behavior. As John Kingsley-Heath, the Nairobi white hunter who was so savagely mauled by a wounded lion in 1961, said afterward, "Once Simba picks his victim he stays with it. A wounded leopard will rush from one member of a party to another, biting each in turn, leaving one and running for the next. A lion takes time to finish what he begins."

Pete heard two shots from Henry's .470, so close together they blurred into each other. Next he saw Poolman bowled aside, saw his rifle go sailing through the air. Henry fell flat on his back at Pete's right, and a crazy flicker of thought ran through Pete's mind: "When we get back to camp tonight I'll razz you plenty for lying there on your fanny while a lion grabs your client!"

"I can only conclude that I had not yet had time to be scared," he told me.

Looking back, he believes the lion was half dead at that point and running blindly for him. Henry had probably hit it both times. By then it likely had three bullets in it, maybe four. But it was still 400 pounds of deadly fury.

It carried Pete backward six or eight feet as he fell. He landed on his side, lying across it, with his left forearm clamped in its jaws. He felt no pain but he was aware of teeth crunching through the bones of his wrist.

He did the wrong thing instinctively. He grabbed the lion's lower jaw with his right hand to keep it from closing

next he saw Poolman bowled aside, saw his rifle go sailing through the air

its mouth. But then he recalls thinking, "He'll bite your fingers off." He yanked his hand away so fast that he cut the skin on the inside of his fingers against the lion's front teeth.

Next he saw Gatia come dodging in. The native shoved the muzzle of his rifle between the lion's body and Pete's and drove two shots into the cat's spine within inches of the man's back. The gun was so close that Pete felt the blast of concussion, and the jolting hammerblows that went through the body of the lion. But the jaws had not relaxed on his arm, and he screamed, "Shoot him again!"

The third shot did it. He felt the jaws loosen and the heavy muscular body go slack under him. He had trouble getting his hand and watch strap untangled from the lion's teeth, and when he pulled free he could not see the hand. It was turned back and the end of the arm bones protruded from the bloody stub that had been his wrist. Luckily the teeth had straddled the main artery and frayed but not severed it. Pete remembers mumbling to himself, "Well, at least I've got a stump left." Then he rolled to his knees and looked around.

What he saw was sheer horror.

Just as the lion smashed into him and he started to fall, he had heard a shot and a muffled cry, and had seen Poolman throw up both arms and topple backward. Henry was lying a few feet away now, his chest and shirt front a mass of blood.

What had happened was almost too fantastic and dreadful to believe. As the lion knocked Henry off his feet and streaked past him, he had twisted around and grabbed it by the tail in a last-ditch attempt to keep it from getting at his client. It pulled him part way to his feet and into line with the young gun bearer David, and at that instant David fired a load of buckshot at pointblank range. It did not touch the lion but it smashed into Henry's chest and killed him instantly.

Pete crawled over to him, felt for pulse and listened for his breathing, but he was dead.

From her place in the hunting car at the foot of the ridge Jean had heard the lion roar (none of the others remembered hearing that, but she did), had heard the shots, seen her husband's hat fly off and Henry fall backward. She came racing up the slope now and took charge, cool and capable.

David was hysterical, but she pulled him together and sent him hurrying down to the car for the medical kit. She washed Pete's arm, poured on antiseptics, bound the hand back in place as best she could, and gave him a couple of codeine tablets.

He was in shock by then and he has no clear recollection of what happened next. He felt no pain, but he does remember a deadly fatigue.

"Some who have heard the story have asked whether we did the right thing," he told me. "I don't know. The decision was of necessity made by Gatia and David, and in the shock and horror of what had happened I believe they did the best they could."

He did not lose consciousness but he must have blacked out on his feet, for the next thing he remembered they were jolting along in the Toyota, with Jean supporting him and Gatia at the wheel.

"Where's Henry?" he mumbled.

"Back there with David," she told him.

The two blacks had talked the thing over in Swahili. Henry was a big man, between 220 and 240, and it was 300 yards to the hunting car. They had decided against trying to carry the body that distance. Maybe they were afraid to remove it until the police came. Instead they took it to the shade of a nearby tree, left David to keep hyenas and vultures away, and Gatia, who had had very little experience at driving (Jean had had none with a 4-wheel-drive vehicle) undertook the long rough trip back to camp.

Gatia tried to drive as fast as he could. A little man, about 5 feet 2, he could not see over the front fender, and he hit rock after rock. The bumps were nerve wracking and Pete kept yelling "pa'le, pa'le," thinking it was the Swahili word for slow. Actually it meant "just then." He should have been saying "po'le, po'le," instead. Gatia kept pouring on coal and they kept hitting rocks.

Steve and Terry had gone out that morning to make a round of leopard baits. They would not be back yet, and that meant there would be nobody at camp who could operate the radio. But a young couple from Texas, Ron and Mary Cauble, were camped nearby, trapping and studying baboons as part of a research project in primate behavior. Gatia headed for their camp.

Pete's wrist watch had stopped at 5:41, when the lion bit into it. It was three hours later when they reached the Caubles. That had been a pretty terrible three hours.

Ron and Mary took over. She contacted the Ker, Downey and Selby headquarters in Nairobi on the radio, and then Ron left to bring in Henry's body, picking up a couple of native military police on the way.

At Oloitokitok, a few miles from the hunting camp, there was an emergency landing strip and a first-aid station manned by a competent Indian intern. Pete was driven there immediately. The safari firm had an aircraft and a doctor on the way at once, and everything humanly possible was done for him. At 1 o'clock that afternoon, about seven hours after the lion attacked, he was in the Nairobi Hospital.

Ron Cauble went out the next morning to have a look at the lion. He found most of it devoured by hyenas. The only thing he could salvage was the skull, and it was from him that Pete learned, many months later, that one of his shots had broken the lower jaw on the right side.

The unlucky David was arrested, and Kenya police authorities made a painstaking investigation, but in the end Henry's death was ruled entirely accidental and the young gun bearer was exonerated. It was, however, an accident that in all likelihood would not have happened with an older and more experienced man, such as Ethia.

Pete's Browning was held by the police for a time, but he got it back through the safari firm after four months.

He spent 18 days in the hospital, and then flew home. His wrist healed surprisingly well, and although his fingers will always be a bit numb, he recovered about three-fourths of the use of his hand.

"I'll never forget that agonizing minute as the lion grabbed me and bore me to the ground," Barrett says today. "I will never forget, either, the sight of Henry Poolman springing in front of me to take the attack himself. I'll always figure he saved my life at the expense of his own. He was one of the best, that man Poolman."

A few months after the tragedy, the East Africa Professional Hunters Association set up an educational fund for Henry's daughter Adelaide, in memory of her father. Pete Barrett turned over to that fund all his proceeds from the story.

"It's a story I never expected to tell," he says. "but so many inaccurate versions have been circulated that I decided it was time to set the record straight. This is how it really happened."

A
Hell of a Way
to Move

HERSCH Neighbor's wife
Eunice huddled deeper in her heavy coat and shifted weight
in the saddle, trying to ease the ache that had crept into her
bones from 36 days of rain, wind and snow. Her thoughts
went back to the home they had left and she felt about the
way a lot of pioneer women must have felt in covered-wagon
days.

The pack outfit, 22 horses in all, was slogging along a
desolate track, slashed through the rugged wilderness of
either north-central Alberta or British Columbia. The
Neighbors weren't sure which. The road, such as it was, was
covered with 18 inches of water. The date was September 30
but there had been cold weather in the mountains, there was
half an inch of ice on top, and the horses were breaking
through at each step. It was hard going but better than
bogging belly deep in the muskeg on either side.

They had hit the road three hours back and had thought
it meant they were close to civilization at last. But then they
had seen the colored markers and knew it for what it was, a

seismic road, gouged through the bush with bulldozers by crews exploring for oil, starting nowhere and going nowhere.

Eunice Neighbor wondered grumpily why they had been such fools as to let themselves in for all that had happened in the last five weeks. But when she started mulling over the reasons that had led up to this cold and miserable day, she grinned at her own grumpiness. If they were doing it over again, she knew their decision would be the same.

Hersch and Eunice had always felt at home in the wilderness. He was born in Oregon in 1906, one of a family of nine, all of them hillsmen, hunters and stockmen. The family moved to Alberta when he was nine and settled on a bush homestead. He went on his first big-game hunt when he was 17, as a wrangler, and started as a guide a year later. He had loved the mountains and bush as far back as he could remember.

His wife was born on a homestead 70 miles west of Edmonton, but left it in 1923, when she was nine years old, and got her education at Prince George, Victoria, and Kirkland, Washington. She went back to Alberta and married Hersch when she was 16, and up to that time she had never touched a gun, knew nothing about the woods and hardly knew one end of a horse from the other. But she learned fast, and for many years they had made a living by running a pack outfit and guiding big-game hunters.

They started out in central Alberta, back in the '30's, but got fenced in by prairie farmers from the dry belt, so they pulled stakes and moved to Tete Jaune Cache in British Columbia, 70 miles west of Jasper.

They put in 13 years of hard work there before they resigned themselves to the fact that they had made a bad choice. The land took too much building up and the wild grass was too soft for good winter feed for horses. Hersch came home at the end of a hard day of logging in the winter of 1953 and said, a little grimly, "We're going to move." Eunice surprised him with a cheerful "Where to?"

"I didn't expect you'd go for it," he said, "but I've been thinking of the Anahim Lake country."

"If it has good grass and winter feed, and good hunting, it'll be better than this," she told him.

They got out maps and plotted a trip. In June they and their 16-year-old son Norris, whom they called Nod, spent three weeks prowling around central-western British Columbia. They saw a lot of good land, all taken, and plenty of frost-bitten land not taken.

They went home and did some more planning. A friend said there was good grassland in the Halfway River area, north of the Peace. "Go take a look on Cypress Creek," he advised. So in October they left home once more and headed north, taking their 13-year-old daughter Sandy this time and leaving Nod behind.

They hired horses and rode a full day over a pack trail to the Halfway. Another day down that river took them to Cypress Creek, which flows out of the Rockies from the west, and there they found what they had been looking for, wild virgin country, plenty of good hard grass, and a beautifull view of the mountains 12 miles to the west.

The move would mean genuine pioneering and a lot of hard work, and they'd be strictly on their own. The only near neighbors would be two bachelors half a mile away. The next nearest would be two others eight miles south, and a fifth 10 miles north. It would be a 25-mile ride by horse east to the Alaska Highway, and another 98 miles down that road to Fort St. John, which would be the closest town for trading and business. But they made their decision, and filed for two quarter sections of land on Cypress Creek, 320 acres for a start.

Moving to a place so remote would pose a few problems. Once they had a cabin finished and ready, they could truck their household goods up the Alaska Highway to a point nearest the new location and take them in the rest of the way by pack horse and wagon. But when it came to moving

their stock Hersch made other plans. They would trail
their horses through the mountains to the Halfway valley,
riding and packing, scheduling the trip for fall and making
a hunt of it. Once they reached the Halfway they'd put the
horses up for the winter and come back to Tete Jaune Cache
to wait for spring, when they could complete the move.

The pack trip would cover 300 miles, nearly all of it
through country devoid of human habitation, the last 200
through a wild and rugged area that they had never seen.
They didn't even have reliable maps of that part. They
picked a route that would hit into the mountains at Mt.
Robson, then follow along the Alberta–British Columbia
border to the headwaters of the Murray River. They'd go
down the Murray to East Pine on the Hart Highway, strike
cross country to the Peace, and follow the Halfway up to
Cypress Creek. They figured 30 days for the trip. They'd be
in familiar country until they reached Kakwa Lake. Beyond
that it would all be new.

Sandy and Nod would go along. Sandy was 14 then, had
finished eighth grade with special merits, and so had won
permission from her school authorities to skip September
and October of her ninth year.

At 17, just under six feet tall and with an irrepressible
sense of humor, Nod had only a little interest in horses or
riding them, but was good natured about it and willing to
learn.

Art Mintz, a young man whom the Neighbors had known
since he was a kid of nine or ten, when he was flunkeying
in a logging camp, and who had wrangled for them the last
few years, would go with them. His dad was a logger and
trapper and Art had grown up in the bush. A born worrier,
he covered every concern with sharp humor and met every
hard knock with a grin and a quip.

Before the time arrived to leave, a friend swelled the
party to six. During the outfitting years at Tete Jaune Cache

the Neighbors had formed a firm friendship with Jim Scott, a rancher and hunter client from Oswego in northeastern Montana. When they wrote Jim and told him of the proposed move he replied that he wanted to go along for the adventure of the thing and for the hunting.

It was his ambition to collect respectable heads of all the big game British Columbia and Alberta had to offer. He had a good start by that time and he saw the 300-mile ride as a golden opportunity.

Hersch led the pack train away from the ranch just before noon on August 26, 1954. The aspens were yellowing and every sign indicated that autumn was at hand. They could expect bad weather in the mountains. But they were bursting with eagerness and anticipation, buoyed up by the knowledge that they were heading into a new life.

They rode the 19 miles to Mt. Robson that afternoon, unpacked, fed the horses, put up the tents and sat down to supper at 7 o'clock. Camp was a cozy and cheerful place. They had three tents, one a pyramid model 12 feet square for cooking and eating. Sandy would sleep in it. Jim, Nod and Art had a 10x10 pyramid to themselves, and Hersch and his wife were using a reflector type, resembling a lean-to, handy and easily warmed with an open fire.

The second day involved a stiff climb of 3,000 feet, up from the wild, boiling Whitehorn River, past Emperor Falls and across a sheer and treacherous rock face at a place that's still called the Flying Trestle, from an ingenious but hair-raising structure that was built there years ago by outfitters packing into the mountains. Nobody who rode the Flying Trestle ever forgot it.

The men who built it drilled holes into the rock face, set long heavy logs in the holes, braced them and used them as the foundation for a log shelf, six feet wide and 100 feet long, with a pole railing on the outside. To top things off, it climbed steeply. It was safe enough, but it was no place for the faint of heart, for as you rode across it you could look over the edge or between the logs of the floor straight down into the churning, rock-strewn Emperor River 1,500 feet below!

That crude structure stayed in use for some 35 years. Then the logs started to rot, and the British Columbia Public Works Department blasted the trestle away and gouged a 10-foot trail the length of the rock face. It's not as picturesque but it's far easier on the nerves.

Six days out with the nights freezing cold, they got into first-class caribou country, high alpine meadows dotted with blue-green lakes and shut in by rugged mountains on all sides. Caribou sign was plentiful, so they stopped and put in a day in camp to give Jim a chance at a head.

He and Hersch got within 500 yards of a band of seven that included one good bull. Hersch stood up, half hidden behind a rock, and waved his hat back and forth. The caribou threw up their heads, stared hard, and then trotted warily in for a closer look. Jim bellied down with his .250-3000 Savage resting across a boulder and dropped the bull with two shots.

Game was getting more plentiful now. They saw caribou and a wolverine, there were fresh grizzly diggings along the trail, and they spotted the first goats of the trip.

On September 3 they reached Boundary Lake, about 70 miles north of the ranch at Tete Jaune Cache, and found another hunting party camped ahead of them, an outfit from Slave Lake, Alberta.

Hersch elected to lay over here and let Jim try for a goat. Art put in the morning shoeing horses, Eunice baked bread and the first cake of the trip.

The other party's outfitter dug out an old map of the Wapiti Lake country and the Murray, that lay ahead, and traced a copy for the Neighbors, marking trails, rivers and turnoffs. "Don't get tangled up and go down the Wapiti River," he warned. "It'll take you east into Alberta."

Jim and Hersch rode into camp at dark. Jim had killed a goat with a good burly head.

They got their first snow on the night of September 6, and when they pulled out the next morning a bitterly cold wind was blowing down from the peaks. They had one high pass to go through and the snow had drifted so deep there that it was difficult to follow the trail and the horses had hard going. Dropping down beyond the pass, through heavy timber, rock jumbles and windfalls, they lost the trail in the snow and cut down the mountain in the wrong place.

About halfway to the bottom a waspish, stiff-legged little pack mare upset over a windfall. She landed on her side on a slanting tangle of logs about four feet off the ground, with her legs uphill. She couldn't get up until she was rolled over with her feet downhill. Hersch and Art and Jim finally managed to get her pack off, and the mare rolled over under her own power, slid down the windfall, fell off and scrambled to her feet, cut and skinned in a dozen places. "This is a hell of a way to move," Hersch admitted when things were straightened out again.

They rode into a meadow beside Kakwa Lake at 6 o'clock that night, bone tired, hungry, cold and discouraged. They were 13 days out from the home ranch now and had made less than 100 miles. The country they knew was behind. Ahead lay more than 200 miles of unfamiliar wilderness, with only the outfitter's old map to go by.

They laid over three days at Kakwa Lake, and the second morning they suffered the first serious mishap of the trip.

Their camp was within hearing distance of a place called Thunder Valley, named for the rumble of its snow slides. Almost any day all summer long you can hear three or four of them roar down from the high slopes. Just as the Neighbor party sat down to breakfast that morning they heard what they thought was a slide starting. But after two or three seconds Art said, "That noise is coming from the wrong direction. It wouldn't be our tent burning down, would it?" He said it so calmly that the others thought he was kidding, but when they lifted the flap of the cook tent and looked out he had hit the nail on the head. The 10x10 tent in which he and Jim and Nod slept was going up in flames.

It was all over in three minutes. Nod grabbed a pail and ran for the hole where they dipped drinking water, and Hersch and Jim stampeded for the burning tent to get the guns and ammunition out. By that time the tent roof was gone, and Nod, arriving with his bucket of water and trying to douse the flames around his dad, succeeded only in pouring Jim's eiderdown bag full. Hersch and Jim came out with the rifles and ammo and other gear, and Hersch started slashing ropes. Art and Eunice dragged what remained of the burning tent off to one side, but there wasn't enough left to be of any use. Luckily they had lost none of their equipment.

Hersch and his wife turned the reflector tent over to Jim and Nod and Art. They spent the next few nights in improvised sprucebough wickiups and managed to keep fairly dry in spite of almost continuous rain. Later, as the weather worsened, they crowded into the cook tent with Sandy.

On September 11 they rode north once more. They reached Torrens Creek the evening of the 13th and holed up for a few days of hunting. This was good sheep country and it would be the last chance Jim would have for a bighorn, which he coveted greatly.

Because of low clouds, fog, rain and snow, it took him four days to score. The fourth afternoon Hersch and he and Art got above the fog, the snow cleared, and when they crawled up to a knife-edged ridge and peered over there were 14 bighorn rams of assorted sizes grazing in a little basin 150 yards below, like sheep on a picture postcard. There was one big one in the bunch with a full curl, and Jim slid his rifle into place and dropped it in its tracks.

It was dark by the time they started back off the mountain, pitch dark with the blackness of a stormy, foggy night. Art and Hersch were carrying heavy loads of meat, Jim the head, and they felt their way down for two hours, stumbling and sliding. They rode into camp an hour before midnight, cold, wet and tired, but very happy.

The party broke camp on Torrens Creek on September 18. An hour out, every semblance of trail disappeared and they confronted a hellish stretch of muskeg and windfall. The horses bogged down, one after another. One of the pack mares got stuck in a small bottomless creek like a cork in a bottle. She stepped in, started to go down, floundered and kept sinking. It wasn't much of a creek and she really fitted tight. In a matter of seconds all that was holding her up was her pack, which was wider than the channel.

They had to work fast. They tied a lariat to her halter, snubbed the other end around the saddle horn on a sturdy horse, and delegated Art to hold it snug and keep the mare from sinking deeper. Hersch untied the diamond hitch holding the pack so it would pop loose if and when they got her partly out. Then, by reaching in to his armpits in sloppy goop, Hersch fastened a second lariat around a hind leg and a third to her tail. With him, Sandy and Eunice pulling on one, Jim and Nod on the other, and Art and his horse leaning into the head rope, they managed to lift her enough to get the pack off. Then everybody pulled like mad again. Eunice was sure they'd break her neck or yank her tail off, but suddenly she came free and they skidded her on her ribs to safety. It had taken two hours to get her out.

Late that afternoon they found enough high ground for a camp, with a little grass for the horses, and called it quits for the night.

They had no more than crawled into their bedrolls when the wind came up, rattling the stovepipe and the lamp that hung on a pole of the cook tent, and threatening to rip the

tents away over their heads. They got up, anchored everything and tightened ropes all around, and finally fell asleep
with the storm still howling. An hour before daylight they
awoke to an eerie quiet and peered out under the tent wall.
There were four inches of snow on the ground and more
coming down.

The three days that followed were the worst Hersch and
his wife had ever put in on a trip. They floundered through
endless bog, leading the horses mile after mile across places
too wet for riding. The horses bogged down and were pulled
out. The packs worked loose, they detoured around one
windfall after another or cut trail where they could not go
around.

To make matters worse they had only the haziest idea
where they were. As Hersch grumbled at supper the third
night, "We may not be lost, but we're damn badly con-
fused."

They got out of the muskeg on September 22, and for
the first time since leaving Boundary Lake 17 days before
came across signs of travel by other outfits. One small
party with a few unshod horses, probably a band of Indians,
had gone through not many days earlier. The other, a fair
sized survey party, had been there back in the summer.
They had traveled north, in the direction Hersch wanted
to go, so he followed their trail. It led finally to a river
flowing north, and the Neighbor outfit camped on it. Ten
minutes after leaving camp the next morning they came to
the worst bog they had seen, a place so wet and shaky that if
you climbed up on a hummock a sickly looking swamp spruce
50 feet away was likely to quiver and quake. There was no
way around, so they plunged in.

Horses sank to their bellies in the mire and trails had to
be cut around windfalls. It took four hours and a half to go
a mile and a half. The horses became so tired and bewildered
that when the party stopped to hack through a windfall they

refused to move until prodded ahead one by one. If one started to bog down he'd give up, tip over and lie there, not even trying to extricate himself.

Years later, the old horses left from that trip would stop and hang their heads if Hersch made more than two mistakes on a trail. They'd retrace their steps twice, but if he tried it a third time they balked and their expression said clearly, "Here we go again!"

The party made three miles that day and it cost seven hours of the hardest work they had done on the trip. A few mornings before, after he had had a hard time finding the horses in a blinding snowstorm, Art had announced, with wry humor, that if he ever got out of the bush this time he was going to quit wrangling.

"Gonna find a chunk of land, build a nice log house, get me 100 hens and settle down," he declared. The next day was stormy and miserable, and around the campfire at night the others heard Art mutter, "Maybe I only want a little piece of ground and a small cabin, and a couple dozen chickens." And that day in the muskeg, trying to thaw out around the lunch fire, he rolled a cigaret, watched morosely as a huge snowflake fell on it and soaked it before he could lick it shut, threw it on the ground and growled, "One hen is enough!"

They got free of the bog a couple of hours before dark, and shortly after that crossed a ridge and got their first look at Wapiti Lake.

Here, the outfitter they had met back at Boundary Lake had warned, the Wapiti River ran east into Alberta. That was not the way they wanted to go. A short distance to the north lay the head of the Murray, which would take them north to the Peace. All they had to do was find it.

They located a good trail along a river they took to be the Wapiti, and followed it. After an hour the trail swung west, away from the river, and everybody was jubilant, thinking they were headed for the Murray. But before long they were back to the same river, crossing and recrossing. There seemed no other way to get through the country. This river continued to run almost due north and if their crude map was any good that meant it was the Murray, so they kept on.

Their supplies were almost gone now. They had planned for a 30-day trip and the 30 days were up. They had no meat left and little of anything else. It seemed ridiculous to think they might go hungry in that country, but they were traveling through very bad muskeg, windfalls and heavy timber, and although moose and bear sign was plentiful they had seen nothing worth shooting for 10 days.

Hersch and Scott left camp on the morning of September 27, with wet snow on the ground, carrying Jim's .250-3000, a .22, and fishing gear. "We'll bring back something for supper," Hersch promised, "but I can't predict just what it will be."

They were still out, about 5 o'clock in the afternoon, when Art Mintz came bounding into the cook tent, where Eunice was trying to scrape a meal together, and blurted, "There's a moose right in camp!"

She grabbed up her .300 Savage and bolted out of the tent. A young bull was feeding in the willows at the edge of the timber, and she dropped him with one shot, not 75 yards from the frying pan.

Art and Nod were still dressing him out when Hersch and Jim rode in, lugging a packsack full of fish and half a dozen blue grouse. Supper that night was a celebration, with moose stew, fried trout and moose steaks.

Late the next afternoon they found an abandoned trapper's cabin on the river bank. From the signs the place had not been used for years, but hanging by a wire from the ridge pole was a 10-pound cloth bag of sugar, wet and drippy but still clean.

They camped, built up a roaring fire to dry themselves out, brewed a huge pail of tea and everybody squeezed a big dollop of sugar sirup into his cup. It was the first sweetening they had had in many days.

They found the trapper's name and address scrawled on the wall of the cabin, and would arrange to repay him for the sugar later on.

The next two days they rode through bush, mud, muskeg and bog, still not sure whether they were following the right river. At dark the second night, miles away across the muskeg to the north, they saw lights twinkling. That, they agreed, had to be the town of East Pine, where the Hart Highway crosses the Murray. They were not lost, after all. They were getting close to the Peace.

Confident they'd be in East Pine the next day, everybody took a bath and put on his last clean clothes, in preparation for a return to civilization. Except for the trapper's abandoned cabin, it had been more than a month since they had seen a house or eaten inside four walls.

The following forenoon, the last day in September, they found the flooded, ice-covered seismic line, gouged through the bush the winter before by an oil exploration crew. They rode it for hours because it was better than the muskeg on either side. About 2 o'clock in the afternoon Hersch halted the pack string at a good camp ground with muskeg on all sides and started to look the place over. Nailed on a tree was a forestry sign that read, "Keep Alberta Green."

They knew the unhappy truth at last. They had followed the Wapiti rather than the Murray, and were no longer in British Columbia. They had strayed a good 100 miles off their route, and in view of the lateness of the season and the kind of country they had come through there was no hope that they could retrace their steps.

"Well, we've moved," Hersch said bitterly. "But it looks as if we moved to the wrong place."

Two hours after they started out the next morning they reached a homesteader's shack, with a line of washing hanging in the yard, the first occupied human habitation they had encountered since leaving the home ranch on August 26. The hamlet of Hinton Trail lay 16 miles ahead, the homesteader told them.

Five miles further on they found a pioneering farmer with some fenced land and an unoccupied house they were welcome to use. They turned the horses out on good grass, moved into the old house and set up their camp stove. That night of October 1, for the first time in two weeks, they slept warm and dry.

They were still 200 miles from their destination on Cypress Creek and it was plain there was no chance of trailing the horses the rest of the way before spring, so they made a deal with the farmer to leave them in his pasture for a couple of weeks. Then he hitched up his team, they loaded their gear into his wagon and the party headed for the little town of Hazelmere, three miles away, with six downcast people plodding along behind, through snow and mud.

As soon as they wrapped up a few details they headed back to Tete Jaune Cache by bus and train, arriving October 7.

Hersch found a wintering place for the horses at Pouce Coupe, just below Dawson Creek. Late the following May he and a helper trailed them up the Alaska Highway to mile 110, then cut directly west to the Halfway and followed it to the new location on Cypress Creek. The stirrups dragged in snow part of the time.

Hersch and the helper started to cut and skid logs for a cabin, but it was far from finished when the time came for Sandy and her mother to move in.

They drove the Neighbor's household gear up the Alaska Highway to Mile 147 by truck, and camped there while the men hauled everything 27 miles into the bush with a team and wagon.

Coming back to the highway for a load on one of the trips, Hersch camped overnight by himself at a halfway point, staying in a tent he had left there for that purpose. He didn't have a rifle along.

He was awakened sometime before midnight by a tearing sound. At that time of year there is no complete darkness in that country. When he raised up in his bedroll he could see, through the white tent wall, a big black bear standing up with its front paws on the roof of the pyramid tent, raking the roof and wall with its claws in an effort to tear its way in.

Hersch admitted afterward that what he did was a foolish thing, but he didn't stop to think of that at the time. He bounded out of bed and punched the bear in the belly with all his might. He must have landed a real haymaker, for the bear let out an astonished "Woof!" and fell over backward like a man knocked down. "My arm went in clear to the elbow," Hersch said later.

The bear didn't stay down. It scrambled to its feet and took off, and Hersch went back to bed. But he was no more than asleep when he heard the sound of ripping canvas once more. That time the bear had bitten through, put its teeth into the edge of a pack box that contained a slab of bacon, and was dragging the box through a big hole in the tent.

Hersch rushed out, grabbed up an ax and threw it. It walloped the bear in the ribs and he ran for the woods again. Hersch lit the gas lamp and kept it burning the rest of the night, and that ended the affair, although he heard the bear prowling in the brush near the tent several times before morning.

The torn wall of the tent was damaged so badly that it had to be replaced. "And I guess the same thing could have happened to me," Hersch said a little sheepishly when he related the story.

Eunice and Sandy rode finally to the site of their new home with four pet cats in sacks on the front of their

he bounded out of bed and
punched the bear in the belly
with all his might

saddles. As Hersch told them, they were about nine months late.

He and Eunice are still there. They own almost 5,000 acres of land now, have a good horse herd and a fine start in cattle, and enough fence strung that it keeps them busy repairing what moose tear down. They wanted wild country and they found it. The latest word I had from them, they are still 23 miles from the nearest phone and that's an old crank model that hangs on the wall.

The long move was worthwhile, but on one thing Hersch Neighbor and his wife are agreed. If they ever move again, they'll hold out for a decent road and a modern van.

White Fury
on the
Barrens

THE weather-beaten trading schooner *Venture,* 43 feet long and auxiliary powered with an ancient Diesel engine, dropped anchor in Long Island Sound on the evening of July 22, 1937.

Not the Long Island Sound you have heard about. This one is a narrow channel of the sea lying between another Long Island and the east shore of Hudson Bay, about 35 miles north of Cape Jones, where the huge funnel of that bay narrows into James Bay, which forms its spout.

For an Arctic trading schooner, the *Venture* carried strange cargo, including 18 humans. Nine of us were clients, sportsmen from the States, the first such party ever to cruise up the Quebec shore of James Bay and Hudson Bay to fish, hunt, photograph and see the country.

Lloyd Melville, from Rydal Bank, Ontario, who had organized the trip and chartered the *Venture* for it, planned to conduct similar guided tours into that remote and fabulously wild country each year from then on, but the plan fell through, and ours was the last as well as the first group to undertake it.

Melville's crew consisted of three guides and a cook. The *Venture* was owned and skippered by Jack Palmquist, the only free trader then operating on James Bay in competition with the Hudson's Bay Company. He had a small trading post at Old Factory, on the coast about halfway between the Eastmain and Fort George Rivers. Married to a mission-educated Cree girl, and speaking Cree as readily as English, he had an inside track with the Indians and was doing all right.

He had a crew of three aboard the *Venture*. Alagkok, the little Eskimo engineer, spoke no English but understood the workings of the throbbing old diesel as a man understands a well-loved wife—and gave it the same affectionate care. The deckhand was a Cree, equally innocent of English, whose name time has erased from my memory. And because no charts existed for the treacherous island-girt passages along that coast, and no white skipper of that day would have dreamed of sailing them without a Cree pilot aboard (and probably wouldn't even today), at Eastmain we had taken on an aged and leather-faced Indian, Bosun Kagaback, as pilot.

Only the Crees knew those waters well enough, from a lifetime of canoe travel, to recall the endless landmarks along the bleak coast, follow the channels and avoid the reefs. Kagaback, who had piloted for years for the Hudson's Bay Company, saw us safely north to Fort George. There we exchanged him for Tommy Lameboy, equally weathered, who knew the coast the rest of the way.

We had left the end of steel on the T & NO Railroad at Moosonee on July 12, when the *Venture* moved down the Moose River into the open waters of James Bay and pointed her nose north. When the wind favored us, we ran under sail. When it didn't, the wheezing diesel pushed us along at a lumbering six knots.

We were headed into a region that only a handful of whites—the men of the Hudson's Bay Company, an occasional free trader, missionaries, Mounties, and now and then a roving prospector—had ever seen. Not a foot of road lay between us and the Arctic ice, not even a blazed trail save for the portages the Crees had cut around the rapids on the big rivers they traveled. If you went into that bleak Land of Midnight Twilight, you went by canoe or ship in summer, by dog team in winter.

Below decks the *Venture* carried our duffle and luggage, tents and camping equipment. Lashed to the rails were four big freight canoes that would carry us to the fishing pools of the barrenland rivers, and also would serve to ferry the clients and guides ashore each night to make camp. There was not room aboard the old 43-footer for 18 to sleep.

I have roamed the back country of this continent for almost 50 years, from the Great Smokies and the diamond-back-infested flatwoods of Florida to the Aleutian Islands of Alaska, but that treeless and empty subarctic land was the most fascinating place I have ever seen.

At Moose Factory, at Eastmain and at Fort George we found big camps of the Crees, down to the posts for the summer from their trapping and hunting grounds along the big rivers of the interior, a few of them living in tents but the great majority in wigwams, as they had lived long before the first white men saw them. The wigwams were big and comfortable, and clean, too.

Consisting of a circular frame of poles, 12 to 20 feet across, they were covered with canvas, sealskins, whatever was available. The floor was carpeted deep with green spruce twigs, a ring of stones in the center contained the fire, and a small opening at the top carried the smoke out. On poles outside hung gear of all kinds, snowshoes, dog harness, frames for drying pelts, and bundles of sphagnum moss that would be used for baby diapers and sanitary napkins, the all-around absorbent cotton of the North. And tied to stakes in front of every wigwam were the gaunt, hungry sled dogs, half-wild, furtive-eyed, crafty thieves, great workers but vicious fighters, ever on the lookout for trouble. Snowshoes and every scrap of harness had to be hung beyond their reach.

On Cape Hope Island, only 125 miles north of the mouth of the Moose, we dropped anchor one morning in front of a drab and cheerless cluster of low-roofed houses, some built of logs, some of rough, unpainted lumber whipsawed by hand from driftwood. This was the home of the Cape Hope Eskimo band, the southernmost of their race on the North American continent, headed by a wise old patriarch named Weteltik.

The smell of seal oil hung over the place, rancid and all-pervading. Whale and seal harpoons were racked by the doors, canoes and boats rested on high pole frames or, if they contained no leather, were drawn up on shore, and big surly dogs ranged the camp.

We went ashore, avoiding the dogs, and were met with a welcome so friendly that I have never forgotten it. We couldn't buy anything, for money had no value there, but we gave away cigarets and traded tennis shoes and knives, soap, tea, sugar and jam, for whale harpoons, mukluks, ivory carvings and snowshoes. The trading was done through two interpreters. Weteltik understood Cree. Palmquist told him in that language what we wanted, and he passed the word on to his people in Eskimo. That morning was one I'll remember all my life.

But of that whole fascinating month, nothing stands forth in my mind more clearly than the trout fishing we found in the wonderful, tumbling rivers of the rocky moors, north of the limit of trees. (We were in that kind of country for more than a week, carrying our tent poles along from camp to camp, and combing the rocky beaches for driftwood to feed our camp and cooking fires.)

The fish were squaretails, the big speckled trout of northern Canada (we caught a few Arctic char too), but they were different in some ways from any of their kind I had ever encountered. They were untutored, uneducated and unwise.

They came of generations that had had no dealing with flies, spinners or any man-made device of treachery, save the nets the roaming Crees set at the mouths of the rivers.

They took whatever was offered, swiftly and recklessly. They rose to flies, wet or dry, they smashed at spinners or the throat latch of another trout. They were no more canny than bluegills in a millpond, and no harder to catch.

One morning, without much hope of getting a response, I tore a narrow strip from a red bandanna handkerchief, knotted it around the shank of my hook, and fed it into a chute of green water at the foot of a pool. A 16-inch fish struck like forked lightning.

The trout ran from 15 to 20 inches in length, heavy-bodied and fat. Many of them weighed three pounds, and they were as rugged in battle as any fish I have ever taken. It was no trick for three or four rods to catch in a morning all the party of 18 needed for a day. Many times two flies on a leader took doubles, and frequently we landed six or eight trout from one pool before the action slacked off. I have never seen any other fishing to match it.

In the summer camp of the Crees at the Fort George Post, where 500 Indians were living in wigwams and tents scattered over a long, level meadow below the red-and-white buildings of the Hudson's Bay Company, we were introduced in a small way to the thing I was chiefly interested in, a polar bear hunt.

One of the Crees brought three white bearskins out of his wigwam and spread them on the grass. He wanted to trade.

They were the pelts of an adult and two fair-sized cubs. When we asked him, through Palmquist, where and how he had killed them, he had quite a story to tell.

Coming down the east coast of Hudson Bay and around

Cape Jones in the spring, he said, he had blundered into the sow and her yearling youngsters. He had run his canoe ashore for the night and his woman was lugging the tent and other gear up to a little hollow above the beach. The Indian himself was still fooling around the canoe when the three bears walked into sight over a low ridge only 30 or 40 yards away.

The female reared up to look things over and didn't like what she saw. She began to growl and swing her head. One of the cubs walked on a few feet, got a noseful of Cree, and squalled in alarm. That did it. The sow let go a hair-lifting bellow of rage and charged.

Luckily for the Indian, he had been watching for seals that afternoon and his rifle still lay in the bottom of the canoe, loaded and uncased. He scrambled for it while the bear was making up her mind, and when she started her rush he was ready for her. He knocked her off her feet with the first shot, finished her with the second, and then killed the cubs.

Those three pelts were the first polar bearskins I had ever seen outside a zoo. Thickly furred, ivory white and lustrous, they whetted my appetite for an ice-bear rug of my own as nothing else had done.

At the end of his recital, the Indian ventured a sentence in English. "Plenty bear this year!" he grunted.

To this day I don't know whether he meant that he had had his fill of them for the time being, or that they were abundant and our chances would be good.

There was no open hunting season for sportsmen on polar bears on that coast then. All game was kept for the natives. If an ice bear was taken by a white man, it had to be under a permit issued to a museum or scientific institution and the bear, or at least its skull, must go for scientific purposes. That did not prevent the hunter from keeping the pelt, however.

Two of us had the coveted permits, calling for two bears apiece. Howard Cooper of Kalamazoo, a friend and hunting partner of mine who died many years ago, would try to collect his bears for a museum in his home city. My permit had been issued to the Cranbrook Institute of Science at Bloomfield Hills, Michigan.

The great white bear of the north (the Eskimos call him Nanook, the Crees Wahb'-es-co) is not always an animal of sea and ice floe. In the brief arctic summer he ranges along the coast and the rocky islands of the polar sea as well, I suppose feeding on mice and lemmings, birds' eggs, berries, and fish and seals, like all bears.

The Crees and Eskimos had told us that bears summered regularly on the islands in Hudson Bay and at the northern end of James Bay, but because 20 to 40 miles of open ocean lay in their way, they rarely hunted them, although the law allowed them to kill any they could.

We found ample proof of what they said, on some of the islands, too. Bear tracks crossed the beaches, holes had been dug in gravel banks for shelter from the summer sun, grass flattened where the animals had bedded, rocks overturned, and other sign was there in abundance. One of the islands— the Crees called it Niska or Grey Goose—had been literally torn up by bears.

A few days after we saw the three pelts at Fort George and heard the Indian's story of how he took them, we reached Long Island Sound, the bleakest and most desolate region we had seen. Treeless islands, rocky shores, moss and arctic willow. We were in polar bear country at last.

The first evening Eskimos paddled out to the Venture to trade fresh-caught char for canned peaches. Through two interpreters, Alagkok and our skipper, they told us there were many bears on a place they called Bear Island, 15 to 30 miles offshore. It did not show on our maps, and even now I am not sure of its correct name.

Cooper and I headed for it the next morning with Palmquist and the crew, leaving the rest of the party camped on Long Island.

When we reached the island the Eskimos had talked about, it proved to be a bleak, rolling tabletop of rock and moss, some two miles long and half as wide, rising steeply in a series of cliffs at the southern end, sloping to the north and ending in a long reef running out into the ocean.

We came in under it in a northwest gale, with a black squall sweeping down on us, and the rocky bottom would not hold the Venture's anchors. We looked in vain for an opening in the ragged, surf-fringed beach, and when none appeared we ran for a smaller island a mile away.

There we found a snug little harbor, covered with a black raft of ducks. We went ashore to have a look at the bigger island with binoculars, and almost at once Howard Cooper spotted what we were hoping to see, a white bear at the foot of the cliffs, alternately lying down and pawing rocks around as if hunting for mice.

The storm and raging seas held us in that harbor for four hours. All that time the bear wandered around in plain sight, either below the cliffs or on the rocky tundra above them. At last our patience was exhausted. If we did not go after him before dark, Tommy Lameboy and Palmquist agreed, he would be likely to leave the island and take to the sea during the night.

There was no hope of crossing to Bear Island in a canoe. We'd have to run the Venture out in plain view and risk spooking him.

He saw or heard us as soon as we cleared our little harbor, and while we beat our slow way across the churning channel he stood near the top of the cliffs and watched us, the only living thing on all that bleak island or in the smoking sea, a bear carved from old ivory, the most unforgettable animal my eyes have ever rested on.

When we were within 300 yards of shore he climbed deliberately up the cliff and galloped off, stopping now and then to look back our way.

Lameboy had the Venture's wheel. At Palmquist's sharp order he ran the schooner within 50 yards of the jagged rocks where the surf was smoking, then turned parallel to the beach. A canoe was trailing at the stern. Tommy and Cooper and I tumbled into it, and somehow we got through the surf and scrambled out on shore, and dragged the freight canoe up beyond reach of the sea. Then we followed the bear up the cliff.

Cooper and I were carrying .300 Savage rifles. At the time we thought them adequate. I wouldn't think so today, not for a bear of that size. But at least we were better off than the old Cree. He had no gun at all.

The bear was out of sight behind the low backbone of the island, and we went after him at a run. But the running was wretchedly hard, over soft moss, around shallow pools and between huge rocks, and before we reached the crest of the ridge I dropped out. Sweat was streaming down my face despite the bitter ice-field wind, and I couldn't get enough air into my lungs. I'd be in no condition to shoot if we met the bear, I concluded. I swung back toward the sea cliffs, thinking he might have turned that way.

I was at the top of the cliff when I heard distant rifle fire. Whirling around, I could see Cooper almost at the far side of the island, alternately shooting and then running a few steps. Another shot thudded and to my total astonishment the slug sang above my head. It had ricocheted off a rock, and the realization hit me that the bear must be somewhere between Cooper and me, or he would not be shooting in my direction.

I swung my head, and sure enough, there was the bear, out of Cooper's range now, coming straight for me at a lumbering run.

there was one shell left in the chamber of the gun and there would be no time for reloading

He did not know I was there. Directly behind me a ravine led down the face of the cliff to the sea, forming a natural bear trail. It was for that he was headed.

I went down on the moss to get out of sight and watched him lope toward me, and I had mixed feelings. I wanted him to come on. This was the thing I had come north for, and the hunt was all in my hands now. We'd be face to face in another minute or two. Unless I stopped him cleanly and in his tracks, there'd be a very one-sided bear-and-man fight.

He was the first game I had ever faced more dangerous than a whitetail deer. I was no expert rifleman, no crack shot, and I couldn't help some small misgivings as to whether I was up to my part of what was coming. Events were to prove I wasn't.

He went out of sight in a shallow dip, and I got to my feet and started after him, afraid he'd turn off and get away. Then he came up on my side of the hollow, and I suddenly realized that a running bear is neither slow nor clumsy. This one was covering ground like a racehorse.

I dropped to one knee, and when I thought he was close enough I threw my first shot. It had no effect and I tried again, with no better result.

The third one stopped him. He stood, whipping his head from side to side, lashing and biting at his own shoulders. When it was all over I learned that my 180-grain softnose had cut across his back under the skin and fat, just too high to break the spine or put him down. It was probably a painful wound, and it turned him into a bundle of explosive white fury, but it did nothing to disable him.

I thought he was badly wounded, and I scrambled erect to finish him. But just as I shot the next time he lurched ahead, and that one missed. Then, for the first time, he saw me.

The whole character of the hunt changed in a fraction of a second. I was no longer hunting the bear. He was hunting me. He dropped his head and came like an overgrown farm dog rushing out of a driveway at a passing car, and I did some desperately fast mental arithmetic.

I had started with five shells in the Savage. I had shot four times. I did the problem in subtraction with the speed of a computer, and did it over again. The answer was the same each time. There was one shell left in the chamber of the gun and there would be no time for reloading.

Instinct told me to drop the rifle and run, but my conscious mind knew better. Everything rested now on that single shell, and I still remember thinking I couldn't possibly kill him in time.

I cannot recall aiming or firing, but at the shot his head went down between his forelegs and he skidded to a stop, rolled up as tight as a shrimp. The bullet had struck him between the eyes, just below the bulge of the forehead, and had expanded so effectively that there was not a piece of unbroken bone bigger than a silver dollar left in his skull. A lightning bolt could not have killed more instantly.

I backed away while I fed five fresh hulls into the rifle. I waited two or three minutes then, feeling a whole lot better. When he did not move or twitch, I walked in with the safety off and prodded him around the head with the muzzle of the Savage. He was as lifeless as the rock he had fallen beside.

The next thing I did was walk back and find the empty cases I had levered out. From them to the bear I paced off exactly 17 steps, 51 feet.

Someone asked me long afterward whether I had actually shot at his head the last time. "Hell, no," I said. "I just shot at the bear." And I guess that was the truth.

I had my white bearskin. I also had nightmares for weeks afterward.

It happened 33 years ago. I have done much hunting since, some with a gun, some with a camera. But I have never again put myself in a situation of that kind, and as long as I live I don't intend to.

The Silent
Hunter

JOHN Lesowski was a kid only nine or ten years old when he acquired the best dog he would ever have. Tip was a Boston Bull and German Shepherd cross, but none of the hounds Lesowski has owned since, and he has had some good ones, could equal the mongrel at the thing he was born to do. That was to hunt cats.

John started him as a pup on ground squirrels and rabbits, but he quickly showed a strong preference for housecats, and from that it was only a short step to bobcats. There were enough of them around Vernon, in British Columbia 100 miles north of the U.S. border, where Lesowski grew up on a farm, to meet the needs of a boy and his dog nicely. Tip and John did all right.

Then the winter after the boy was 12 he decided to become a cougar hunter. He had read everything about it he could get his hands on, and most of the stories said that cougar hunters led their dogs on leash until they hit a fresh track, so he decided that was what he would do.

171

He was on snowshoes and he led Tip for four hours. In that short space of time he learned a great deal about cougar hunting that he had never seen in a story. Every time he started one way around a tree the dog went the other. If John climbed over a windfall Tip crawled under. Finally John unbuckled his collar and said, "Go get 'em!"

The dog found a fresh track—he must have known about it all along—and just 30 minutes after he was turned loose he had a big tom cougar up a tree. John got there as fast as he could, and he says now that nothing that has happened to him on a hunt since could begin to match the next minute for thrills.

The boy hunter was a little under-gunned, carrying a .22, but if he was short on rifle he was long on confidence. The cat wasn't up very high. John clipped him at the butt of an ear and he came down just as dead as any bobcat. Before the day was over Tip treed a second cougar, a smaller tom, and his boss killed that one, too. That was the beginning of a lifetime of cougar hunting, for both boy and dog. Tip has been dead many years, but Lesowski is still at it.

At first it was clandestine. John started playing hooky from school to do it. He'd cache his .22 the day before, leave for school in the morning with Tip trailing along, pick up the rifle, and away they'd go. When his mother got wise she sold the dog to people living 12 miles away, on the other side of the Shuswap River. It took Tip six months to find his way back. The new owner came after him, took him home, turned him loose, and that time he was back at the Lesowski house the next morning. When John promised to play no more hooky the man gave the dog back to him.

Tip would hunt anything John put him on, bobcat, lynx, cougar or bear. Lesowski took 65 cougars with him, but when Tip was getting old and not so quick on his feet he ran one in deep snow and overtook it on the ground. The cat killed Tip with one swat of a paw.

"For my part, I expect to go on cougar hunting as long as

I can follow dogs," John says. "I'm 44 now, and that means I've been doing it for 32 years. I've put in the hardest days of my life on such hunts, walking until I was sure my next step would be my last, then walking 10 or 15 more miles back to my car, long after darkness had fallen. More times than I can remember, after a day like that, I've started out again at daylight, too. And I have enjoyed every minute of it."

Lesowski is a British Columbia conservation officer, living with his wife and two girls, Gail, 13, and Joyce, 12, at Williams Lake, 250 miles north of Vancouver. Before he went on that job he worked for the British Columbia Fish and Game Branch for nine years as a predatory animal hunter. He has not kept a complete score of his cougar kills, but they total over 100, and the big cats are his foremost interest where wildlife affairs are concerned.

For him no other trophy animal in British Columbia, where he has lived his 44 years and done all his hunting, can hold a candle to them. The mere sight of a big one's track— on new snow some are the size of small saucers—is all it takes to start his heart beating double time. Those great round pad marks tell a story that tugs at any hunter's imagination. Here, in the black of night, walked one of the most stealthy and mysterious animals in North America, a magnificent cat, padding the dark timber on noiseless feet, furtive and silent, a cat that few humans ever see unless they follow dogs to the end of his track.

"So far as I'm concerned there are more thrills, excitement and anticipation in hunting him than in going after moose, caribou, mountain goats or any other game I have tried," Lesowski told me. "No matter how well a man knows his dogs he can never be sure just what sort of cougar he is after until he gets to the tree, or what will happen at the finish. Hound men are an incurable lot anyway, and once this hunting gets in the blood there's nothing quite like it."

On top of the suspense and action of the hunt, the hunter

who kills one of the big cats has a trophy that rates among the most impressive and beautiful he can take. There is nothing more breath-taking in a trophy room than a full mount of a big tom cougar. It speaks of wild country, rugged mountains, deep woods and shadowy trails. Even a cougar rug is something to look at twice. It's hardly a wonder that the pioneers liked to use the pelts for couch or bed covers, and sometimes even for lap robes.

Speaking of the cougar as a trophy, one thing that surprises many hunters, and causes frequent arguments, is his honest weight. He is smaller than his reputation would indicate. Full grown and in good condition, the toms average from about 135 pounds up to 165. The biggest Lesowski ever put on scales was 7 feet 3 inches long and weighed 187 pounds. Most females range from 75 to 135.

Over the years a few real whopper toms have been reliably recorded. Teddy Roosevelt killed one near Meeker, Colorado, in 1901 that weighed 227. The skull of that one stood in first place on the Boone and Crockett record list until after 1964, when it was topped by a skull taken in Wayne County, Utah. Another, killed in Colorado in 1927, weighed 217 pounds field dressed. But these are rare exceptions.

The lion is totally unpredictable, and no two hunts are the same. Lesowski has known one to kill a seasoned hound one day, then tree ahead of a green pup the next.

"I could train a poodle to hunt cougars if he had the nose for it, and if he'd bark he'd tree most of 'em," John says. "But sooner or later he'd also overtake one that didn't feel like climbing, and when that happened I'd have to get another poodle. With good dogs, some are pushovers, like those first two Tip treed for me, but most of the time they're anything but."

A big fat tom, carrying surplus weight, is usually short-winded once he's jumped and pushed hard. If he has recently eaten all the deer or elk or moose he can hold and is too full to run, he's likely to tree within a quarter mile. But a gaunt female with an empty belly may be good for five or ten miles, through broken rimrock, rough canyons, thick timber, the worst going she can find. And if dogs are put down on a track to cold trail and the cat hears them coming and lines out with a good start, both the hounds and the hunter can expect a lot of exercise before they look at that cougar in a tree.

In the late winter of 1962, in the Black Creek area along the Horsefly River 50 miles east of Williams Lake, a cougar track was seen near a remote country school. Alarmed for the safety of the children, the neighborhood wanted the cat hunted down, and Lesowski was asked to go after it.

He took two friends along, Manley Hanks, a guide, and Fred Jones, a rancher and trapper who also did some guiding, both from Horsefly. They had three dogs, two of John's and one of Fred's.

There was 18 inches of snow on the ground, making it necessary to use snowshoes. They picked up the tracks a mile and a half from the school. The prints indicated a big tom, but were too old to turn the dogs loose on. If they did that the hounds would go out of hearing and the cougar would go out of the country.

The three men walked all that day without getting close enough to warn the cougar that he was being followed, and when they got back to Fred's ranch after dark they had put 25 miles behind them. Right after daylight the next morning they picked up where they had left off.

That turned out to be an unusually interesting day of tracking. The cougar, still unaware that anyone was after him, swam the Horsefly River three times. He'd jump off a shelf of ice along shore, cross the open channel in the middle and climb out on the ice on the far side. Each time the hunters had to look for a place where the river was frozen all the way across, in order to follow.

That day, also, that cat proved that a cougar will feed on carrion readily if he needs to. They found where he had dug seven different moose heads, left by hunters the previous fall, out from under the snow and eaten a snack from each of them.

That was another 25-mile day, but the men were closing in now. When they left the track at dark the cougar was not far ahead, in an area where it seemed likely he'd stay for a day or two. They drove out the third morning in Fred's jeep and made a big circle around that area. No track came out. They went back, took the trail and followed it, confident they would jump him.

They caught up with him in late afternoon, finding his first kill, a moose calf. There were fresh tracks all over the place and the dogs went frantic. Turned loose, they started him less than half a mile away.

He headed downhill in an area of open timber and John saw him 300 yards away, running straight for him. The cat came within 30 yards, climbed six feet off the ground in a big pine, and stood looking back in the direction of the dogs.

Lesowski had been guilty of an oversight that morning. When he climbed into the jeep he had left his rifle in the car that had been used the day before. He was armed now with nothing but a small hand ax.

His favorite cougar gun, incidentally, is a Browning pump-action .22. It's light, easy to pack, and all the rifle he needs. He uses long-rifle hollow-points, and if he wants to save a skull intact for measuring he places his shot in the lungs. Hit there most cats hang on until they wilt and come down dead. But the shot he prefers, to make sure his dogs don't get clawed up, is in the front of the head, between the eyes and ears and a half inch off center. A .22 hollow-point there kills so quickly that the cat often hangs in a fork and it's necessary to climb to get him down.

In addition to his rifle, on all his cougar hunts John carries a compass, camera, knife, hand ax and rope, plus food and a tin to boil water in. The days are likely to be long.

When that big tom went six feet up the pine and stopped,

having no gun Lesowski yapped like a dog. He had never seen a lion climb any faster. The cat went up on the tree in long jumps with bark flying, until it was about 30 feet off the ground. Then it stopped and looked down to see where the extra dog had come from.

"I'll never forget the look on his face when he discovered what had done that barking right on top of him," John told me.

The three hounds were there in a minute, and then Fred and Manley came along with their .22's and shot the cat out. They skinned him, hiked to the nearest ranch, and the rancher drove them back to their jeep. They got home in time for a late supper. In those three days they had snow-shoed between 65 and 75 miles.

"Any animal that can give three men and three dogs a hunt of that kind is no small potatoes," Lesowski summed things up.

In almost any gathering of hunters you can start a lively argument by bringing up the subject of how much damage the cougar does to a deer population. Many sportsmen rate him the mortal foe of whitetails and muleys, and even of elk and moose. This attitude, coupled with the hostility stockmen feel toward him because of his raids on sheep, cattle and even horses, has been reflected over the years in year-round open seasons and in the cougar bounties that have long been paid in many places.

On the other hand, most game managers and even some hunters believe that the big cats are necessary to a healthy deer herd, that by helping to keep antlered game in balance with its food supply they render a major service. "In rough country and wilderness areas the lion is the deer's best friend," Jack O'Connor wrote in *Outdoor Life* a number of years ago. John Lesowski agrees. Today the cougar is fast winning recognition as an important game animal.

One thing John is sure of. Cougars do not "chase deer out of the country," as hunters often contend. He has found deer feeding as close as 75 yards to a lion that was sleeping after a kill, and they must have known the cat was there.

While there is no denying the big cat's fondness for venison and his skill in hunting it, it is far from his only food. In many areas rabbits are his bread and butter instead. In seven years of cougar hunting in the Caribou District of British Columbia, Lesowski kept a record of the stomach contents of 39 of the animals, all killed in the fall and winter months. Rabbits made up the biggest share, 26 per cent. Deer meat was second, at 23 per cent. Then came carrion, 12 per cent, and moose, domestic sheep and porcupines, each making up 8 per cent. In two cases the cougars had eaten other cougars.

They do not hesitate to turn cannibal if given the right opportunity. Lesowski has found two clearcut instances of it. In the first, near Horsefly in December of 1960, he skinned a male and a week later killed a female that had been feeding on the carcass for several days. She was in good condition and there were plenty of deer and moose in the area, so hunger could hardly have accounted for her behavior.

In the second instance a big cougar deliberately killed and fed on a smaller one. That happened in March of 1961, with 14 inches of snow on the ground, along the Horsefly River. The tracks told the whole story.

Both animals were toms. The big one had trailed his victim for some distance, both had swum the river, and once the pursuer got close enough he made a typical cougar rush. They fought briefly at the edge of an opening, left a little blood on the snow, then separated. The smaller tom ran about 50 yards and walked on in a big circle. The other one crept to the top of a knoll, waylaid him and attacked again. That time they fought viciously over a 40-foot circle, trampling down bushes and breaking willow branches. The small cougar lay there, his neck broken and a third of him eaten.

Manley Hanks and John treed the big one only 150

yards away, after he had stayed near his kill for two days. He had suffered only one claw cut in the fight, on his chest. He was 87 inches long, his victim 78, but the cat that had done the killing was the older and heavier of the two. As in the other case, there were plenty of deer and moose around to be had for the taking.

Actually, the cougar eats almost anything he comes across, from grasshoppers to moose, and including squirrels, rabbits, beavers, skunks, turkeys, fish, and on occasion even bobcats, lynx and coyotes. Frequently he also displays a liking for mutton, beef and colt meat if they are available.

In turn, the big cat himself is said to be good eating. John told me he had tried it only once, but he certainly enjoyed it that time. He had put in a hard day, from daylight until almost dark, following a cougar in 18 inches of snow. The dogs finally treed, and he shot and skinned it, but by that time darkness had fallen and he was too tired to hike back to his jeep, 25 miles away by road, so he camped under a tree for the night.

He had carried no lunch and had eaten nothing since breakfast. He was taking the cougar head home, along with the pelt, and he finally cut out the tongue and boiled it over his fire.

"It was the best piece of meat I ever ate, only there wasn't enough of it," he recalls.

One of the great mysteries about the cougar is his skittishness where humans are concerned. Shy and secretive in the extreme, he is one of the least frequently seen animals in the woods, and even when he is treed or brought to bay by dogs he displays little of the slashing fury of other big cats, and it's close to impossible to provoke him into fighting back at a man. He's capable of doing terrible damage but just refuses to deal it out.

In many places guides make it a practice to climb into a tree with a treed lion, work a loop of rope over his head, pull him off his perch, lower him to the ground, tie him up and take him home alive. It's hardly a wonder that he has acquired a reputation for cowardice, that he is sometimes called the gutless wonder.

Yet the belief that man has nothing to fear from him, regardless of circumstances, is a mistaken one. A female cougar protecting her young is likely to be dangerous, and every now and then extreme hunger goads one of the big cats into making a bold and determined attack on a human. This is especially likely to happen in the case of a disabled animal that has been injured or stuck full of porcupine quills and is no longer able to hunt its natural prey. Lesowski has checked out three such cases of unprovoked attack that have occurred in British Columbia in the last 30 years.

In October of 1942 Jack Carson, a trapper living on Horsefly Lake, was taking in winter supplies for his trapline between that lake and Quesnel. His main cabin was four miles north of Horsefly Lake and he was making two trips a day, packing supplies to it.

Moose were rutting, and he carried his rifle, a 6.5mm Mannlicher, on all his trips. But when several days went by without seeing a moose, he concluded that the rifle was excess baggage. To make his loads lighter, he'd leave it behind. At the last minute, however, luckily for him he changed his mind, picked it up and took it along.

He had covered about half of the 4-mile hike to the lake when he heard a sudden loud racket in thick brush and young cedar just ahead, and realized that some large animal was coming straight for him.

There were no big trees handy for protection, but he stepped behind a small lodgepole pine and waited. His first thought was that he was being rushed by a surely bull moose. Then he caught a glimpse of something tawny and decided it was an off-color deer. The next thing he knew a big cougar came tearing out of the brush only three or four steps away and jumped at his face. The small pine was between them.

The cat slammed into it, dropped to the ground at his feet, and he threw his rifle up for a shot.

But the day was rainy, and back at the cabin Carson had cleaned and dried the gun—and neglected to bolt a shell into the chamber. The hammer clicked now on an empty rifle.

He thinks the cougar did not quite have the guts to finish her attack from the foot of the tree. Instead she bounded up on a windfall 15 feet away and crouched, readying herself for another spring.

"Her big long tail was really lashing," Jack recalls.

But before she could pounce again he had a shell in the rifle and drove a softpoint into her head. She fell off the windfall so dead she never moved a muscle. "It takes quite a while to tell the story," Carson said long afterward, "but I'd bet that from the time I first heard brush crack until she was dead wasn't more than four or five seconds."

The cougar was a big female, more than 7 feet long, and in prime condition. But cougars breed the year around, like domestic cats, and the young are born at all seasons. Although it was October, when Jack skinned this one he found her udders full of milk. Her kits were probably nearby, and it was Lesowski's theory that she attacked out of maternal instinct, to protect them. That would also account for her noisy rush through the thicket, highly unusual cougar behavior and probably intended to frighten the man away.

Whether she would actually have completed the attack if she had not been shot remains an unanswered question— but Jack Carson had no doubts on that score, and the other cases bear him out.

The next one happened at Victoria Lake, near the north end of Vancouver Island, in March of 1953. Two men, Buck Richmond, manager of a lumber mill at Port Alice, and Gerald Walters, a woodsman and guide then working for Richmond as a millwright, now dead, were fishing on the lake. They went ashore for lunch, built a fire, and Walters,

the man met the attack with a smashing blow of his fist on the cat's nose

43 at the time, walked into the timber for wood. He was bending over to pick up dry branches when he saw a cougar crouched behind a log, ready to spring. It spit and launched itself.

The man met the attack with a smashing blow of his fist on the cat's nose, hard enough to knock it to the ground and break his own finger. The cougar, a female, grabbed one knee in her teeth and clawed that leg from hip to ankle. Walters got her by the throat and screamed for help. At first Richmond thought he was yelling for fun, but when he caught the words, "A cougar has got me," he grabbed a hand ax and ran to his partner's aid.

When he got there man and cougar were rolling and twisting on the ground. Walters was trying desperately to strangle the cat and she was biting and clawing at his hands. For a few seconds Richmond couldn't use his hatchet. Then he got an opening and drove the blade into the middle of of the cougar's back, all the way through her spine. Even that did not break up the fight, but Walters managed to twist her head to one side and three hard blows with the back of the ax ended the affair. The lion was 5 feet 7 inches long, very thin, on the verge of starvation and probably crazed by hunger.

The most recent attack came in March of 1965. Jim Baker, a 43-year-old rancher living near Loon Lake a few miles east of Clinton, was building fence with the help of a 15-year-old boy, John Simpkins, who had quit school to work for him because he thought he'd like ranch life.

The boy was about 60 feet downhill from Baker when the rancher saw the head of a cougar emerge from behind a big juniper clump between them, only a few steps from young Simpkins. "There's a cougar behind you!" he yelled. The cat jumped before the boy could turn his head, clearing 16 feet in a single leap. It landed on his back and knocked him flat.

Tracks showed afterward that the cougar had stalked its prey exactly as it would have stalked a deer. It had come around the hill in an open area with few trees, taking advantage of every bit of cover and creeping within striking distance behind the juniper clump.

The startled youth threw up his hand to protect his face and throat. The cougar bit through the hand, then went for the head above the eyes, tearing at skin and scalp. Baker, knowing that one bite in the throat would be the end, shouted to Simpkins to keep his chin down and at the same time started for them.

He jumped astride the cat and did his best to pull it off, but it would not let go its hold. Baker then jerked out a pocket knife and jabbed the blade deep into its throat. He missed his mark, the jugular vein, but the knife wound was too much for the cougar. It dropped Simpkins, ran off a few feet and crouched behind a brush pile. The rancher grabbed

Baker then jerked
out a pocket knife
and jabbed the blade
deep into its throat

up a hammer and started for it, and when he was only four feet away it whirled and scratched its way up a tree.

The boy was bleeding badly, and Baker rushed him to a hospital at Ashcroft. It took between 30 and 40 stitches to close the wounds on his face, head and arm, but he came out of the hospital at the end of 10 days in pretty good shape.

It was after dark when Jim Baker got home from his trip to the hospital that night. The next morning he went back to the scene with a neighbor, but the cat was gone.

Twenty-four hours later Frank Richter, a conservation officer from Kamloops, and John Lesowski undertook to hunt it down. They picked up the track more than a mile from the place where the cougar had leaped on young Simpkins. The animal had lain under a tree there, but the ground was half bare and patched with crusted snow, and the dogs could not follow the track.

Late that afternoon, however, the hunters got an unexpected break when Richter saw a gaunt, smallish cougar cross the road about half a mile from the scene of the attack. Thy put four dogs down and the cat treed only 100 yards from the road.

It was a female about three years old, no more than skin and bones. More than six feet long, she should have weighed 100 to 125 pounds. Instead she weighed 70, and examination showed she was starving. There had been a severe shortage of rabbits around there that winter and the cougars were all hungry. One had killed a goat in a yard near Baker's place in full daylight only a short time before.

It's Lesowski's belief that cougar litters born in times of rabbit abundance learn to hunt rabbits but not deer, and if a rabbit die-off occurs these young cats get pretty hungry before they find out how to go on a venison diet. John thinks they are the ones that come into dooryards and kill dogs and goats. He has known them actually to starve to death in a deer area. He was sure that this female was one of that kind, driven by extreme hunger to attack young Simpkins.

Such happenings are rare, and hunger accounts for most of them. Normally man has little to fear from the big stealthy cat. But that doesn't make him any less interesting. He does not need to be a potential man-killer to qualify as a great game animal. There are plenty of other things about him to satisfy the hunter.

"I don't expect I'll ever hunt any of the other big cats, such as tigers, leopards or lions, or even jaguars," John Lesowski says. "But as long as there are cougars in my home mountains to furnish excitement for me and my dogs, I won't complain."

Death
Came
Running

IT began as a fishing trip into the back country of Alberta's Jasper National Park. The way the three men planned it, it looked about as dangerous as a game of dominoes. But it ended in an ordeal almost too terrible to believe. Steve Rose, Dave Slutker and Leonard Jeck came back from that trip with injuries and scars they will carry to their graves.

Rose was a Los Angeles art dealer, 44 at the time, who liked all kinds of hunting, sheep first and foremost, and liked fishing almost as well.

Slutker, a former outfitter at Brule just outside Jasper Park, and Rose were partners in a mail-order fur business at Edmonton, dealing in the furs of the north, polar bear, grizzly and black bear skins and rugs, timber and arctic wolf, wolverine, lynx and others.

Rose had been working unusually hard in the spring of 1968 and had lost his elderly mother after a lingering illness of two years. Too, he had always had a strong desire to get into the mountains in early summer. So when Slutker phoned from Edmonton and invited him to come up for a week or two of fishing, packing and camping he needed no urging.

He caught a flight from Los Angeles to Vancouver, transferred and went on non-stop to Edmonton. Dave was waiting at the airport there on the afternoon of May 25, and they left for Jasper by car the next morning. Jeck, a friend of Dave's whom he had engaged to outfit and guide them for 10 or 12 days, would meet them there.

Dave could not have picked a better man. Leonard Jeck was 8 or 10 years older than Rose, with more than 30 years of outfitting, trail riding and guiding under his belt. Quiet, unassuming, level-headed, he was exactly the kind you'd like to have along in case of trouble. And although they didn't know it, there was bad trouble ahead.

Jeck had just brought his horses off the winter range and was holding them at a camp below Snake Indian Falls on the Snake Indian River an hour and a half north of Jasper by pickup. They would start the pack trip from there.

At that point their plans suffered a jolt. Leonard had learned only that day that the Snake Indian, where they intended to do their fishing, would not be open until June 15. The park wardens had not yet gotten their horses for the summer, and probably had delayed the opening because they were concerned about tourists getting into trouble in a remote area where they'd be hard to reach.

So Rose and Slutker had a choice. They could carry through their plans with Jeck and go fishless, or go somewhere else for fishing. Dave and Steve enjoyed trout fishing well enough, but this time it was really secondary to getting off in the mountains for a week or two. Also, Leonard had his horses ready for them and his crew had shoes on the ones they were to use. They told him they'd go ahead with the pack trip even though they couldn't fish.

The three drove up to the horse camp the next morning. The wranglers had a big tent up, a stone fire pit built, and a rope corral for the horses. Dave and Steve pitched their tent, and spent the next few days helping with the stock, riding, taking pictures and just loafing.

Then they loaded three pack horses, saddled and took the main trail up along the Snake Indian. Five or six miles above the Willow Creek Ranger Station, not yet manned for the summer, they found a spot for a fly camp, a beautiful location on the river, with a half-moon meadow for the horses and a point of trees to cut the wind.

"I'll see that place in my mind and hear the lonesome sound of the horse bells 20 years from now," Rose told me.

They knew they were in bear country. All of Jasper Park is prime grizzly range. But they didn't give it much thought. They were experienced woodsmen, with many years and many hunts in grizzly country behind them. They had seen no grizzly tracks, and didn't feel any real concern about bears, although they did take the usual precautions, burning garbage, leaving no scraps or cans around, and moving their meat and bacon some distance out of camp.

There was one thing about the situation that was new to Rose. Because they were in the park, they could not carry firearms. It was his first experience in a place of that kind without a gun, and he didn't altogether like it.

The second morning they saddled early and headed for the high country. They were in a corner of the park that Jeck had not seen, but one of his wranglers had cooked for a party there 10 years before, and he had told Leonard about two high lakes that were supposed to have good fishing. Leonard wanted to get a look at them, with future trips in mind. It would be a hard ride, for the snow was still deep in places, but the early-summer days were getting long and they thought they could make it back to the fly camp before dark.

There was a trail of sorts for a ways, up a creek, but as

they climbed they encountered more snow and rougher going, so they finally decided to leave the horses in the creek bottom and go ahead on foot.

They hiked for an hour and a half, topping out on the crest of a steep saddle. By that time Leonard and Steve were separated from Dave. He was only 27, and still given to running up mountains. Steve and Leonard were setting a little slower pace. They could see Dave on a ridge above timberline, 400 to 500 yards ahead.

There was a small, spruce-covered basin beyond the saddle, and they started across it. Rose stopped to take a picture and Jeck walked on. He had just gone out of sight in the timber when he yelled at the top of his lungs, and in the same instant Steve heard a bear growl. Then he saw Leonard and a honey-blond grizzly rolling down through the spruce, 30 feet away.

When they had a chance to piece the story together later on, they agreed that the bear's attack was not premeditated. She and Leonard had come face to face at 5 feet while she was running full tilt through the timber, with two cubs right behind her. It was Steve's theory that she had caught a whiff of man scent but had not located them, and was clearing out when she and Leonard bumped into each other. Had she planned the attack, almost certainly she would have sent the cubs up a tree or left them somewhere out of the way.

Not that it made any difference. Premeditated or not, that attack was as good an example as I know about of what is likely to happen when a man and grizzly surprise each other at close quarters. The bear didn't hesitate a second. She simply kept running the way she was headed, grabbed Jeck by the upper leg and took him along.

When Rose heard her loud growl and Leonard's screams, and saw the two of them rolling in a heap, his blood ran pretty cold. He knew his partner was in deadly danger, and in all likelihood he and Dave were too, although Slutker was

*she simply kept running the way she was headed, grabbed
Jeck by the upper leg and took him along*

out of harm's way at the moment. The only weapons any of
them had were folding pocket knives.

Steve froze where he was. He was sure Leonard would
play dead, and might escape with a few bites and a light
working over. Steve hadn't seen cubs, but if there were any
along, as he suspected, the bear might leave in a minute or
two and lead them off.

But he didn't stay frozen more than a few seconds. He
realized very quickly that if Jeck had tried to play dead he
had given that up. The grizzly was pressing her attack
savagely, and from the sound of the battle and what Rose
could see he could tell that Leonard was fighting for his life,
trying to fend her off with his bare hands and the canvas
case of his spotting scope.

Steve was standing beside a scrubby timberline spruce, not
more than 20 feet tall, with thick branches all the way to the
ground, and he clambered into it. If he got up where he
could see the bear, he reasoned, maybe he could draw her off
Leonard by yelling at her. Probably instinct also told him

that if he succeeded he would be better off in the tree than facing her on the ground, although he didn't really think that scraggly spruce would stop her.

It didn't. Rose scrambled up 12 or 15 feet and yelled at the top of his voice. Then he saw her coming, making a beeline and running hellbent. The tree barely slowed her. She climbed like an overgrown squirrel, not grabbing the trunk but using the branches like ladder rungs.

The man was braced and ready, and when she was just below him he stomped her in the face with both boots. She didn't even flinch, and before he could pull his feet back onto a branch he felt her jaws crush into his lower leg.

She got her teeth into him solidly and yanked and shook in an attempt to pull him down. When he hung on with his hands and arms, she let go, grabbed him higher in the leg and let herself fall out of the tree. That time she took him along. They went crashing down through the branches together and hit the ground with a good hard thump.

That loosened her hold and Steve rolled over on his face, pulled his old hunting jacket over his back and head and prepared to take his turn at playing dead.

She grabbed him in the leg again, mauled him around, and then moved up to his back and shoulders. She kept biting, making puncture wounds and letting go, holding him down with her paws and taking time to select deliberately the place for each bite.

She was working herself into a terrible fury, maybe from the smell and taste of blood, and all of a sudden she grabbed his left sohulder, ripped out a bite of flesh and ate it. At that point Rose decided he had played dead long enough.

He yelled at her—Dave said afterward the screams were the most terrifying he had ever heard—and reached for his knife. It was in a back pocket on the right side and he went for it with his right hand. The instant he moved that arm the grizzly pounced on it. She bit deep into the shoulder and tore out a bite and then another. Steve was lying on his belly, with his head turned that way, and he could watch her tear at him. Their faces were no more than six inches apart, and he will remember as long as he lives the fetid stench of her breath, mixed with the smell of his own blood.

He rolled enough to reach up with his left arm, grab her by the nose and twist it with every ounce of strength he had. It didn't faze her. She grabbed into his shoulder once more and he felt bone break as she ripped away a piece of the shoulder blade. Blood streamed down the right arm, and he could no longer use it.

he stomped her in the
face with both boots

Up to that instant he had not thought about the bear killing him. His whole concern had been for the pain and for ways of fighting her off. Now it dawned on him all of a sudden that maybe he wasn't going to fight her off. Another bite or two would tear away his right arm, and if the main artery hadn't already been severed it would be then. That could end only one way, whether he died under her jaws or bled to death after she walked away.

Desperate men do desperate things, and Steve tried the only tactic he could think of. He rammed the fingers of his left hand up her nostrils as far as they would go.

He never knew whether that did any good or whether something else took her attention. Anyway, she let go of him, twisted her head aside and looked up the hill. Then she leaped off him and started that way at a dead run.

There, barreling through the spruce, came Slutker, carrying a club and running to meet her headon. He had heard the noise of the fight and was charging down to do what he could, armed only with a chunk of wood he had grabbed up.

"It was a brave decision, and it says a great deal for the kind of man he is," Steve told me.

Neither Jeck nor Rose was doing any yelling at that point, and Dave was not sure just where they were. He was shouting "Where are you? Where are you?" as he ran. Then he saw the bear coming for him around a tree less than 10 steps away. There was no chance to dodge her, no sense trying to run. She was too close and coming too fast. Dave braced himself and belted her in the face with his club, but the blow had no effect.

She sent him sprawling and went for his face in a wicked, slashing attack.

"The next thing I knew I was lying on my back, looking up at her," he said afterward. "She took a bite from just below my eye to the jaw under my ear. I remember hearing the bones crack as she closed her jaws, and I thought to myself, 'Oh God, no, not in the face!'"

Dave still does not know why the right side of his face

was not ripped entirely away. He managed to get hold of her tongue with his left hand and pulled with all his strength. She dropped him and jerked her head back, giving him time to roll over and cover the back of his head with his hands. He got one bite through the left hand that punched a hole between the first two fingers. Then he felt her front paws on his back and heard her growling, and he recalled thinking, "She's going to take my head off!"

She had opened him up between the eyes and down through the nose to the upper lip, crushed in his cheek bone and eye socket, and left a jagged hole in the right side of his face that you could have laid an orange in.

It was Steve's belief at the time that she inflicted that terrible wound with a murderous blow of a front paw as she came up to Dave. Steve even thought he saw Dave take the blow and go down as if sledged, rolling from the force of it. But Dave was positive that was not the way it happened, and Dr. J. M. Alton, who did the initial plastic work on him at Edmonton and who had a great deal of knowledge about bear attacks and their consequences, told him it would have been impossible for a blow from a paw to cause the type of damage he suffered.

The bear did not do much biting or mauling after that first lightning onslaught. Dave attempted to play dead, even tried to hold his breath. For a few seconds he felt her claws dig into his shoulder, and then suddenly she was gone.

To Rose it looked as if she lay down on him briefly, the way a bear does on its kill. She was growling and looking back toward Steve, and he kept thinking, "Oh, my God, here she comes again."

But she was no longer interested in him. Maybe she thought that part of her job was finished. Suddenly she jumped to her feet and came straight for him, and his heart came up in his throat, but she ran across his legs without looking at him, tore on past Jeck and went out of sight. She had broken off the fight as suddenly as she began it.

They never knew what made her leave in that abrupt

fashion, but the logical explanation seemed to be that her cubs had moved out. Having sensed that she had killed or disabled all three of the men, suddenly she decided to follow the youngsters.

Steve lay for a couple of minutes where she had mauled him, trying to pull himself out of the shock. Then he crawled a few feet up the slope and called to Dave.

Slutker was on his feet, weaving, half his face crushed in or torn away, pouring blood, a dreadful sight, but he walked slowly to Rose. His first words were ,"Steve, we're in a hell of a spot." Then he looked around. "Where's Leonard?"

Steve pointed down the hill. "Down there," he said. "But I don't know whether he's alive or dead." He had heard no sound from Jeck since the bear left him. But now Leonard settled that question in person. He came hobbling out of the timber, limping badly on both legs and moving very slowly.

It would be hard to imagine three men in a worse fix. Jeck was bitten severely on the legs and arms; Slutker was groggy from the wound on the face, blinded in one eye and the other full of blood; Rose had lost a lot of blood, was still bleeding badly, and could barely move his left leg.

The way back to the horses lay through rocks and fallen timber and down into a steep canyon. There was no trail. It had taken an hour and a half to hike to the place where the bear had attacked. The three would be lucky if they made as good time going back, and they shared the feeling that if they did not reach help before nightfall they would never make it. They wasted no time feeling sorry for themselves, however. They were in poor shape to help each other, but somehow it had to be done.

Steve tried crawling on all fours for about 10 yards but he could see he'd never make it that way, so he stood up and started to walk in spite of the agonizing pain.

He went ahead, leading Dave, and Leonard brought up the rear, shouting directions. When they started down into the canyon it was pure hell. They slipped and fell, got up and staggered on. They stopped to rest only four times in all, and then for only a minute or two.

Leonard's sense of direction proved fantastic. They hit the creek at the log where they had crossed it going in. By that time Steve was suffering from extreme thirst, probably as a result of the blood he had lost. He stopped for a long drink, and then they limped on to the horses.

Steve took his down jacket off the saddle and with Dave's help got it over his right shoulder and buttoned it as tight as he could. It would check the bleeding, and he'd need it for warmth once shock set in. He knew that was inevitable.

They got on the horses and Leonard took the lead. Dave could barely see to follow him, and Steve was in the worst shape of all, with both arms disabled and no way to control his horse. The horse gave him a pretty rough trip, jamming his torn legs against trees and bouncing off ledges to land hard on its front feet and send sickening waves of agony through the injured man. He hurt all over, but his right shoulder was the worst. The pain was excruciating every minute of that three-hour ride, and it seemed more like three days to him.

Leonard sang to keep their spirits up, and Dave did some praying. Every stream they came to Dave climbed off his horse and filled his hat with water for Steve, and each time Rose gulped down the whole hat full.

Dave was jerking the saddle off his horse by the time Steve rode into camp. Leonard left his saddled. He was the only one who knew the exact way to the Willow Creek Ranger Station, he had the best horse and was in the best condition to ride. If he could break in there he could use the phone to summon help.

He was shaking now like a half-drowned puppy. Dave built a small fire and gave him a chocolate bar to eat, and he took 15 minutes to warm up. Steve got a bottle of Bufferin, all the medicine they had, out of his shaving kit and they split it three ways. Then Steve kicked off his boots and crawled into his bag. Dave did the same, and Leonard rode off.

They had reached the camp at 6 o'clock. Jeck left before 6:30. If all went well, and if a helicopter was available at Hinton, 20 miles east of the park boundary on the road to Edmonton, as they believed, they would be out of the mountains by dark. All Dave and Steve could do was wait and hope. Steve pulled the canvas water bucket over by his bag and went on drinking, and they talked to keep each other awake. They were afraid to sleep. If Leonard failed to raise help and came back, they would have to undertake the long ride out, and if they slept and stiffened up that would be too much for them. Steve realized later that he could not have made it. By the time he reached a hospital a third of his blood was gone, and he could not have survived more riding.

At 9 o'clock he and Dave heard a helicopter coming. Their hearts sank when it droned over and kept going. They didn't guess that Jeck, hurt as he was, was in the chopper, guiding it. He spotted the camp and the pilot turned back and landed in the meadow. The first man out was Dr. Michael Todd of Hinton.

Leonard had made it to the ranger station in less than an hour, used his knife to get the lock off, and called the nearest park warden. The warden caught Robert Southworth, pilot of the helicopter, just as he was tying down for the night. Bob picked up Dr. Todd, they flew to the ranger station, squeezed Jeck into the two-man bubble with them, and headed for the injured men.

Dr. Todd administered shots to ease the pain. There was too little daylight left for Bob Southworth to make two flights back to Hinton. Instead he would take Dave and Leonard as far as the Seldom Inn Ranger Station at the end of the Jasper road, and then come back for Steve. Mickey McGuire, the chief park warden, was already on his way to the ranger station in a station wagon pressed into service as an ambulance, bringing a thermos jug of hot coffee and warm blankets. He'd take the two partners out.

Dr. Todd stayed with Steve. The 'copter was back in less than half an hour, but by that time it was getting dark. They couldn't risk getting Rose into the bubble, the way he was bleeding, so they put him on a stretcher, still in his bag, lashed it to the landing runners and lifted out of the meadow for the hour's flight to the Community Hospital at Hinton. They landed there just before 11 that night, 9½ hours after the bear attack.

The hospital was small but very efficient, staffed by four young Scottish medics, Dr. Todd, Dr. Duncan Murray, Dr. Ian Reid, and Dr. Ronald Fraser, and by excellent nurses. They were waiting for Steve, with blood donors available, and the operating room and everything in readiness.

They wheeled him into surgery at 11 o'clock and told him afterward that he was taken out between 3:30 and 4 the next morning.

McGuire rushed Dave and Leonard to a hospital at Jasper, arriving at midnight, and they were patched up there.

The aftermath? Not altogether happy, but not as bad as it might have been. Jeck had more than 30 deep bites in his legs, back and arms, and two claw wounds on his chest, but he recovered in good shape. Slutker's skull was fractured above the eye socket, his cheek bone smashed and the eyelid torn. He was moved to Edmonton for plastic surgery early the following June. The surgeons did a great job, restoring the eye socket and putting back in place more than 40 small pieces of cheek bone.

Rose had suffered serious bites on the left leg, the left shoulder and back, with some muscles torn out of the left arm, and very bad damage to the right shoulder. The bear had ripped away the muscles that enabled him to lift his arm on that side. His left arm and leg recovered fully, but there was some permanent damage to the right arm.

Months afterward Steve summed up his thinking about the whole affair this way:

"I can't see that we were to blame in any way. It was an

accident, pure and simple. We were veteran outdoorsmen, taking every normal precaution. We could make the same trip 1,000 times in safety, or go back tomorrow and encounter the same kind of trouble. Maybe if you go into bear country enough times your luck is bound to run out.

"I can understand officials, either in this country or Canada, not wanting tourists running around the national parks with guns. But a sidearm would have saved us. Even with a .22 I could have killed the bear when she had me by the leg in the tree or was chewing my back.

"I feel strongly that sidearms should be allowed in the back country of certain parks for the sake of safety. The wardens in Jasper carry rifles for their own protection. Why should visitors be denied the same right? A man is entitled to protect his life, in a national park as well as anywhere else, and few if any would abuse the privilege by trying to shoot elk or sheep with a pistol.

"At the very least, I believe licensed guides should be allowed to carry guns in such parks, to protect the members of the party they are guiding.

"I can make one guarantee. Any time I go into grizzly country from now on I'll have a short-barreled .44 Magnum along, laws or no laws. If I can't take the gun I won't go. I don't want grizzlies done away with, but after what we went through I put humans ahead of bears."

Terror
in the
North

WHEN Olive Goodwin married the young trapper Walter Reamer in the fall of 1920, their first home was a primitive 10 x 10 trapper's shack in Alberta 30 miles north of Athabasca Landing, on the river of the same name.

It was a wild and lonely place but it was also good fur country, with fox, lynx, beaver and bear, and there was plenty of game. Walter put out a trapline, and killed enough deer and moose for food. They lived on meat and bannock, which Olive baked on a little rusty camp stove.

She accompanied Walter everywhere he went. They had a dog team of sorts, two scrubs that weren't worth much but could pull a load of traps and other gear on a homemade toboggan. The country was beautiful, the trapline kept them busy, they were in love, and Olive had never been happier in her 19 years. She was a frontier trapper's wife and that was exactly what she wanted to be.

She was the daughter of a trapper and homesteader, too, so isolation and hardship were not new to her. Her mother

201

had died when she was eight. The family was living then on the Sturgeon River in Alberta 25 miles north of Edmonton, having moved from Wisconsin a few months before.

After her account of the privations and dangers of her early years appeared in *Outdoor Life,* in May of 1969, a neighbor who had known the Goodwin family in Wisconsin and still remembered the hewn-log house in which they lived wrote the magazine to say: "Olive Fredrickson is a brave pioneer woman, and she came by her courage honestly. Her father, Archie Goodwin, was probably the greatest hunter and pioneer that ever lived in Clark County, Wisconsin."

At the time Olive's mother died, her father and three brothers, Elmer, Will and Menzo, had gone north to Lesser Slave Lake for the winter, looking for a place to homestead in good fur country where they could trap and live off the land. She was alone at home with her mother. She couldn't go to school, for the mother was not well enough to be left by herself. She had brought four girls and eight boys into the world and raised them, and her health and strength were gone.

There was no railroad north of Edmonton at that time, and no way to send word of her death to the father even if the others had known his exact whereabouts, which they didn't. Olive's sister Maud and her husband came to stay with the 8-year-old girl, and it was almost five months before the father and the boys got a message from the Mounties, saying that the mother was gone. Then it took them another month to come the 180 miles home, following the old Klondike Gold Trail by team and wagon, through muskeg so bad that some days they did well to make two miles.

The following June the Goodwins set out for the Peace River country, with two teams and wagons, taking all their possessions, including a crate with 10 chickens. But they never got to the Peace.

That was a hard trip, even harder on stock than on

people, much of it across creeks and through muskeg where they had to build pole bridges and lay corduroy as they went. Others had tried it ahead of them, and at many of the creek crossings they saw the remains of horses and oxen half sunk in the mud. Some had been there for years and only a few bones were left. Other carcasses were still covered with dried hide. The mosquitoes, horse flies, blackflies, deer flies and bot flies, hoof rot, and a disease called swamp fever, had proven too much for the poor brutes. From a camp on a low hill one noon the Goodwins counted 21 horses that had died within the last month or so.

"The pioneers in the Peace and Athabasca River valleys paid dear for their new homes," Olive said long afterward.

The family stopped at the end of summer, when they got as far as Tomato Creek, a small tributary of the Athabasca. Olive never knew how it got its name, for in shady places there was frost a foot down in the muskeg all summer, and there were few nights when water didn't freeze. You could no more grow tomatoes there than on the moon, she recalled. But they did find excellent grass for the horses, vetch and peavine belly deep on a horse on the poplar ridges, plenty of deer and moose, and blueberries and cranberries everywhere. The first day they camped there her father and the boys went hunting and her brother John killed a moose with a rack that his long-barreled .303 British couldn't reach across.

By Christmas of that year they had put up a big one-room log cabin with an open fire on the dirt floor for heat, pole bunks along the wall, and grain sacks stuffed with hay for mattresses. They were only three miles from the Athabasca, which many people followed on the long trek north to take up land, and where freight teams hauled supplies and mail on the river ice all winter. The father soon built a bigger house, and barns to shelter stock, and the place became a stopover point for men, women, children, horses, mules and oxen. Teams were stabled and fed for $1 apiece, and Olive remembered seeing as many as 60 of them in the barns in one night. Goodwin's Halfway House, as the place came to be called, was soon known all through that country.

There was no school within 45 miles, but Olive—at that time she preferred her middle name of Alta—began studying from old schoolbooks her brothers had brought along and did the best she could to get some education.

There was a great chance to make money in the halfway-house business, and in trapping the surrounding country for muskrats, weasels, mink, foxes and a few lynx, so the Goodwins never completed their move to the Peace. As the years passed they trapped, raised black and silver foxes, took care of a garden and chickens, and raised cattle and horses and sold them to the settlers. In 1917 the father was remarried, to an old school chum.

Three years later a young trapper named Walter Reamer stopped at the Halfway House one day and stayed overnight. He and Olive played a violin and guitar all evening, and she said later that it was a case of love at first sight. Reamer went to work for a neighbor near the Goodwin place, and in the fall they were married and struck out together.

They stayed in the tiny trapper's cabin only until Christmas. Then the young husband grew restless and decided to go down to Bonacord, where he knew farmers they could work for.

The fact was, Walter Reamer was afflicted with a fatal wanderlust. For him there was always some other place where game and fur were more plentiful, opportunities better.

"I loved him very much, but I have to admit he had itchy feet," Olive told me long afterward.

Her two older brothers, John and Lea, had opposed the marriage because of that, but their objections did no good. Walter's restlessness was to account for much moving around in the brief years of the marriage, and in the end it led him indirectly to his death.

In the first 16 months after they were married they moved four times: north to a trapline, to the big farm at Bonacord, to a coal mining job, and then to another farm. At the two farms Walter made $20 a month, doing chores and cutting wood and fence rails, and his wife helped in the house for their room and board. While he worked in the coal mine she stayed with a widow a few miles away, earning her own keep, and seeing him only on Saturdays and Sundays.

In February 1922 their first baby, also named Olive, was born in Edmonton. Olive was in the hospital three days before and 14 days after the birth. The couple stayed on with an elderly couple in Edmonton another two weeks so she could be near a doctor. Then Walter met a man in town who was ready to go back down to Fort McMurray, on the Clearwater at its confluence with the Athabasca, where he had worked previously and been paid $4 a day. He said Walter could get a job there, and $4 a day meant a small fortune in that country at that time. So as soon as Olive was strong enough, when their little daughter was a month old, they headed back to the raw frontier.

They got on a train on the Great Waterways Railroad, which ran from Edmonton to the end of steel at the tiny settlement of Waterways, on the Clearwater four miles above Fort McMurray. They would make that last short leg of the journey by horses and sleigh on the river ice.

What a train trip that was! They crawled along, terribly slow, and where the tracks crossed big stretches of muskeg they could look out the window and see the mucky ground tremble and shake like open water. At one place a boxcar had been derailed and only about two feet of it showed above the slimy ooze. Olive shivered at the sight of it and she still shivered years afterward, remembering it.

At Fort McMurray they moved in with one of her brothers, Frank, in two rooms above his dance hall. The place was jumping, but it was a welcome change for the young wife after her years in the bush. There were women for neighbors, children, good lively music on dance nights, people coming and going beneath the kitchen window.

Walter's first job there was driving a team of five dogs down-river to Fort MacKay, taking along the businessman who owned the dogs. That was a team to make you look twice. Actually, all but one were pure-bred timber wolves, big gray brutes that were forever backing up to get slack in their chains so that if somebody walked close enough they could spring forward and grab him.

The one that wasn't a wolf was a big red dog named Smiler. He'd curl up his lip and wag his tail when anyone approached him, and he seemed extra pleased when he was being harnessed for a trip. Not so the wolves. Or if they were they never showed it. But once in harness they were hard workers, and tired far less easily than dogs.

Sled wolves were in common use there in the north at that time, and most of them were hard characters. The owners got them by digging them out of dens as pups, and they never completely lost their wolf ways. Olive saw a small cocker spaniel come out from behind a lumber pile near Frank's team one day. The two nearest wolves backed up until their chains were slack, and when the cocker trotted within reach they lunged and killed him before he could yelp. He was torn in two and swallowed in just a few gulps. After that she didn't wonder Frank had warned her that if he was away and she was feeding his team, she was to throw the food to them from a safe distance and never get close.

He brought his lead wolf, Dan, upstairs to their rooms on a chain one day to give his sister a real close look. The animal stood as high as her chest and weighed more than she did, but Frank assured her he was as gentle as a kitten so long as his boss had hold of the chain.

She had baked bread that day and put two loaves in a box under the table to cool. The wolf smelled it, and almost before they knew what was happening, he skidded Frank across the floor and went after the bread. Frank pulled and kicked and yelled, but Dan didn't raise his head until he had gulped down both loaves. Used to being fed only once a day, and forever hungry, those sled wolves were expert pilferers and could put away extra food in a hurry if they got the chance.

Walter got back from his downriver trip in the nick of time. There were wide streams of water running between the solid ice in mid-river and the shore by the time he returned, and Frank had to go out in a small boat and bring him and the dogs to the bank. Olive had worried for two or three days that the ice would start moving. She knew if it did and he was out on it he'd certainly drown.

He got home on a Friday afternoon. On Sunday the two of them went for a walk on a trail that followed the Athabasca as far as Horse Creek, with Walter carrying the baby. All of a sudden they heard a thunderous noise upriver, and looking that way they could see a pile of ice like a small mountain springing up in mid-stream.

Olive had lived along the Athabasca long enough to know what that meant. The river ice had started to move, and a jam was forming in the rapids a half mile above. She knew the awesome power of that ice, and knew they needed to get back to Fort McMurray without losing a second. They were in no actual danger, for if the ice cut them off on the trail they could climb the tar-sand hills back from the river, but those hills were brushy and rough and that would mean a very hard hike, especially with the baby. Walter wasn't as concerned as his wife was, for he had never lived close to a big north-country river, but he took her word for it and they started to hurry back.

They had not gone a quarter mile when the jam began moving slowly down, and with blasts like the crash of cannon the 3-foot-thick ice ahead of it, where they were, started to break and go. The Athabasca was over a half mile wide there, but there was not room in the channel for that huge, moving mountain of ice. The whole groaning, cracking mass ground and shoved its way along with unbelievable force, tearing trees out by the roots, gouging away tons of river-bank, and where the shore was low pushing up onto the land, flattening brush and tipping trees in a mashed, tangled rubble.

At one point they found it thrusting onto the shore for 400 feet, and they made a long rough detour up the hill, and then clawed their way through thick stuff back to the trail.

Back at Fort McMurray they met a sight that was hard to believe. A huge ridge of ice was piling up on a 3-acre island in the middle of the river, plowing and churning trees, earth and rock until the whole island was ground away. Then the ice stopped moving, save for a muddy channel 100 feet wide on their side. Another jam had formed. That jam backed the ice flow a mile up the Clearwater, tearing boats apart, knocking down houses and wrecking a sawmill. Many people took refuge on the hill behind the settlement. But within an hour the pent-up force of the mighty river broke the jam and the ice moved once more. The great piles that were left on the banks soon melted in the warmth of the spring sun and the whole thing was forgotten.

A big stern-wheeler steamboat, the *Slavie,* was being built near the sawmill and was nearly ready for launching now. Walter got a job there toting planks. Hard work but good pay, and Olive was busy and happy, cooking, keeping house and taking care of the baby.

But at the end of six days her husband quit the job and almost broke her heart when he announced that he had signed up with a road-building gang to work on a portage road that was being built around 14 miles of rapids on the Slave River, between Fort Fitzgerald and Fort Smith. That meant going another 250 miles down north, close to 400 by

river, the way they'd travel, far away from the nearest
doctor, to a lonely outpost where she would be almost the
only white woman. Her brother Frank urged her to stay
behind, but Walter wanted her to go with him and she had
always believed that a wife belonged with her husband.

They would make the long trip down the Athabasca and
across the lake of the same name aboard a scow, one of
two pushed ahead of a big motorboat. Theirs would be
loaded with flour and other food stuff at one end, a team
of horses and hay and oats at the other. Their bed would
be a pile of hay in the center, with blankets spread over it.
They couldn't know it ahead of time, of course, but they
would lose one man and a sled dog before the trip was
finished.

"If I had been older I probably would have refused to
go," Olive recalled later, "but I was only 21, and I wanted
very much to be where my husband was."

It was May now, and ducks and geese were as plentiful as
she had ever seen them anywhere. The whole country
seemed alive with them, in the air and on the water. The
scenery along the Athabasca was beautiful and all told it
was a pleasant trip. But it was also scary.

The river was full of driftwood and big chunks of ice,
and the scow banged into them time after time. But the
skipper, Joe Bird, was an experienced boatman who knew
every turn and bar as he knew the back of his hand, and he
kept them out of serious trouble.

A big Hudson's Bay Company steamer churning down
the river ahead, within sight each time they rounded a
bend, didn't fare so well. It was also towing two heavy
scows, one lashed on either side, and in trying to dodge a
big raft of logs and ice, it crowded too close to shore. The
scow on the right rammed into the bank with a pile-driver
blow that broke it wide open, and the four horses it carried were in the icy water in seconds. One of the crew cut
their ropes and wound up in the river with them, but he

grabbed one by the tail and was pulled out when the horse climbed the bank.

There was no room for the horses on the second scow, so the crew went ashore and cleared a lane through the piled-up ice on the bank, to let them get to the grassy slopes above the river. They'd be rounded up again after repairs were made.

Bird stopped his boat to offer help, and no one noticed when a Husky belonging to Jim Wood, the boss of the road crew Walter was to work with, jumped overboard. He was a $100 sled dog that Jim was taking to Fort Fitzgerald to sell. His chain let him reach the water but wasn't long enough for him to swim ashore, and when the tow started on the poor dog was dragged under the front end of a scow and drowned.

At the mouth of the river, where it empties into Lake Athabasca, the tow had to cross 19 miles of open water to Fort Chipewyan, where the Slave River goes out. But a strong wind from the east had piled the western half of the lake full of ice. Big chunks and broken fields of it were grinding and groaning, and there was nothing to do but camp on shore and wait for the wind to change.

That took two days. They started out as soon as the ice had cleared sufficiently, but a bitterly cold west wind drove them aground on a sandbar where they were stuck for hours, while the men worked frantically with poles trying to free the heavy scows. And once they were afloat again they had to turn back into the Athabasca for shelter.

They waited another two days, and by that time the Hudson's Bay steamboat caught up with them. The smashed scow had been patched up and the four horses were riding in it again. The gas-powered boat that was pushing the scow with the Reamers aboard had one advantage over the big stern-wheeler. Powered with steam, the latter had to tie up at the bank every now and then to take on a load of cordwood for fuel. Bird didn't.

The wind changed, and he decided it would raise the water high enough to see them over the sandbars. They'd race the ice floes to Chipewyan. Almost before Olive knew what was happening she saw the Hudson's Bay sternwheeler out in the lake, and everybody in her outfit was scurrying to get started. The wind was churning Lake Athabasca into terribly high seas, and off to the east they could see a white line of ice drifting slowly but inexorably toward them. That was no place to be, on a scow pushed by a motorboat, and she was scared out of her boots.

A mile offshore the rough water began to smash the two scows together, and they heard boards break and saw water seeping through. They stopped and wallowed in the seas while sacks of flour were piled over the cracks to plug the leak.

Capt. Bird took the scows in tow now, one behind the other. That kept them from banging into one another, but when Walter and Olive looked up from the rear one as the one ahead climbed to the crest of a wave it was like looking up the slope of a gray mountain. The next minute they'd be up on the crest, staring down at the other scow and the boat. The horses had a hard time keeping their footing and they were as frightened as the young wife was. They reared and stomped and that made things even worse.

Within minutes Walter and Olive were miserably seasick. And every time they rose on a sea, she could see that towering wall of ice drifting closer and closer. From water level it looked much closer than it was, and she gave up all hope of making it across the lake. She was sure the scows would swamp or they'd be crushed beneath tons of ice, and she called herself a hundred kinds of fool for bringing the baby into such a situation. If Walter was as worried as she was he didn't talk about it, maybe because he was too busy pumping water out of the leaky scow.

Four miles off the north shore of the lake they came into the lee of a big island that held back the great wall of ice,

*the horses had a hard time keeping their footing and they
were as frightened as the young wife was*

and none too soon. Floating cakes were closing in around
them now and the scow smacked into those floes time after
time with a crack like a pistol shot.

The mouth of the Slave at Fort Chipewyan is a bad place
to get into even in good weather, with bars and rocks, and
the tow arrived in the dusk of a wild and hellish night.
There is no real darkness in that country in late May, June
and July, just a few hours of twilight, then daybreak again.
Olive was tucked under the blankets with the baby when the
sound of shouting brought her to her feet, just in time to see
a rope tangle around a man's legs on the deck of the boat
and yank him into the water and ice alongside.

They didn't see him again. Either he was crushed to

death or the bitterly cold water finished him almost instantly. The tow nudged its way on into the river, dodging rocks and ice, and when Olive looked out again they were in quiet water between high, rock-strewn banks, with the buildings of Fort Chipewyan shining clean and white on a granite cliff to the left.

"I don't think I've ever seen a more welcome sight," she told me. "I drew a real breath for the first time since we had come out into Lake Athabasca."

The men kept watch for the body of the lost crewman the rest of that night, but he was never found.

At 10 the next morning their tow and the big Hudson's Bay steamboat were under way again, down the Slave. That is a mighty river. Between Chipewyan and the place where the Peace runs into it, it averages as much as two miles wide, dotted with islands and strewn with sandbars. It's a beautiful river, but the boat pilots had no use for that stretch because the bars were forever shifting. Channels that were wide and deep one year did not exist the next, and the first boat through each season put up stakes with small flags to guide those that followed.

Five miles downriver that morning the big stern-wheeler went hard aground on a sandbar. Her paddle wheels churned the water at full speed in reverse, but the boat did not budge an inch. Bird felt his way cautiously around and went on, and that same evening he tied up at Fort Fitzgerald, with 14 miles of rapids ahead, too rough to be navigated.

The first day at Fitzgerald the Reamers watched as odd a performance as they had ever seen, sled dogs and big northern pike or jackfish competing for table scraps thrown into the river after meals on the steamboat. The boat had worked off the bar and caught up again by then.

The water was boiling with fish turning and dodging among the swimming dogs, and Olive expected them to grab a husky's foot or tail but it didn't happen. The Slave teamed with jackfish, and probably because the water was so muddy from the high water and ice they were swarming up every clear creek in packed, hungry schools. That was the season when the Indians caught and dried their summer's supply of fish, for themselves and their dogs.

Reamer and his wife moved into a tent two miles north of the Fort, and when an improvident Indian offered him two half-starved dogs for $25 (good sled dogs were selling for $60 to $100 apiece), he snapped them up, much to Olive's delight. She knew that meant he was looking ahead to a winter of trapping after the road job ended. She had had all the moving she wanted.

They moved once more that summer, into a small cabin close to where the road crew was working, about halfway to

Fort Smith, which is located at the lower end of the rapids that begin at Fitzgerald. Walter and the other men put that cabin up in one Sunday. It was only 10 x 12, with the bark still on the logs, a pole-and-sod roof, and a dirt floor with roots and stubs sticking up. But it would do, for they'd be living in it only through July and part of August, and Olive was completely happy once more.

They were less than half a mile from one of the wildest rapids on the Slave, and the roar of the water was like low thunder day and night. A few times on a Sunday they pulled fly nets over their heads, covered the baby with a specially-made net, and walked down to the river to watch it pound driftwood and logs to pieces against huge rocks.

"Looking back, I suppose that was as good a summer as I had ever had," Olive says today. "Now that the dangers of our long trip north from Fort McMurray was past, I realized that we had had a ringside seat for one of the great spectacles of the north, the annual breakup of the ice, the age-old prelude to the Arctic spring. It had been a majestic thing to see, but it had also been terrifying and I had no wish ever to witness it again."

What she wanted now was to get back to McMurray and enjoy a winter of such comforts as that lonely little outpost afforded.

Winter
of
Starvation

THE scow was heavy and cumbersome, an old 30-footer that Walter Reamer and his young wife Olive had bought at Fort Fitzgerald, on the Slave River in the far north of Alberta. But they didn't have much plunder; and with only two grownups, a baby and a pair of sled dogs on board, it rode high. The deep steady current of the Slave pushed them north far faster than a man could have walked on shore.

The scow had oars and now and then Reamer grew impatient and used them for a short distance, but there was no need for it. Mostly he just steered enough to hold to the middle of the channel, and they watched the early-fall scenery slip past along the banks or played with their 6-month-old daughter, also named Olive. When they weren't cuddling her, she slept as contented as a kitten in the small cardboard box that served for her bed.

Muskrat sign was plentiful along the river, and there was lots of old beaver work, lodges and the evidence of dams, but nothing recent. The beaver had been trapped out of that country then, but have since made a comeback and are abundant again now. The Reamers saw deer and moose tracks on the sandbars, and flocks of ptarmigan fed in the willows on the river bottoms. Wherever there was green grass along the shore, snow geese pastured by the hundreds. The Reamers were rarely out of hearing of those wild voices, either by day or during the half-light of the short Arctic night.

Where the Salt River came into the Slave they went ashore at a camp where Indians were drying fish. A cluster of smoke-blackened tents stood on the bank; men, women and children were all over the place; and gaunt sled dogs were tethered to stakes, their wild and eerie howling echoing across the river. Fish by the hundreds, split open, were drying on pole racks. Mostly jackfish or northern pike, and goldeyes, with a few big "coney fish" mixed in. These were inconnu, known as the sheefish in many places in the Arctic, weighing an average of 8 to 12 pounds.

When Reamer and his wife left the camp the Indians gave them enough fish for their evening meal, for themselves and their two dogs. They had come to a land of plenty, they agreed, a dream country for a young trapper and his family. Fortunately they had no inkling of what lay ahead.

The time was late August of 1922. The trip had come about when Walter met two trappers, Nels Nelson and Pete Anderson, at Fort Fitzgerald. He had worked through the short summer with a road crew building a portage road between Fort Fitzgerald and Fort Smith, around 14 miles of wicked rapids on the Slave. The road job was finished about the middle of August, and then along came Pete and Nels.

They had trapped the fall before down the Slave at Grand Detour in Northwest Territories, 100 miles upriver from Great Slave Lake. They had come out before Christmas, they said, with 1,600 muskat skins that brought $1.50 apiece. There were lakes all over the country between the Slave and the Little Buffalo, they told Walter, and every one of those lakes crawled with marsh rats.

Reamer was a rover, and also a trapper at heart above everything else. For him stories of that kind were like wild tales of a gold strike. He gave up then and there all thought of his plan to go back to Fort McMurray, on the Athabasca River 250 miles south, where his wife had been looking forward to the presence of other white women, a few frontier comforts, and a doctor in case she or the baby needed one. The three of them, Walter decided, would spend the winter trapping on those rich fur grounds.

They bought the scow and 34 single-spring traps, a pair of 3-foot snowshoes and enough babiche (rawhide) to make a larger pair. The small ones were for Olive. Walter would fashion his own before snow came. They also bought 400 pounds of flour, 50 pounds of white sugar, and four 50-pound sacks of potatoes. Olive remembered that they paid $12 for each of those sacks. Coal oil was $2 a gallon at Fitzgerald. They added beans, rice, salt pork, oatmeal and baking powder, salt, tea, and cornmeal for the dogs, and the grub list was complete.

The scow was hauled across the 14-mile portage, and the Mounties at Fort Smith checked the supplies to make sure they were adequate, a standard procedure then with anyone going into Northwest Territories for the winter. It was a sensible requirement, too, for the winters there are long and cold and the hardships can be terribly severe, as the Reamers were to learn.

They loaded the scow and shoved off on August 23, on the long slow trip down the Slave to their trapping grounds. They were in completely unfamiliar country, for it was the first time either of them had been that far north. So far as they knew there'd be no whites within 50 miles of where they were going. They had no idea where or what their winter home would be like. But they were on the way into what Walter had been told was good fur country, and he was completely happy. Olive didn't face quite as cheerfully as he did the prospect of wintering with a child not yet a year old, hundreds of miles from the nearest doctor.

Nels and Pete had said to look for an old sawdust pile where a sawmill had once stood, on the west shore of the river, and settle down around there some place. They passed the sawdust pile on the fourth day of floating. Nels had also described another landmark, a high cut bank some distance below the old mill site, with a tumbledown cabin perched on the very edge of the bank where the shore had caved away in times of high water.

They found the cabin exactly as he had described it, half rotted away, forlorn and lonely looking. Just below the high bank, whoever had lived there at one time had made themselves a good boat landing, and it was just what Reamer was looking for. They tied up the scow, let the two dogs loose for a run, got the tent up and carried their supplies and outfit up the bank. It was close to midnight when they finished. They tied the dogs to trees and turned in.

They were no more than asleep when Olive was awakened by some animal gnawing on the slab of salt pork that they had brought into the tent for safekeeping. At first she thought one of the dogs had gotten loose, but as her eyes grew used to the dim light in the tent she made out a large skunk instead.

The tent was only a 9 x 12, and the skunk was working on the pork within three feet of her face. She shook Walter awake and they tried to drive the animal off, but he wouldn't budge.

"I'll have to shoot him or we won't have any pork left," Walter said finally. They knew it wasn't a very good idea but they had no choice.

"I can report that shooting a skunk inside a tent is a big mistake," Olive says now. "Whoever invented tear gas simply copied an idea that skunks have used for thousands of years."

Walter's rifle cracked. It wouldn't be truthful to say the air turned blue, for it was too dusky in the tent to distinguish colors. But it certainly turned something. Their eyes started to water, they were half blinded, and began to gag. Olive grabbed the baby and fumbled her way outside. After a minute or so Walter stumbled out behind her, dragging a dead skunk. He threw it over the river bank, and they hauled their bedding outside, spread it under a big spruce, and spent the rest of the night in the open. Luckily they were tired enough to sleep anywhere.

The next morning they moved the tent a few hundred feet down the hill and carried all their belongings over to it. But it was many days before the overpowering smell of skunk subsided, and Olive told her husband more than once, somewhat reproachfully, that his way of saving a slab of salt pork was worse than useless. The pork smelled almost as bad as the tent.

Next they started work on a log cabin, 12 x 16, for a winter home. Walter cut and notched the trees and together they carried them up to the site and rolled them into place. An Indian woman at Fort Fitzgerald had given Olive a small hammock for the baby. She slung it between two trees, put little Olive in it, tucked mosquito net carefully around her to keep off the millions of mosquitoes and blackflies; and the child slept and cooed and amused herself while her parents worked.

In two weeks the cabin was up, windows in and door hung, and a bunk bed built. Olive cut hay with a butcher knife for a mattress, built cupboards out of wooden packing boxes, and she and Walter settled down in the nicest house of their own that they had had since they were married.

There was one small drawback. They had left the bark on the logs, and as soon as their stove warmed the place big black spruce beetles came out from under that bark. They bit savagely, and Olive was more afraid of them than she would have been of a bear. After all, she had been used to bears all her life, but not to beetles.

It was still too early to start trapping, so Walter took trips each day to scout the country, look for game and fur

sign and locate the lakes where the muskrats were. It took
only a few of these trips for him to realize that he had
picked the wrong place for winter headquarters. He found
little sign of fox, lynx or coyote, and the nearest lake on that
side of the river was 10 miles away. This was not the place
that had been described by the two trappers back at Fitzgerald, and Reamer was plainly worried. He'd sit in the
evenings, thinking hard, and wouldn't even hear his wife
when she spoke to him.

They had built a tiny, cranky canoe, nine feet long, using
willow trunks hewed flat on one side for the ribs and frame.
Walter sawed the planks, a quarter inch thick, out of a birch
log with a crosscut saw. They were only six or eight inches
wide, and it took a lot of them to complete the job. The
planking was covered with canvas, four coats of paint were
put on, and they had a serviceable one-man canoe. But after
one trip in it, with Walter and the baby, Olive decided firmly
that it was not a family craft. From then on, she promised
herself, she would stay ashore until they got a better boat.

They made that one trip, down the Slave, to look for
muskrat country. Four miles below their cabin they found
a lovely clear creek running in, and stopped to catch jackfish.
They tried fishing from the canoe but it was too unsafe, so
they got out on the sandy shore and started to fish from
the beach.

Olive decided to use two lines. She stuck one pole in the
ground and picked up the second, and when she turned
around she had a 9-pound pike on the first one. She dropped
the other outfit, but had no more than started to haul her
catch in when the second pole started to slide toward the
water. She had a 7-pounder on that line. She yelled for help,
and before Walter could get her second fish in he was fast
to a 4-pounder of his own. They fished with one line apiece
after that. Olive caught 18 big jackfish about as fast as she
could take them off the hook, and Walter did as well. When
they loaded the catch into the canoe and started back upriver, the gunwales were hardly more than an inch above the

water. It was then that Olive resolved not to go out in that craft again.

She made jackfish booyah, a favorite dish of theirs, for supper that night. Booyah is a common term all through the north country for soup or stew. Probably the name comes from the French bouillon, or maybe from bouillabaisse, the famous fish soup of France. To make it with jackfish you scale and clean the fish, strip the skin off in one piece like a sock, and lay it aside for later use. Boil the whole fish in salt water for 10 or 15 minutes, until the meat flakes off the bones easily. Mix the meat, fresh mashed potatoes and dry bread crumbs, and stuff it all into the uncooked skin. Tie the ends, put it back in the salt water and cook until it is thoroughly heated through.

The next morning Olive suggested to Walter that he scout for lakes on the opposite side of the river. Perhaps they had misunderstood Nels Nelson's directions. The Slave was a mile wide, and her heart was in her throat while she watched her husband paddle across in that miserable little canoe. But he came back in late afternoon and said there was no end to the marshy country he had found, dotted with small lakes, with muskrat houses on all of them.

The Reamers knew then that they had built their cabin on the wrong side of the river. It would be dangerous to cross as long as the water was open, and once the Slave started to freeze over, and while it was breaking up in the spring, Walter could not get across at all. Those were the best times to trap. Heartsick as Olive was at the idea of leaving the place they had fixed up so nicely, there was no choice.

They had torn the scow apart to make doors and windows. That left only the canoe, and it was not adequate for the move to the other shore, so she suggested to Walter that he build a boat. After he was marooned across the river by a windstorm and had to stay overnight without food or bedding, he agreed.

It was a clumsy boat, without much taper at the bow, for they had no way to bend the heavy boards of the scow, but it was far better than the canoe. They moved to the west side of the Slave and started another cabin. Planning to live in it only until November, when the lakes froze and they'd have to quit trapping, they threw it up hurriedly, of small green logs, using the doors and windows from their first place. It was soon finished, and about October 1 they put their traps out.

Circumstances altered their plans, and they stayed on in that rough little cabin until spring. For one thing, there was far more fur on the west side of the river, mink as well as muskrats. There was also more firewood handy and the cabin stood in a thick grove of spruce, where it was sheltered from the wind.

The trapping prospects looked good, but now they faced another problem. Wild meat was scarce enough to cause worry. There was not a moose or deer track anywhere. Caribou came through now and then, crossing from one range of hills to another, and timber wolves followed them, but the caribou could not be relied on for a meat supply.

It was at least 60 miles from the Little Buffalo River to the moss-covered hills east of the Slave, and before winter closed in they had named that belt of scrub timber and swampy lakes Starvation Wilderness. Snow came to stay on October 10, and after that the whole country lay white and lifeless, without even the chickadees and Canada jays they had expected to see in the winter woods.

Trapping was good. They were looking at the traps twice a day, and coming back to camp with as many as a dozen muskrats. They would hike out to the lakes together. Then Olive would take the baby and the dog team with a small toboggan and cover half the line. Walter would go over the other half with a packsack, skinning his rats as he took them from the traps. They'd meet at midday, and on the way back to camp he would cover his wife's end of the line, she would take his. That afforded a change of scenery and also give the rats time to fill the traps again.

They trapped until the first of November, when the lakes

froze and the temperature dropped too low for them to be out in the wind and cold. From December until the end of March it rarely climbed as high as 10 below zero, and there were days when it went to 65 below. The wind was like a knife, and the Reamers huddled in their poorly chinked shack and tried to cut enough spruce and willow to keep warm.

Spruce and balsam pitch dripped from the roof poles and fouled and matted Olive's long, auburn curls that Walter liked so much, until in desperation she took the scissors one day when he was out looking at fox traps and cut them as short as she could. He was so upset when he came home that she saw his face turn gray, but bobbed hair came into style soon after that and she never afterward let hers grow long again.

They managed through that bitter winter until February. By then they knew they would run out of food long before June, when they had planned to catch the first steamboat coming up the Slave from the arctic. They had known since October, too, that Olive was pregnant again. Their second baby would be born in July. They didn't dare to wait for the boat, knowing that before the end of winter they would have nothing to eat.

They were in no shape for the 60-mile trip out to Fort Smith. Their two dogs were old, half starved, and not strong enough to pull Olive and the baby on the sled. The infant could ride but she would have to walk. Nor did they have suitable clothing for cold of 40 and 50 below. But they outfitted themselves as best they could.

Olive made a parka for herself out of an old blanket and covered it with canvas. Walter had only buckskin pants and moccasins, a sweater and a wool jacket over everything. What they lacked were fur parkas and fur-lined moccasins. But as their food dwindled and no moose or caribou tracks, not even a sign of rabbits, marred the clean snow around them, they grimly made ready for the trip. Walter would leave Olive and the baby at Fort Smith and come back to the camp in time to trap again as soon as the lakes opened.

They put hot water in a water bottle, heated stones, wrapped the baby in their whole bedroll of four blankets with the stones and water bottle beside her, and struck out up the Slave. The empty toboggan was all the dogs could pull.

It was bitterly cold, probably around 40 below, the going was hard, and they made poor time. Mail was being carried up and down the Slave off and on that winter by dog team, and the teams had packed a pretty good trail on the ice, but snow had drifted it over and the Reamers couldn't follow it. When they left it they were plodding through two feet of soft snow.

The dogs pulled willingly enough for a while but the heavy going was too much for them. After about 15 miles they began to give out. They stopped frequently, and more than once they lay down in the snow. Walter urged them on and pushed all he could on the toboggan handles to help, but he and his wife both knew they weren't going to go much farther. They tried to hurry, knowing darkness was not far off, but there was not enough strength left in either the woman or the dogs for that.

The winter days are very short there in the north, and by 3:30 in the afternoon dusk was beginning to come down. The dogs followed the mail team's trail across the river to the east bank—and there was a little cabin with smoke curling out of the chimney.

"I can't remember that I was ever gladder to see a human habitation," Olive recalls.

The cabin belonged to two young trappers and the Reamers pulled in thinking they would stay the night there. But there wasn't room to walk between the stove, beds and table, and it was plain that short of a life-or-death matter the trappers couldn't put them up. They had tea and bannock, and were told that four miles farther up the Slave another trapper, Bert Bennett, had a comfortable cabin

*Walter went ahead
to break trail and
pull them along*

at the sawdust pile they had passed on the way downriver back in August. They rested a little while, and started for Bennett's place, with the early darkness thickening over the frozen wilderness. Olive didn't feel as if she could go 500 feet, much less four miles.

That was a terrible hike. Each mile of the four seemed like 10. The dogs stopped every few yards to lie down in their harness, and Walter went ahead to break trail and pull them along with a short length of rope while his wife pushed on the toboggan handles for a change. It was too dark for him to see where he was putting his snowshoes, and he must have fallen 100 times. Olive had pain stabbing at her legs, back and all through her body. She realized finally that she was leaning on the toboggan handles more than she was pushing.

"It seemed that the easiest thing to do would be to walk off into the snow and lie down and sleep forever," she told me long afterward.

But there was the baby to think of. Olive could hear her

whimper now and then, and wondered vaguely whether she was freezing. There was nothing to be done about it if she was. She wasn't hungry, for she had been fed at the trapper's cabin, and the mother didn't dare open the bedroll she was wrapped in to look at her.

"I just kept putting one foot ahead of the other, stumbling and staggering along, exhausted and terribly cold, until I lost all track of where we were or how far we had come," is the way Olive recalls the last mile.

A shout from Walter brought her out of her stupor. "Hello, there!" he yelled. She looked ahead and could see a square of light shining out of a window. Oh, God, what a welcome sight!

Afterward she could not remember the trapper Bennett opening the door, or her and the baby being carried into the warmth of the cabin. The first thing she recalled was Walter pulling off her coat and moccasins. Then somebody set a bowl of hot soup in front of her and her husband shook her and told her to eat.

In a daze she watched Bennett take off the baby's rabbit-skin coat and start to feed her. They said afterward that she cried, "No, don't take her coat off. She'll freeze!" but Olive had no memory of that. She did not even realize that they were safe and warm inside four walls. The next thing she knew gray daylight was filtering in the window of the cabin, and Walter was telling her to get up for breakfast.

She was too stiff and sore to make it, but he pulled her out of bed and made her move her legs and body. It's surprising how much power of recovery a human has at 21. She was four months pregnant, had run and walked 23 miles the day before in deep snow—and when Bennett looked at his thermometer that morning it was 61 below! The wonder was that the three of them had not frozen to death on the trail.

They knew now that they could not make it out to Fort Smith with their dogs and outfit. It would be dangerous and

she realized that she was leaning on the toboggan more than she was pushing

foolhardy to try. Luckily, Bennett had extra supplies that he could spare. He sold them flour and beans enough to see them through, and even loaned Walter 24 good muskrat traps. The hospitality and helpfulness of people in the far north then were hard to beat.

They stayed there three days, while little Olive reveled in a big board floor to toddle around on and her mother regained strength. At the end of that time the family was as good as new and the dogs had been stoked with enough food that they were in better shape than when they began the terrible trip upriver. Walter and Olive Reamer were ready to go back to their cabin and see the winter out. With muskrats at $1.50 each, there was good money to be made as soon as the lakes started to open. When the first boat came up the Slave they would be waiting for it, sitting pretty. Or so they thought.

Bennett advised them to go back to their cabin by a different route, not to follow the mail team's trail on the river. They could save five miles, he said, by taking a cutoff through the bush on what is called in that country a river snigh, a channel or small creek made when the Slave was in flood in early summer.

They started out on a clear morning, with the sun shining through a thin haze of frost. Wind had drifted and packed the snow solidly enough that they seldom broke through, and the going was easy. They pulled up in front of their lonely little cabin just as it was coming full dark—and not more than 200 feet from the door was a fresh moose track cutting across the snow. Had they been home that moose would have meant meat for the rest of the winter, and the dogs needed it even more than they did.

Today, almost 50 years later, the woman who was young Olive Reamer still remembers that as one of the most heartbreaking minutes of her life. "But it was a good thing we couldn't foresee what was coming next," she adds.

Nightmare
Spring

THE moose track led off into
scrubby spruce, away from the river.

Walter Reamer and his young wife Olive had found it at
dark the night before, when they drove their two gaunt sled
dogs in at the end of a heartbreaking trip 23 miles up the
Slave and 23 back, in a futile attempt to get out to Fort
Smith on the border between Northwest Territories and
Alberta, before the two of them and their infant daughter
died of hunger at their remote trapline camp.

The moose had walked within 200 feet of the cabin.
If Reamer could kill it, it would mean meat for most of the
remaining weeks of winter, and the bones and leavings also
would supply urgently needed food for the dogs. Walter
poked shells into his wife's old .25/35 Winchester carbine,
the best rifle they had, and took the track right after breakfast. He had a rifle of his own, a .303 Savage, but it was in
bad condition, hardly safe for shooting, and he had very
little ammunition for it.

He followed the moose all that day without catching

sight of it, made a fire and camped under a spruce tree in below-zero cold that night, and took the trail again at daylight the next morning. But the moose was traveling through the country and kept going, and by early afternoon Walter had to give up. His home-made snowshoes were wearing out, and he was getting so far from camp that he did not dare to keep on. He got back to the cabin after dark, tired and sick with disappointment, and Olive felt as bad as he did. That was the only moose track they had seen, and the closest they had come to killing fresh meat, through the whole winter.

They did not see or hear a living thing except each other and the dogs, and three foxes that Walter trapped, until the end of March. It seemed as if all the game, even rabbits, had left the area or died off. Neither of the Reamers had ever seen a winter wilderness as lifeless and still as that country along the Slave.

They fed the three fox carcasses to the dogs, and the animals were starved enough to gulp the smelly fox meat down with relish. The beans and flour that Bert Bennett, a neighboring trapper, had sold them were running low, and they were eating less than half of what they wanted.

In desperation, toward the first of April they decided to start mink and muskrat trapping, despite the fact that the lakes and marshes were still covered with three or four feet of ironhard ice. It wasn't so much that they wanted fur as that they needed the muskrats desperately for food for themselves and the dogs. None of them would last much longer without a supply of meat.

They made a trip to the nearest lake, where they had trapped before freezeup, taking little Olive, the baby, on the toboggan—and found the shallow, swampy lake frozen solidly to the bottom. Not a muskrat was left alive. They went on to two or three other lakes farther away, and the situation was the same. When they turned the dogs back toward camp that afternoon Walter and Olive were about as disheartened and worried as two people could get.

A few days after they packed up the little food they had left, their tent, bedding and traps, and went eight miles west to some bigger lakes that Walter had found while he was tracking the moose.

They put up the tent at the first lake, found water under the ice, cut into muskrat houses and caught a few rats. That eased the pinch of hunger, but they were not taking enough for themselves and the dogs and at last Walter made the unhappy announcement that the dogs would have to be destroyed. Although Olive realized that that was kinder than to let them starve, the idea broke her heart and she coaxed him to wait a few more days in the hope that the weather would turn warmer and trapping would pick up.

Instead, it turned bitterly cold and stayed that way for eight days. Before the end of the cold spell the dogs were so hungry they whined and howled for food almost continuously, and finally Walter shot them. It had to be done, but his wife cried until she was sick.

Less than a week after that the weather broke. The sun came out warm and bright, the snow started to melt and the lakes opened up around the shores. The Reamers began trapping and shooting muskrats by the dozens. If the night was cold and ice formed their luck fell off. Some days they took only five or six pelts, but one day before the fur spree was over they took 70. Walter followed the trapline from daylight to dark, and Olive was kept busy every minute skinning rats and stretching the pelts, making stretchers by bending willow sticks into shape.

They were living on muskrat meat and having enough to eat for the first time that winter. Olive boiled it and gave her little daughter the broth from her bottle, and she thrived on it.

When spring comes to the North it comes with a rush. Suddenly it is sunny day after day, and the days are long and warm. But the short dark hours of the spring nights are often cold, and it was hard to keep warm in the tent, even with a fire in the tiny stove.

They were wet most of the time, from wading out into the icy water to retrieve rats they shot, and their clothing did not have time to dry thoroughly overnight. But they were taking a rich harvest of pelts and saw no reason to complain. After the hunger and hardships of the winter this trapline springtime was a welcome season indeed.

They continued trapping while the snow melted and the creeks rose and became treacherous little rivers. Walter and his wife agreed that they'd stay camped at this lake until May 10. Then they would hike back to their cabin, go up the Slave to Bert Bennett's place by rowboat, and there catch the first steamer of the season to Fort Smith.

But things don't always go as people plan them. On the morning of May 2 Olive was baking bannock in the little stovepipe oven in the tent. She stepped outside to look for Walter, saw him coming a quarter mile up the lake, took the baby by the hand and walked to meet him. Little Olive was toddling all over now.

There were rats swimming in the open water along the shore and she kept back far enough not to frighten them. Every now and then Walter would stop and pick off one with his Remington .22. When they met, his wife took part of his load of fresh pelts and the three started back.

All of a sudden they heard ammunition exploding at a terrible rate, and then smoke and flames rolled up around the tent. Walter dropped his sack of fur and ran, and Olive grabbed her daughter and hurried after him. When she got to the tent her husband was dragging out charred food stuff and burning pieces of blankets. She grabbed the things as he pulled them out and doused them in the lake.

It was all over in 10 minutes. A tent disintegrates fast in a fire.

What they had saved would have made a very small bundle. Two or three half-burned pieces of blanket, a few matches in their pockets and in a waterproof container. Walter's .22 that he had been shooting rats with was safe,

smoke and flames rolled up around the tent

Olive's .25/35 had been standing outside the tent. There were four shells in its magazine, and Walter had a box for the .22 in his pocket. The rest of their ammunition was gone. They also pulled a scorched .22 Stevens of Olive's out of the burned tent. It was damaged, but looked as if it could be fired. They didn't even have a piece of canvas big enough to wrap the baby in if rain came.

Most of their rat pelts had been hanging in a tree outside the tent and were safe. They had lost only 10 or 12 that were inside drying. But one of the possessions Olive loved most was gone, the violin her brother Lea had given her for her sixteenth birthday.

"Right then that birthday seemed a long time back, somehow," she recalls.

Of their food they had salvaged about four cups of flour,

wet and mixed with cinders, a pound or so of beans and a little bannock. For the baby, luckily, there were a few cans of condensed milk left undamaged.

That handful of supplies would have to see them through, with muskrat meat, until they could reach Bennett's cabin. That meant a hard hike of eight or 10 miles without dogs, through flooded and difficult country, and then 23 miles in a crude and clumsy rowboat against the spring current of the mighty Slave. Worst of all, they could not make the trip upriver until the Slave broke up, and they had no way to forecast when that would happen.

They knew the ice went out of the Athabasca around the middle of May, but they asked each other hopelessly when the breakup was due on the Slave.

Things looked very grim. Olive was expecting her second baby in less than two months. There'd be a rough time ahead. But there was no use sitting by the ruins of the tent and worrying about it. The thing to do now was get started.

They hung their traps in trees where they could be found the following fall, ate their bannock and a good meal of muskrat they had roasted earlier, rolled the baby in the patches of bedding and lay down under a tree to rest for a few hours. They did not dare to spare matches for a fire. The few they had must be hoarded for times of genuine need.

When they awoke they made up their loads and were ready to start. Olive wrapped her daughter in the blanket pieces and tied her in with babiche, to be carried on her mother's back, Indian style. The little toddler was so thin she wasn't very heavy. Next, Olive rolled one cooking pot, knives, forks, spoons, a cup and the baby bottle in a scorched scrap of blanket and tied it all on behind. They tied the two .22's and the .25/35 together in one bundle. Olive would carry that like a suitcase.

Walter's load would consist of the dry muskrat pelts, about 250 in all, their stove—it weighed only 10 pounds—

and three lengths of stovepipe. He had fashioned a home-made packsack, big and roomy, from a gunny sack and rope. By shoving as many rat skins down in the bottom as the sack would hold, nose down, then telescoping a second tier inside those and continuing the process until the sack was jammed to the top, they managed to pack their total catch. A fur buyer back at her father's Halfway House had showed Olive that trick years before.

They left the burned-out camp with her carrying all she could handle and Walter packing a load of close to 110 pounds. In the late winter they had traveled eight miles coming to that lake from their cabin. Now they must cover between 16 and 20 going back. Every creek was roaring full and two or three times its usual width. They detoured miles to find places where they could wade across, and then had to follow the streams back to their blazed trail to avoid getting lost. Many times Walter had to make three trips through the swollen and icy creeks, one with his pack, one with the baby and his wife's load, and a third to help her across.

It took two days of the hardest kind of travel to get back to the cabin. At the end of the first day they stopped, made a shelterless camp under a clump of spruce and roasted a muskrat they had brought along. Near this place they had cached several rat carcasses on a high rack of poles earlier, hanging them so they would dry, against possible future need. After supper Walter went to get them.

He came back looking very glum. A wolverine had raided the cache and there was not a rat left. They went without breakfast and their noon meal the second day, but in the middle of that afternoon Olive shot a small muskrat in a slough. It wasn't big enough to make a good meal for one hungry person, let alone three, but they stopped and cooked it on the spot and divided it up.

It was midnight when they trudged wearily up to their cabin, tired, discouraged and hungry. But at least they had a roof over their heads again, and four walls to keep out the cold at night. Going to bed supperless didn't seem too bad.

When daylight came, Olive got up and picked out all the dried beans she could find, where she had discarded culls during the winter. She also scraped every empty flour sack for the little flour that remained. Then she cooked the beans and baked a bannock from the flour, dirt and all.

One look at the Slave that morning confirmed their worst fears. Water was running between the ice and shore. They coudln't get out on the river, and wouldn't have dared if they could. There was no hope of following the shore up to Bennett's place, either, because of the many large creeks that came in. They had no choice but to wait for the ice to go out.

Walter started to calk the rowboat and cover the seams with pitch. Olive put in the time hunting, looking for muskrats, ducks, squirrels, even small birds, anything edible. Her total kill the next five days consisted of three red squirrels. It wasn't much, but it helped.

Then the worst disaster of all struck. On May 10, with ice still solid in the river, Walter and his wife split up to hunt. He took the baby piggy-back and went in one direction, Olive in the other. He was carrying his Remington .22, and she had the fire-damaged Stevens that they had salvaged from the burned tent. Those were the only guns for which there was sufficient ammunition now.

Olive scared up a flock of mallards, but they flushed out of range. Then, at the edge of a small muskeg a half mile north of camp, she saw a rabbit hunched under a clump of brush, the first one she had seen since fall. She had never wanted game more than she wanted that rabbit. She rested the .22 against a small tree and pulled the trigger. All she remembered afterward was fire in her face, blinding light, then a numbness in her nose and eyes.

She never knew how long she leaned against that tree. She couldn't see, her ears rang, and there was terrible pain from the bridge of her nose through her right eye and clear around to her ear. Slowly the weakness went out of her legs, and she stamped the ground in agony. She couldn't get her eye wiped dry and the more she wiped it the worse it hurt.

At first she didn't know what had happened. Then she remembered that she had tried to shoot a rabbit. She felt around on the ground and found the gun. Next she looked for the rabbit, but there was nothing under the bush. Then she started to wonder if she would be able to find her way home, half blinded as she was.

She knew that she was straight north of the cabin, so she started walking in the direction she thought was south, stumbling along, blundering into trees and falling over rough places. She could see enough with her left eye to know that her right hand was red with blood, and each time she wiped her cheek and chin the hand got more bloody. Once she heard ducks quack nearby, and thoughtlessly stopped to see whether she could make them out well enough for a shot, not realizing that in all likelihood her rifle was beyond firing. But she couldn't see farther than she could reach her arms in front of her, so she stumbled on and by some stroke of luck found the cabin.

Walter was picking a duck he had killed. Little Olive came running to meet her mother, and then Olive heard her husband cry, "Oh, my God, what happened to you?"

She let him ease her down and then for the first time she was aware of severe pain in her right hand. She held it up and he looked quickly and mumbled, "Twenty-two shell. It's full of pieces of .22 shell. Your gun must have blown back."

He picked fragments of shell out of that hand and out of her nose for the next two days. Luckily the eye had escaped with nothing worse than powder burns. He kept washing it out with clean water, and Olive felt her way around the cabin with the help of the other eye. Although the injured eye recovered, she never regained full sight in it.

For both the Reamers, the 11 days between May 10,

when she had the accident with the gun, and the time when the ice finally went out of the Slave, were a lagging nightmare of hunger and worry, mostly hunger.

Because they were so short of matches, they kept plenty of wood on hand and fed the fire at intervals all night, never letting it go out. Olive found a roll of wire and set snares for ducks, rabbits, muskrats, anything she might catch. In all, she snared two red squirrels and a blackbird. They peeled trees and scraped off and ate the inner bark. They pulled dead slough grass along the edge of the water and ate the tender yellow shoots below. One day Olive saw a fool hen, a spruce grouse, perched on the low branch of a tree. She hurried to rig a snare on a pole, reached up and dropped it over the bird's head and jerked her to the ground. That was the best meal they had all that time, and for once little Olive got all the broth she wanted.

Hunger cramps kept the parents awake at night, and when they slept they dreamed troubled dreams of food. In Olive's case being seven months pregnant didn't make things any better. Right then she needed to eat for two. Each night they slept less, each day they became weaker, and the baby's whimpering for food tore the father and mother apart. Walter cursed himself over and over for bringing his wife and youngster down the Slave. He vowed that if they got out alive he was through with the North for good, but somehow Olive doubted that.

If only they had brought a few traps back from the tent camp they could have caught muskrats or ducks. But they had counted on the cache of dried rat carcasses that the wolverine had robbed, and left all their traps behind.

They were down to two shells now, for Olive's .25/35. The .22 ammunition was gone. Before that happened Walter had thrown the Stevens away to make sure his wife wouldn't be tempted into firing it again.

For three days their only food was what they called spruce tea. Olive stripped green needles off and boiled them, and they drank a few spoonfuls every couple of hours. It eased the hunger cramps and seemed to provide some strength, but a few times it also caused severe nausea.

Little Olive was no longer running around the cabin. She sat quiet and played listlessly with whatever was at hand. There was no color in her lips and cheeks and her eyes looked hollow and dull.

"I can't put into words how worried and afraid Walter and I were," Olive told me.

They had left their fishhooks at the cabin on the east side of the Slave when they moved the previous fall, but now they made crude hooks by bending safety pins and tried fishing in the open water along the shore of the river, using pieces of red yarn for bait. The catch totaled one very small jackfish.

On May 17 Walter killed a big mallard drake with the last shell for the .25/35, and they feasted. They even cleaned and washed the entrails, cooked them and saved them for the next day. They set aside all of the broth for the baby and she had the first good meal she had had in many days.

The day after that Olive tapped a small birch tree (they were few and far between in that area) for sap. It tasted good, but they had only half a cup to divide among the three of them.

At last, at 10 o'clock on the morning of May 21, the ice in the Slave began to move. By midnight it was gone and the water was rolling past their door, and at 3 in the morning of the 22nd (it was light all night now) they shoved their little boat into the river and were on their way to Bennett's.

It was dangerous to try traveling so soon after the ice went out, for chunks of stranded ice weighing many tons kept sliding off the banks and drifting down with the current, but they had no choice.

Walter rowed and Olive sat in the stern and paddled, and steered away from floating ice. In their condition it was killing work, for to avoid the worst of the ice they had to stay well out from the bank and buck the current.

Their closest call came the first day. Rowing close to shore, they saw a huge block of ice come sliding off a pile 40 feet high and crash into the water almost alongside them. The force of it literally lifted the rowboat into the air and sent it flying. They wound up 150 feet out, in the swiftest part of the current, right side up only because they had happened to be pointed in the right direction when the ice thundered down.

Little Olive had the last of the duck soup that day. Her mother and father drank spruce tea and gathered and ate slough-grass roots. They also drank water often because it seemed to ease their hunger, and they kept rowing until they gave out.

It took six days to make the 23-mile trip up the Slave to Bert Bennett's cabin, and they were as dreadful as any days the Reamers could remember. They pulled to shore at Bennett's place at midnight on May 27, dirty, ragged, starving, and burned so black by wind and sun that they hardly recognized their own reflections when they looked in a mirror. In those six days Walter and Olive had eaten nothing but spruce tea, grass roots, and the inner bark of trees.

A Mr. and Mrs. King from Fort Smith were at Bennett's. They had come down on the ice in March. She gave each of the Reamers half a biscuit and a couple of spoonsful of stewed apricots, but the food was too much for their stomachs. They awakened three hours later with dreadful cramps and were miserably sick for the next 12 hours. It was four days before Olive was well enough to be out of bed, but Mrs. King fed her a few spoonsful of canned soup and cream every hour, and at the end of that time she felt fine. By then Walter and the baby had bounced back until they were as good as new, too.

Bennett and the Kings fixed the family up with clothing,

and they waited out a comfortable and happy month, until the *Miss Mackenzie* came up the Slave on her first trip of the year. They boarded her near the end of June, and the trip to Fort Smith was perfect.

Reamer sold his furs there. He had 560 muskrat pelts, 27 mink, three red foxes, four skunks and a few weasels. The fox pelts brought $25 each, the mink $10. The Northwest Territories Store had grubstaked him when he left for the trapline the previous August. He paid off the debt, and had $1,060 left in cash. He and his wife agreed that they had never seen any money that came harder.

They went by portage road from Fort Smith to Fort Fitzgerald, and then took the stern-wheeler *Slavie,* the same boat that Walter had worked on when it was being built a year earlier. They went up the Slave, across Lake Athabasca and up the Athabasca River to Fort McMurray. They were reversing the route they had traveled on their trip of hardship and danger right after the ice went out the spring before.

There were some 300 passengers on the *Slavie,* and they were a picturesque lot, mostly a mixture of white trappers coming out at the end of winter and Indians on their way to collect treaty money from the Government.

At Fort McMurray a doctor removed the last two slivers of .22 shell from Olive's nose, and then they boarded a train for Edmonton, on the way to Bellingham, Washington, where Walter's family lived and where their second daughter, Vala, was born on July 18, four days after they arrived.

She was a scrawny, blue-gray baby, weighing only 3½ pounds, and for three weeks the attending doctor did not think either she or the mother would live. But they made it through, and Vala grew to be a healthy, pretty girl.

Walter went back to his trapline in the fall but Olive had had enough of the North. She would never again winter in a trapper's shack with her two little girls if she could help it. She stayed behind in Washington, and soon got a job cook-

ing at a camp where her brother-in-law, Ed Coreau, and his
son Jim were taking out cedar poles.

She worked there until early in 1928. Walter came back
from the fur country many times, but he never had a suitable
place for a wife and children to live in. Olive still loved him
very much but she could no longer follow him into the bush
when fall came and the trapline called. She understood that
that call was something he could not resist, but the life of
hardship was not fair to her children. The last time she saw
him was just before Christmas of 1927, when he left once
more for the North. Their third baby, Louis had been born
that September.

The pole camp closed shortly after Christmas, and in
May Olive went to Vanderhoof, British Columbia. But the
job she had there, looking after a small farm, lasted only
two weeks.

She had $500 saved up, enough for a stake, and she began
looking for a homestead. She found exactly what she wanted,
on the Stuart River 40 miles down from Fort St. James,
160 acres of good river-bottom land. Clearing it would be
hard work, but she was no stranger to that. There were
neighbors close by, a school just three miles away for the
children, and she fell in love with the place the first time
she saw it.

Neighbors pitched in and helped her build a small log
house, and in June of 1928 she moved in with her family.
There, less than a month later, one of the neighbors, Jack
Hamilton, came with a telegram from the Mounties to tell
her that Walter was dead. He had drowned in a lake on the
Northwest Territories–Alberta border. His canoe had cap-
sized in a windstorm.

Not quite 27, Olive Reamer was a widow with three small
children, an uncleared homestead and an old .30-30 Winchester.

"I'd have to hunt and farm for our living, but I knew that
somehow we'd make out," she says now, looking back across
the 40-odd years.

She
Had to Have
Moose

THE canoe was a 30-foot dugout that the Indians had "given" to the young widow, Olive Reamer. They'd be along in the fall to claim payment in potatoes.

It had been hollowed out from a big cottonwood with a hand ax, but the tree wasn't straight to begin with and the canoe had inherited the characteristics of its parent. Otherwise the Indians would not have parted with it. As a result it was not only heavy and unwieldy but also so cranky you hardly dared to look over the side unless your hair was parted in the middle.

Mrs. Reamer was in the stern, paddling. Her 6-year-old daughter, also named Olive, was wedged firmly in the bow. Between them were Vala, 5, and the baby, Louis, 2. They were going moose hunting and since there was no one to leave the children with they would have to go as a family.

They were not hunting for fun. It was early summer, and the crop of vegetables the young mother had planted in the garden was growing but there was nothing ready for use as yet. The family was out of food.

The moose season wouldn't open until fall, but at that time British Columbia game regulations allowed a prospector to get a permit and kill a moose any time he needed one for food. Olive was not a prospector and, anyway, she had no way to go into town for the permit unless she walked 27 miles each way. But she and her babies were as hungry as any prospector would ever be, and they had to have something to eat.

"I was sure the good Lord would forgive me and I hoped the game warden would too, if he found out about it," Olive told me long afterward.

So that hot, windless July day, shortly before her 28th birthday, when fly season was getting real bad, she told the youngsters, "We've got to go and try to kill a moose." She knew moose would be coming down to the river on that kind of day to rid themselves of flies and mosquitoes. She had never shot a moose, but necessity is the mother of a lot of new experiences and she decided she could do it if she got the chance. She got little Olive and Louis and Vala ready, loaded them into the big clumsy canoe, poked four shells, all she had, into her old .30-30 Winchester Model 94, and started upstream against the quiet current of the Stuart River.

It had been a little more than a year since the June day in 1928 when a neighbor, Jack Hamilton, had come to the lonely homestead 40 miles down the Stuart from Fort St. James, in the mountain country of central British Columbia, with a telegram for Olive from the RCMP at Edmonton, breaking the news that her trapper-husband, Walter Reamer, had drowned in Leland Lake on the Alberta–Northwest Territories border when his canoe tipped over in a hard windstorm.

Forty years later, Olive Reamer still remembered raising her hand to her eyes to wipe away the fog that suddenly clouded them, and Hamilton leading her to a chair by the kitchen table and saying, "You'd better sit down, Mrs. Reamer."

She looked around at her three children. Olive, the 5-year-old, stood wide-eyed, not quite taking it all in. Vala was playing with her little white kitten and Louis lay on his back reaching for his toes. What was to become of them and her?

Little Olive leaned her head against her mother's skirt and began to cry softly for her daddy, and the young widow felt a lump in her chest that made it hard to breathe.

"But that was not the time for tears," she told me. "If I cried I'd do it out of the children's sight."

"Will you be all right?" Jack Hamilton asked before he left.

"I'll be all right," she told him firmly.

All right? She wondered. She was 26, a trapper's widow with three little children, 160 acres of brush-grown land, almost none of it cleared, a small log house—and precious little else.

That was just before the start of the great depression, the period that Canadians of that generation still call the dirty thirties. There was no allowance for dependent children then. Olive knew she could get a small sum of relief money each month, maybe about $12 for the four of them, but she did not dare to ask for it. Her children Olive and Louis had been born in Canada, Vala in the United States, as she had, and she was afraid that if she appealed for help she or Vala or both of them might be sent back to that country. In the very first hours of her grief and loneliness she vowed she would never let that happen, no matter what. It was the four Reamers alone now, to fight a world of privation and hunger, but at least they would stay together.

She was the daughter as well as the wife of a trapper. Her mother had died when she was eight. They had been a happy family, but always poor folk with no money to speak of, and after she married Walter Reamer his trapline didn't bring in much. She had never known anything but a hard life, but now she was thankful for it, knowing that she was better able to face the hardship that lay ahead than most women would be.

"I don't think I looked the part," she said to me years later. And looking at snapshots of the pretty girl she had been, I was quick to agree. "I was no backwoods frump, untidy and slovenly," she went on, her eyes flashing with pride. "I was small, 5 feet 2, and weighed 112, all good solid muscle. And if I do say it, when I had the proper clothes on and was out dancing and dining I could compete with the best of them in looks." She certainly could.

There were plenty of moose around the homestead, some deer, black bears, wolves, rabbits, grouse, foxes, mink and muskrats. The young frontier widow would become a farmer, hunter and trapper on her own, she decided.

She had a little money on hand to buy food with. She owned no horses, but she dug potatoes, raked hay, did anything she could for her few neighbors to pay for the use of a team, and by the next spring she had managed to clear the brush and trees from a few acres of good land. Little Olive was housekeeper, cook and baby sitter while her mother worked outside. Olive planted a vegetable garden and started a hay meadow. She hunted grouse and rabbits, and the first winter the neighbors helped out with a gift of moose meat. The family managed to eke out a living. It was all hard work, day in and day out, the mother dragging herself off to bed when dark came and crawling out at daylight to begin another day, but at least she and her youngsters had something to eat.

Then, in July of 1929, their food gave out. She couldn't bring herself to go deeper in debt to her neighbors, and that was when, in desperation, she decided on the out-of-season moose hunt. With the few odds and ends they had left, they could make out on moose meat until the garden stuff started to ripen.

They hadn't gone far up the Stuart before she began to see moose tracks along shore, and worn moose paths coming down to the river. Then they rounded a bend, and a big cow was standing out on a grassy point, dunking her ungainly head and coming up with mouthfuls of weeds.

Olive didn't want to kill a cow and maybe leave a calf to starve, but she had never been more tempted in her life than she was right then. That big animal meant meat enough to last the family the rest of the summer, and by canning it she could keep every pound from spoiling. She paddled carefully ahead, whispering warnings to the kids to sit still and keep quiet. The closer she got the more she wanted that moose. The cow finally saw them and looked their way, while the hunter wrestled with her conscience.

She never knew what the outcome would have been, for about the time she was getting near enough to shoot, little Olive let out a squeal of pure delight and an awkward red-brown moose calf raised up out of the tall grass. That settled it.

The children were all talking at once now and the cow grunted to her youngster and waded out, ready to swim the river. She was only 200 feet away at that point, and all of a sudden she decided she didn't like the canoe there. Her ears went back, the hair on her shoulders stood up, and her grunts took on a very unfriendly tone.

Olive stuck her paddle in the mud and waited, wondering just what she would do if the moose came for them. There was no chance that she could maneuver the cumbersome dugout out of the way. But she quieted the youngsters with a sharp warning, and after a minute the cow led her calf into deep water and they struck out for the opposite side of the river, where they waded ashore and walked up a moose trail out of sight.

A half mile farther up the river Olive landed and took Louis piggy back. Then, carrying her gun, she led the way very quietly across a grassy point where she thought moose might be feeding. She didn't see any, however, and now the kids began to complain that they were getting very hungry. Their mother was hungry, too. They sat down on the bank to rest and she saw a good rainbow trout swimming in shallow water.

She always carried a few flies and fishhooks in her hat-

band, and now she tied a fly to a length of string and threw
it out, using the string as a handline. The trout took the
hook on about the fifth cast and she hauled it in. She fished
a little longer and caught two squawfish. They hit back to
the canoe then. She built a fire and broiled the rainbow and
one of the squawfish on sticks. The kids divided the trout,
she ate the squawfish. As a rule they have a muddy flavor,
and she had really caught those two for dog food, but to her
surprise that one tasted very much all right.

A little farther up the Stuart they came on two yearling
mule deer, with stubby spikes of antlers in the velvet, watching from a cut bank, but they spooked the instant Olive saw
them and disappeared in the brush. A little later the same
thing happened with two bull moose. They saw the canoe
and ran into the willows while she was reaching for her gun,
and she remembers that she was so disappointed and discouraged she wanted to bawl. That made four moose they
had seen, counting the calf, without getting a shot, and she
decided that killing one was going to be a lot harder than
she had thought. And her arms were so tired from paddling
the heavy dugout that they felt ready to drop out of the
sockets.

She had brought a .22 along, as well as the .30-30, and a
little while after that she used it to shoot a grouse that was
watching from the bank. She had about given up hope of
getting a moose, and was ready to turn back for the long
paddle home, when she saw what looked like the back of one,
standing almost submerged, in the shade of some cottonwoods up ahead. She shushed the kids and eased the canoe
on for a better look, and sure enough, it was a young bull,
probably a yearling. Just the right size for what she wanted.

The moose was feeding, pulling up weeds from the bottom
and putting his head completely under each time he went
down for a mouthful. Olive paddled as close as she dared,
and warned her two little girls to put ther hands over their
ears and keep down as low as they could, for she had to

shoot over their heads. She put the front bead of the Winchester just behind the bull's shoulder, at the top of the water, and when he raised his head she let him have it. He went down with a great splash, and she told the kids they could raise up and look.

Luckily, the young bull did not die right there in deep, muddy water. Getting him ashore for dressing would have been a very hard chore. When Olive got close with the dugout he was trying to drag himself out on the bank. Her shot had broken his back. She crowded him with the canoe, feeling sorry for him all the while, and as soon as she had him all the way on dry land she finished him with a shot in the head.

She had always hated to kill anything, and by that time she was close to tears from pity for the moose. Then she saw little Olive leaning against a tree, crying her heart out, and Vala and Louis with their faces all screwed up in tears, and she felt worse than ever. But she reminded herself that it had to be done to feed the children, and she wiped her own eyes and explained to them as best she could. About that time a porcupine came waddling along, and that took their minds off the moose.

Dressing a moose, even a yearling bull, is no fun. She went at it now, and it was about as hard a job as she had ever tackled. The kids tried to help, but only succeeded in getting in the way. While she worked she couldn't help worrying about her out-of-season kill. What would happen if she were found out? Would the game warden be as understanding as she hoped?

When the job was done she built a small fire and boiled the partridge she had shot, and a few pieces of moose meat, for their supper, giving little Louis the broth in his bottle. She felt better after she ate. She loaded the meat into the dugout and started home, but it was full dark now, and she was so tired that she soon decided not to go on.

They went ashore, spread out a piece of canvas, part

she put the front bead of the Winchester just behind the bull's shoulder

under and part over them, and tried to sleep. The mosquitoes were so bad that the mother finally gave up. She sat over the children the rest of the night, switching mosquitoes off with a willow branch. Daylight came about 4 o'clock, and they got on the way again. Olive Reamer never forgot that early-morning trip back to her home place. Her hands were black with mosquitoes the whole way, and the torment was almost too much to endure.

Joel Hammond, a neighbor, had given her some flour that he had made by grinding his own wheat in a hand mill, and the first thing she did was build a fire and make a batch of hot cakes. The flour was coarse and dusty, but with moose steak and greens fried in moose fat, those cakes made a real good meal. Then she went to work canning meat.

That was the only moose she ever killed out of season. When hunting season rolled around that fall she got a homesteader's free permit and went after a winter's supply of meat. It came even harder that time.

The first one she tried for she wounded with a shot that cut through the tip of his lungs. He got away in thick brush and she took her dog Chum and followed him. Chum drove him back into the river and he swam across and stood wheezing and coughing on the opposite side, too far off for Olive to use her last remaining shell on him. Chum swam the river in pursuit, and started to fight him in shallow water.

Another neighbor, Ross Finley, who lived on the quarter section next to hers, heard the shooting and came to lend a hand. He loaded little Olive and her mother into the dugout and they paddled across to where the dog was badgering the moose. Finley used Olive's last shell when they got close, but missed, and the bull, fighting mad by now, came for the canoe, throwing his head this way and that. Olive was badly scared, for neither she nor the child could swim a stroke and she knew that one blow from the moose's horns would roll the dugout over like a pulpwood bolt.

She moved fast with the bow paddle, and the moose

missed them by less than a foot as she swung the canoe away from him. He was in deep water now and Chum was riding on his shoulders and biting at the back of his neck. The dog took his attention for a second or two, and Olive reached down and grabbed Finley's .22 that was lying in the bottom of the dugout. She shot him at the butt of an ear, with the gun almost touching him. He sank quietly out of sight, leaving Chum floating in the water. The dog was so worn out from the ruckus that he had to be helped to shore.

They tried hard to locate the dead moose, but the current carried it swiftly downriver and it was days before they found it, lying in shallow water at the mouth of a creek, the meat spoiled.

There were plenty more around, however. They could be heard fighting at night, grunting and snorting, and sometimes their horns would clash with a noise as loud as an ax hitting a hollow log. In the early mornings Olive saw as many as five at one time along the weedy river shore. She waited and picked the one she wanted, and that time she killed him with no trouble.

The Stuart was full of ducks and geese that fall and there were grouse everywhere. She had plenty of ammunition for the .22 and always a few .30-30 shells around. She canned everything she killed, and no longer worried about a meat shortage. Life was beginning to sort itself out for her the way she wanted it to.

"A few unmarried men came around and tried to shine up to me, but I wasn't interested," she recalls. "All I wanted was to get more land cleared and buy a cow or two and a team of horses of my own." The young homestead widow was proving to herself that she could take care of her family and make the grade.

But before the winter was over she faced another crisis. By February most of their food was gone except for the canned meat and a few cans of vegetables. They had used the last of the hand-ground flour that Joel Hammond had given her, and were desperately in need of groceries. She had no money but she decided to walk the 27 miles to Vanderhoof, on the Prince George–Prince Rupert railroad, and try to get the supplies she needed on credit. She knew she could pay for them with potatoes the next fall, for by that time she had enough land cleared to grow a bigger potato crop than they needed for themselves.

She left the three children with the George Vinsons, neighbors a mile and a half downriver, and started out on a cold, wintry morning. She had a road to follow, but only a few teams and sleighs had traveled it and the walking was hard, in deep snow. Two miles out of Vanderhoof she finally hitched a ride.

She had no luck getting credit against her potato crop. Those were hard times, and the merchants couldn't afford much generosity. She tried first to buy badly needed rubbers for herself and the kids. They were the cheapest foot gear available. But the store turned her down.

A kindly woman who ran a restaurant did better by her, however. She provided a good dinner, and when Olive put her down for 50 pounds of potatoes she just smiled and shoved a chocolate bar into the young mother's pocket. She got the potatoes when the time came, anyway.

Another storekeeper said he couldn't let Olive have things on credit, but he gave her $2 in cash and told her to do the best she could with it. She knew where part of it was going. For the oatmeal and sugar she had promised her children. But she could see no way to pay for another meal for herself, or a room for the night, and she walked around Vanderhoof thinking of how wet and cold their feet would be in the slush of the spring thaw, about as heart-broken as she had ever been in her life.

Finally she decided to make one more attempt. Some of her neighbors on the Stuart River traded at a store at Finmoore, 19 miles east of Vanderhoof. She also had a friend there, Mrs. John Holter. She would walk the railroad track to Finmoore and try her luck. At the time she didn't know how far it was, and she expected a hike of only 10 miles or so.

It was almost dark when she started. The railroad ties were crusted with ice and the walking was very bad. Her clothes were not enough for the cold night, either. They consisted of denim overalls, men's work socks, Indian moccasins and an old wool sweater with the elbows out, worn under a denim jacket.

She had never been brave in the dark, any time or any place, and that walk was an ordeal. All she could think of were the hobos she had heard stories about, the railroad bums, and she was afraid of every shadow.

She got to the lonely little station at Hulatt, 15 miles from Vanderhoof, at midnight, and asked the stationmaster if she could rest until daylight. She lay down on the floor by the big pot-bellied stove. It was warm and cozy and she was worn out. She started to drift off to sleep, but then she began to worry about the children and the likelihood that if she was later in getting home than she had promised they might come back to the house and get into trouble starting a fire. Things were hard enough without having the place burned down. She got up and trudged away along the track once more.

It was 2 in the morning when she reached the Holter place. Mrs. Holter fixed her a sandwich and a cup of hot milk, and she fell into bed. Her friend shook her awake at 9 o'clock, as she had been told to do. Those scant seven hours of sleep were all Olive had in more than 36.

Mrs. Holter loaned her another $2, and she went to the general store and struck it rich. The proprietor, Percy Moore, stared at her in disbelief when she poured out her hard-luck story. "You've walked from the Stuart River since yesterday morning," he exclaimed. "That's 46 miles!"

"No, 44," she corrected him. "I got a ride the last two miles into Vanderhoof." Then she added, "I've got 14 more to walk home before dark tonight, too."

The first thing he let her have, on credit, was three pair of rubbers she needed so desperately. Then he took care of her grocery list. Eight pounds of oatmeal, three of rice, five of beans, five of sugar and, for a bonus, a 3-pound pail of strawberry jam. That was a luxury she had not dreamed of. She plodded away from Finmoore at 10 o'clock that morning with almost 30 pounds in a packsack on her back, but never before or since was she as glad to carry a load.

Three inches of wet snow had fallen that morning, and the 14-mile walk was endless, each mile longer than the one before. The pack got heavier and heavier, and some time in the afternoon she began to stumble and fall. She was so tired by that time, and her back ached so cruelly from the weight of the pack, that she wanted only to lie in the snow and go to sleep. But she knew better. Time after time she drove herself back to her feet and staggered on, slipping and sliding and falling again.

To this day she does not know what time it was when she reached home, but it was long after dark. Chum met her in the yard, and no human being was ever more glad to fumble at the latch of his own door. She slid out of the pack, pulled off her wet moccasins and socks, and rolled into bed with her clothes on. The last thing she remembered was calling the dog up to lie at her feet for warmth.

The children awakened her at noon the next day, fed her breakfast, and rubbed some of the soreness out of her swollen legs and feet.

When she harvested her potato crop the next fall she paid off her debt to Percy Moore in full, except for one item.

"There was no way to pay him, ever, for his kindness to me when I was broke and had three hungry children at home," she told me.

She made many more trips to Finmoore in the years before she left the Stuart, for she did most of her trading at his store, and when time got better he and his wife and daughter often came out to her farm and bought vegetables and eggs from her. She still remembers walking back to his place the next year carrying six dressed chickens, selling them for 50 cents apiece, spending the money for food, and packing it home.

"Three dollars bought quite a heavy load in those days, too," she recalls.

The Wolves
Were
the Worst

THINGS went on about the same for the young frontier widow, Olive Reamer, the second summer after her trapper husband drowned. She plowed 50 acres of land for a neighbor, Jack Hamilton, that spring. Her two little girls, Olive and Vala, were six and five now, and Louis, the baby, was past two. The girls cleared and burned brush for Hamilton, and they all picked strawberries and raspberries for Joel Hammond, another neighbor. They got more work putting up hay and digging potatoes, and made enough money to buy a cow. They had lots of milk and butter after that. Olive also bought 30 hens and they had all the eggs they wanted.

Vegetables and wild fruit were plentiful. She sold potatoes and garden stuff and bought the other groceries they needed. The Reamers were doing very well, all as healthy as young deer and just about as lively. The mother even built a woodshed, splitting the shakes for the roof herself, out of blocks she cut with a crosscut saw.

Two summers after that she traded two cows and a calf for a team of horses, wild and ornery as mules, but once they were tamed down they proved a good work team. Land clearing and the rest of the work went a lot better after that.

When it came time to kill a moose for the winter's meat the second fall (young Olive and Vala had started to school by that time, in spite of a 3-mile walk along the Stuart River each way) the mother knew exactly what to do, or at least she thought she did. She left the three kids in the house one evening when a cold drizzle of rain was falling, paddled her big 30-foot dugout very quietly up the river to Bear Creek, and spotted a huge bull standing in the water at the mouth of the creek.

She had to stand up in the canoe to see enough of him to shoot. Her rifle was an old .30-30 Winchester Model 94, and she wondered what would happen when it went off. It didn't kick much, but that heavy, Indian-made dugout would tip over if you breathed on it real hard. She finally pulled the trigger anyway, and the moose fell like a ton of brick. Somewhat to her surprise, the canoe stayed right side up, too. But when she paddled to where the animal had dropped, he wasn't there. She looked around, saw a streak of blood leading up from the water toward the timber, and the next thing she knew a very wild-eyed and ugly moose was looking down at her from the top of the bank 30 feet feet away.

She dropped the paddle and grabbed the gun, but before she could get the sights on him he lifted his nose in the air and let out the worst groaning noise she had ever heard. It made every hair on her head stand on end. She shot too soon, through thick willows, and missed him. He whirled and ran and the next she saw of him he was going along a hillside at very long range. She held the .30-30 about two feet over his shoulder and touched it off, and he bunched himself up but kept going.

Olive found a good blood track, but it was raining hard by then and getting dark, so she quit and went home. The next morning she put Chum, her big dog, on the track and he found the moose dead not far from where she had turned back the night before. Two good shots had gone into him, one high in the shoulder, the other above a kidney and up into his ribs. The second hit was probably an accident, at that range, but at the time Olive felt pretty well satisfied with her shooting.

Before she left the Stuart, she had two more moose experiences that she will never forget. She climbed on one of her horses one morning in May to ride six miles to an abandoned hay meadow where a man by the name of Jim Fedderly had lived long before. They called it Fedderly's Meadow. Nobody had cut the hay for many years and Olive thought they might cut and stack it to help out with their winter feeding. She left the children at home.

She had ridden about five miles when she pulled her horse up to look at some flowers beside the trail. She decided to climb off, and had one foot out of the stirrup, when the horse threw up his head, blasted out a frightened snort, and then Olive heard a strange noise almost like a growl behind her. She looked over her shoulder, and not more than 15 feet away stood a cow moose, ears flattened back against her neck and her hair all standing up, at the point of lunging for the horse and rider. No animal had ever looked meaner.

The cow lunged, the woman heaved herself back into the saddle, and the horse jumped so hard he almost threw her off. He didn't quite get clear. The cow clouted him on the hips with her forefeet, hard enough that his hind quarters went almost to the ground, but didn't do him any serious damage. When they were safely out of reach Olive looked back and could see a newborn moose calf, still wet, lying where the cow had started her rush.

The next day she rode back to the hay meadow to scout out a road into it. She tied her horse Shorty where he could graze on blue-joint, and sat down at the edge of the timber to rest. Pretty soon she heard a moose snort on the far side of the meadow. She knew that would spook Shorty after what had happened the day before, so she untied him and climbed back in the saddle in a hurry. By that time he was crow-hopping and prancing like a purebred stallion, and when she looked across the meadow again she saw a cow moose and her calf come running out of the brush, with two big timber wolves after them.

One wolf fooled around in front of the cow, just out of reach of her front feet, and while Olive watched helplessly the other one went after the calf, hamstrung it with one bite and pulled it down. Then it turned its attention to the cow, diving in and grabbing her by the hind legs.

Olive's blood was boiling, and she did her best to force Shorty across the meadow and break the thing up, but he'd have none of that. He pranced and waltzed the other way, and she began to shout to scare the wolves off. They ran into the brush and she rode a circle around the two moose, yelling at the top of her lungs, hoping she could spook those two gray devils out of the neighborhood. Then she hit for home to get a gun.

"I didn't have to urge Shorty," she recalls. "He did his level best the whole way. I suppose he thought the moose and the wolves were both after him."

She drank a glass of milk while her girls put her saddle on Ben, their other horse. Then she loaded the old Winchester and rode back to Fedderly's Meadow as fast as the fresh horse could go. But when she got there she had been gone two hours in all, and she was too late.

She heard the cow moose blow her nose while she was still in the timber. She tied Ben and ran as fast and quietly as she could to the edge of the open, and it's hard to put into words the sight that met her eyes.

The cow was still fighting for her calf, but there wasn't much fight left in her. Her entrails were half torn out. They dragged on the ground as she turned this way and that, trying to trample the wolves with her front feet. But she was too near death to move fast enough. The hamstrung calf still lay off to one side, helpless, where Olive had seen it last.

The cow's hind legs failed and she went down on her haunches while the woman was sneaking from tree to tree to get within good gun range.

"I wanted to be very sure of hitting something when I shot," Olive told me.

When she reached the place she had picked, one wolf was lapping blood at the cow's flank and the other was actually sitting on her hind quarters, his red tongue lolling out from exertion. Olive was so furious while she made the last few yards of her stalk that she gritted her teeth until they hurt.

She drew a bead on the wolf that was sitting on the moose, and when the gun cracked he flew up in the air as if a bomb had hit him. The shot tore out his whole back just behind the shoulders and he was dead when he struck the ground.

The second one made a bad mistake. He didn't know where the rifle shot had come from and he ran straight toward Olive. She kept her sights on him and let him come until he swerved, 200 feet away, to streak for the brush.

when the gun cracked the wolf flew up in the air as if a bomb had hit him

Her shot cut across his chest, blew a hole in him and broke both front legs. At that she had to follow his blood trail for 400 feet through rose brambles and scrub trees. He was still trying to crawl off, but he was almost dead so she let him suffer and saved the one shell she had left for the cow moose. After that was taken care of, she put the calf out of its misery with her belt ax. For a woman who disliked killing things, she had had quite a day. But she never felt the slightest regret where the two wolves were concerned. She made a vow then and there that she would shoot any wolf she laid eyes on the rest of her life if she could.

She still hates wolves. She has seen a lot of their work since, on caribou and deer and other moose, and she is convinced that they kill for fun as well as for hunger. They run and play their victims as renegade dogs do sheep. She has known them to leave a kill, full fed, pull down the next animal they came to and go on without feeding. If they run across a bunch of deer or caribou they don't even take time to finish a kill, she relates. They pull it down and disable it, and go after another and another until they get tired. If there are one or two old wolves in the pack, with poor teeth, they'll stay with the first kill, eat all they want, and then catch up with the rest. Every now and then the pack turns on those decrepit oldtimers, too, and tears them to bits.

"You don't often catch an old, broken-down timber wolf in a trap, and I doubt one ever dies of old age," Olive told me. "I have no use for 'em, and of all the deviltry I have known them to be guilty of none has ever haunted me down through the years more than the savagery of that pair in Fedderly's Meadow that spring day."

A while after that a pack gave her one of the worst frights she ever had, too, and that did nothing to endear the wolf tribe to her.

The years passed quickly, and the fall came when she had five tons of potatoes to dig, and sold them at $2 a hundredweight. She had real money then, for the first time.

Then the man who hauled the potatoes to a gold-mining company at Germansen Landing, 150 miles north of the Reamer place on the Stuart, brought back word that the mining camp wanted to hire a woman cook and would pay good wages.

The family hated to leave the homestead, for they had come to love everything about it by that time, but Olive knew the work would be easier than farming and the pay better, and Louis and the girls would have other people around them, even kids of their own ages to play with. So they sold some of their stock, left the rest with a neighbor, and got ready to move to Germansen Landing.

But the morning they were to leave Vala came down with whooping cough, and a day later young Olive and Louis also were sick with it. It was a month later, on October 25, before they were well enough to travel. By that time, because the boss of the camp had not gotten the message the mother sent him, another cook had been hired, but she didn't know that.

They got a ride north, but the truck developed troubles and when they got as far as a desolate place called Groundhog, 35 miles from their destination—it wasn't even a wide spot in the road, just woods and mountains in the middle of a big burn—the driver dropped them off with their outfit, a loaf of bread and three cans of beans, to wait for a second truck that he said would be along the next morning.

They had a tent and a small ax, and there was plenty of dry firewood in the burn. They got the tent up all right, but Olive had had whooping cough along with her children and it had left her with a touch of pleurisy. Chopping wood proved a tough chore, but she had no choice, for the snow was six inches deep and the weather cold. The kids slept soundly that night but she lay awake, worried that grizzlies might find their little camp.

No truck came the next day or the next. One went by going the wrong way, toward Fort St. James, and she flagged it down and told the driver they were nearly out of food. He left bread and a little canned stuff, but when they did not see another vehicle by noon the next day they rolled their bedding and the tent, Olive put them on her back, and they trudged off on foot. The kids were still weak from their sickness and they made poor time. Night overtook them and they went on for an hour or two by moonlight, but the children played out, so the mother chopped green spruce branches and laid out the bedding. The night was clear and she didn't bother with the tent. Dry wood was plentiful again, and she sat up beside the fire and fed it until the first gray hint of daylight began to show. Then she roused Olive, Vala and Louis, they ate what food was left, and started on.

They had not walked 10 minutes when a timber wolf howled, up on the mountain to one side of them. Another answered from the other side, and then there seemed to be wolves howling in every direction. It wasn't more than another five minutes before Olive saw two shadows slinking along through the brush only a short way off the road, keeping pace with them, and then she caught a glimpse of another behind them.

Shivers ran up and down her spine, and she wished fervently that they had stayed beside their fire until full daylight, but it was too late for wishing to do any good. They would have to keep on and hope the wolves wouldn't muster enough nerve to close in. All Olive could think of was the way she had seen those two go after the cow moose. She was carrying her .30-30 and was ready, but didn't dare use the rifle unless she had to, for fear shooting might provoke an attack.

They walked on a mile and a half and her blood ran cold every minute. Every now and then she'd get a glimpse of a shadowy form in the brush to one side, or see a wolf lope across the road back of them, furtive and sinister. She was desperate with fear, and finally told the kids she was going to use the rifle the next chance she got. But still she held off, scared of the consequences.

The morning brightened slowly and it seemed full daylight would never come. But at last it did, and then all of a sudden the wolves were gone. She didn't see them leave; they just melted out of sight and weren't around any more. A short distance farther on she found the explanation. The fresh tracks of three caribou crossed the road, heading east toward the Wolverine Mountains. The wolves had picked up the caribou scent before they reached the tracks, and had taken off like hounds after a rabbit. Off to the right of the road their tracks covered those of the caribou, going at a full run. Olive counted the sign, and there were seven in the pack. She shuddered to think of the horrid death that awaited the caribou when those seven caught up to them, but she couldn't help being thankful that they had pulled the pack away from the children and herself.

"I guess in a wolf's book caribou are safer game than people, even a woman and three kids," she says. "In all the years I have lived in the mountains of British Columbia, where wolves are still fairly numerous, I have never known of an authenticated case of an actual wolf attack on humans. That's more than I can say for either bears or cougars, incidentally. But it is a fairly common occurrence for a pack to follow people as they did us that morning, and if they are made bold by hunger they'll crowd in within 30 or 40 feet, too. So far as I'm concerned that's too close.

"Maybe we were in no real danger from those seven that skulked along after us for that mile and a half, but being trailed in that fashion is a hair-raising experience and I've never been more frightened in my life. Even if they don't hurt you they can scare you half to death."

The Chinese cook who had been hired at the gold camp when Olive failed to show up on time was a good one, and couldn't very well be dismissed to make room for her. So there the Reamers were, stranded in a mining camp, with everything back at the homestead disposed of. They were all tired out from the trip north, and the young mother was so discouraged she could have cried her eyes out.

The boss of the camp put them up in an empty house, and the first night mice played tag across the beds and all over the floor. But the next morning they were staked to firewood and the supplies they needed, and Olive was offered a job doing washings for the miners. She accepted, they cleaned the house up and made it livable, and the rest of the winter she washed clothes by hand on a washboard every day, with the girls helping. They stayed on there until the gold camp closed the following fall, and by that time she had enough of a stake to go to Prince George, where she got work.

That all happened a good many years ago, but the woman who was Olive Reamer still recalls in vivid detail the scare those wolves gave her that cold morning, and she still hates wolves.

She has no liking for eagles, either. In her opinion, they are as merciless as wolves with anything they can handle, including fawns and moose calves, partridge, ducks and geese. Olive and her present husband once watched a pair even make a successful attack on a yearling mule deer.

They were on a fishing and camping trip on the Stuart River that time, years after she had moved away from the homestead. They rounded a bend in their boat and two eagles were swooping down on the young buck at the water's edge, one after another. They must have surprised it drinking and stunned it sufficiently with the first blow they struck that it could not fight them off. It ran this way and that, stumbling to its knees, backing into brush and logs, rearing on its hind legs to strike out with its forefeet, but never able to connect.

Olive's husband John rowed as hard as he could, hoping to break up the attack, but before they could get within gun range the deer went down in the mud with both eagles on top of it, and couldn't get up. John rammed the boat ashore, grabbed his rifle and ran along the bank. The birds flew off, but were reluctant to leave and lit in a tree nearby. John shot one and the other then cleared out. He killed it the next morning. When they got to the deer its head was torn and bloody, it was holding its neck at a twisted angle, and seemed dazed. It was badly hurt as well as completely exhausted.

They carried it to the boat, took it back to camp, and nursed it as you would a pet lamb for two days and two nights before it recovered. It showed no fear of them, but finally, when John hit a dry tree a hard whack with the ax in cutting firewood for supper, it suddenly seemed to remember that it was a wild deer and bounded out of sight in the brush.

That was a very unusual incident, for the buck was good sized for a yearling. It's close to unheard of for eagles to attack a full grown deer, but this pair must have caught their victim unawares and they were certainly intent on killing him.

Looking back on her life of hardship and privation and struggle, the woman who was a young trapper's widow will tell you today that everything turned out at least as well as she hoped, maybe better. She had the sad misfortune to lose Louis not many years after he started school, from spinal meningitis. But Olive and Vala grew into pretty, fun-loving young women and made happy marriages when the time came.

Shortly after young Olive was married, to an airline captain, her mother was working in Prince George when she met a big, gentle, soft-spoken man named John Fredrickson. Big John, his friends called him, and it fitted him to a T.

"Things got to a point where I couldn't dance with him without seeing stars," Olive told me long afterward, "and after a year we were married. The rest of my life has been very good indeed."

She and John still love hunting, fishing, camping, prospecting, anything that has to do with the outdoors. They also love the back country of northern British Columbia, and have made some fine trips into it.

They lived for a time at Vanderhoof, but in 1968 moved to Okanagan Falls, 35 miles north of the U.S. border.

"When we kill a moose now it's because we want to, not because we have to have meat," Olive Fredrickson says. "But when I think about it, those early years on the homestead, when our winter meals depended on my hunting, weren't half bad."

In
the Jaws
of a Bear

THE grizzly came to the bait at dusk, a medium-sized sow that would have weighed 350 to 400 pounds. She walked in arrogantly, swinging her head and sniffing the air but showing no caution, and when she reached the ripe horse carcass she started to feed at once.

The bait was in a clearing on the bank of a small creek, and the hunters had fixed their blind on a hillside about 175 yards away. That's close enough for a good shot but far enough that a bear is not likely to wind you.

There were four in the blind; Jess Spragg, the outfitter, the two clients, Martin Sokolosky and A. J. Rod, and Bert Bell, the packer. They didn't expect more than one bear, so Sokolosky and Rod had flipped for the shot and Martin had won. Bell had done what is usually done in the West in a case of that kind, spit on a flat stone and tossed it. Martin had picked the wet side and that was the one that came up.

His rifle was custom-built, in .264 Magnum caliber. In Bert's judgment that was a pretty light dose of medicine for a grizzly, and the way things turned out he was right.

Martin took a rest and smashed his shot into the bear's left shoulder. Through the glasses it looked very good. She stood stock still for a second, as if stunned, then turned and bounded into the timber. Martin touched off a second shot as she went out of sight, but they learned later that that one only grazed her across the rump, no more than cutting the skin.

Spragg and Bell had two rules where wounded grizzlies were concerned. First, you never trail 'em alone. And above all, you never follow one at night. It was too dark now to look for this bear, and they felt sure she'd be dead before she had gone more than a few hundred yards, so the four headed back to camp.

They were camped in an open park as flat as your hand, with timbered mountains crowding close on both sides, on Mountain Creek a few miles east of Yellowstone Park. That country is all wide level valleys and timbered slopes, and it would be hard to find a prettier place.

There were 10 in the party. Rod and Sokolosky had their wives along, and Spragg's crew consisted, in addition to him and Bert, of two guides, John McGrew and Jim Bales, Gene Wolford, the cook, and Dave Rhinehart, the young wrangler. Sokolosky, a manufacturer of oil-well equipment at Houston, Texas, had lived for a time in Montana, and he and Rod, a Houston businessman with oil wells on the side, had hunted with Jess before.

Bell had signed on with Spragg as a packer for the 1967 season. He grew up at Cody and had wrangled horses, packed and guided since before he was 15. He was 37 that fall. When he was not off in the mountains, he worked at the Husky oil refinery at Cody, and he also ran 40 head of whiteface cattle on a ranch as a sideline. But when hunting time rolled around his other work had to take a back seat.

They rode away from Holm Lodge, the jumping-off place for Jess's big-game hunts, on the Shoshone River 40 miles west of Cody, early on the morning of September 9 and headed up Eagle Creek trail. They had 27 miles to ride, uphill most of the way, but expected to reach camp before sundown.

The camp had been set up the week before, and Wolford, the cook, was there waiting. Jess, Martin and A. J. went on ahead. They'd stop at Eagle Creek Meadows, about half way, and catch enough cutthroats for breakfast the next morning. Bert was bringing up the rear with the pack string.

Jess and the two hunters were fishing when Bert's party rode through the meadows, about noon, and started the climb to Eagle Creek Divide. The pass is 9,200 feet high, and as Bell's string hit the top, light snow began to fall. They couldn't have asked for anything better. Snow would mean tracking and a good hunt.

Just beyond the divide they pulled up to rest the horses and eat lunch. The snow kept coming down like a feather blanket, and the high country got prettier and quieter as it turned white. The sky cleared during the afternoon, and the sun was only a breath above the mountains when they rode into camp, with the welcoming smell of wood smoke drifting from the cook tent. There were seven tents up, all told, and there was a permanent corral for the horses.

Wolford was one of the best camp cooks Bert had ever known (he died that December), and he outdid himself that night, with turkey, corn on the cob, tossed salad and pumpkin pie.

Everybody took things fairly easy the next day, resting from the long ride. Bert shod a couple of horses and the rest cut wood—it takes a lot to keep seven tents warm—and looked over the country.

Everything pointed to a good hunt. The game trails in the vicinity of camp showed plenty of use, and bears had worked on both of the decrepit old horses that had been shot earlier for grizzly bait. There were fresh bear tracks, rubbing marks on trees, and brush and leaves raked up around the baits, too.

"We'll kill a couple of grizzlies before we leave," Jess predicted.

The sky had turned overcast again and light snow was falling the second morning, and it sounded as if every bull elk in those mountains was bugling. Before noon Martin and A. J. had looked over several bands, found two bulls they were satisfied with, and each had a fine animal down. It had been a great morning, with all the action any hunter could ask for.

They put in the afternoon dressing the two elk, caping out the heads, quartering the meat and getting it and the horns to camp.

Late the next day they went out to check the bear baits again, Martin and Bert to one, his wife and John to the other. The one had been freshly worked on, so Martin and the packer hunched down in the blind and waited. It wasn't long before they saw a big grizzly moving in, but he was careful and Martin couldn't get a shot. The bear circled the bait, keeping back in the brush, got wind of them, whirled and took off. They had tied the horses about a quarter mile away, and he ran in that direction. Bert smelled trouble.

"If he gets close to those horses you and I will have to walk to camp," he told Martin.

That was exactly what happened. The bear all but ran into them, and they broke loose and lit out. Martin and Bell were left with a rough hike of almost three miles.

About that time they heard shots coming from the direction of the other bait. "Bet my wife has been lucky," Martin said. Sure enough, when they hobbled into camp just before dark she and John were there and everybody was celebrating. She had killed a good grizzly.

McGrew and Bert went out to peel its pelt off the next morning. The bear had been rolling around on the dead horse, and it was a job that called for a strong stomach, but they finally got it done.

Late that afternoon Sokolosky, Rod, Jess and Bell headed for the other bait. They tied their horses a good half mile away this time, not relishing the idea of another walk back to camp, and Injuned into the blind, careful not to show themselves or make any commotion.

They sat there until dusk, when the sow grizzly came in and Martin walloped her in the shoulder.

They got an early start the next morning, leaving camp before sunup. There was tracking snow on the ground, but it was a bright, clear morning and they knew the snow wouldn't last long.

Martin and Jess, Dave Rhinehart, the wrangler, and Bert rode out to look for the bear. They tied their horses near the bait and took the blood trail. It was a good one, but one thing bothered them. The grizzly had gone uphill. A badly wounded bear will take the easiest route, and in that country that's down, not up. They began to wonder whether this sow was hurt as bad as they had thought.

They tracked her for a mile. She had stopped a few times, but moved on and didn't seem to be having much trouble traveling. Then they came on the bed where she had spent the night, and things began to look better. There was a lot of blood, including big clots that she had coughed up. That meant a lung shot. They'd find her and finish her now.

Her tracks circled away from the bed in two directions. She must have walked out, come back and left again. Jess and Martin took one track, Dave and Bert the other.

"If you find her don't kill her," Jess instructed. "Back off and whistle us in. We'll let Martin finish what he started. And keep your eyes open. She just might set a trap for you."

Dave Rhinehart had no rifle. Martin was having some trouble with a knee, and as they separated he handed his .264 to the wrangler. "If we find her I'll borrow Jess's rifle," he said. "One gun is all we need." For Bell, that was to mean the difference between life and death.

Dave and he had not trailed the bear far before they concluded that they had picked the right track. They also realized that they were dealing now with a very sick grizzly. There was a fresh blood trail, and she had turned and was going downhill, meandering in and out of thickets. Her steps were getting shorter and she was lurching from side to side. They could even see where she had dragged her toes. She was getting weak and they didn't think they had much farther to go.

She came to a small creek and plunged straight across, not bothering to pick her way, and the two men pulled up short. A wounded bear will backtrack time after time to get wind of anything that may be following it.

"She knows more about us right now than we know about her," Bert told Dave.

They sat down on the bank of the creek to look things over. There was a patch of windfalls on the far side that was just about right for a hurt grizzly to hole up in. They studied that spot for 15 minutes, using the scope on Sokolosky's rifle. But a bear, lying behind a log and watching its back trail, shows only its nose and eyes, and maybe the top of its ears. They could find nothing that looked like a patch of hair.

The sun was melting the tracks fast and they didn't dare lose any more time. Just across the creek there were a couple of trees that looked OK for climbing.

"Let's get up into them and see what we can see from there," Bell suggested. The situation was getting hairy but there didn't seem to be any better way of handling it, so they splashed across and started for the trees. They never reached them.

Bert had not felt any concern about the bear winding them, for he was sure she already knew where they were. But he hadn't figured on winding her, either, and what happened next was the last thing he expected. The breeze shifted and he smelled bear, plain and strong.

Then he heard a noise in the windfall, and when he swung around she was coming over a log 30 yards away, head low, running full tilt and growling as she came, as deadly looking as anything he had ever seen.

His rifle was a converted sporter, an old Enfield .30/06 that he had bought second-hand 12 or 15 years before. He had done all his hunting with it since, and carried it on most of his pack trips. It was beat up and scruffy looking, but it still shot all right. A packer and guide gives his rifle hard use and doesn't fire it often, and Bert figured this old relic was all the gun he needed. Of late, however, it had developed a major fault. The safety had turned stiff and hard to operate.

He hit that safety now and it didn't budge. He pushed it hard three or four times, but it still held the trigger firmly locked, and about that time things started to stand still for him.

"There was nobody on that mountain but the grizzly and Bell," he said afterward. "My heart was in my throat and there was an empty feeling in the bottom of my stomach, the way a boy's pocket feels when he loses his jackknife."

He was still pulling at the dead trigger of the rifle when the bear was so close that all he could see in the sights were her huge head and shoulders. Then she hit him like an avalanche, the gun sailed out of his hands and they went down in a tangled heap. Bert fell face to the ground and she grabbed his left side just below the ribs, the way a hound grabs a coon, and bit down hard.

He still doesn't remember that there was much pain right then, but it must have hurt for he heard himself yell above the savage snarling of the bear. She didn't stop her strangled growling and grunting until she was dead, but as far as Bert knows he yelled only that one time. She hadn't been on carrion, and he didn't smell her, but he will never forget the way she sounded.

Thoughts go through a man's mind like flashes of light-

ning at a time like that. At least they did in his case. He had
a wife, Joan, and three youngsters at home. John was 13,
Marvis 11 and Keith 4. The first thing he thought was, "Oh,
God, I'll never see Joan and the kids again." Then, "I'm
not dead yet, I'll put up a fight!" And after that, "I hope
Dave doesn't leave to go for help."

He twisted his head to one side and his eyes searched for
the wrangler. Rhinehart was standing about 20 yards away,
and Bell saw him raise his rifle and then wait for a clear
chance.

Bert's side was burning like fire. The bear still kept her
hold there, and he knew she'd tear his insides out unless he
could break her grip. He twisted around enough to grab for
her jaws, forced both hands between them and jerked as
hard as he could.

He still does not know whether he actually pried her jaws
apart, or whether she forgot his belly when he shoved his
hands into her mouth and went to work on them instead.
Anyway, he tugged with all his strength and felt her grip
on his side loosen. Then he could feel her chewing his hands
as if she were feeding on them. That was all right with him.
He even had the crazy thought that he'd let her have them.
He could live without hands, but he wouldn't last long if she
ripped out what was under his rib cage.

Dave hadn't shot, and when Bert looked toward him
again he was still trying to get a clear target and it seemed
to Bert that he was looking right up the barrel of the rifle.
Then the wrangler fired, so close that the blast of the gun
seemed to blow Bell's hair off.

So far as he could tell the bear didn't even flinch, and he
thought, "Dear God, he missed!" But he was wrong about
that.

The grizzly had her rump to Dave, and they learned
afterward that the bullet from the .264 went in her lower
back, just missing the spine, opened up and came out of her
stomach. They even found the mushroomed slug in the

*he twisted around enough to grab for her jaws, forced both
hands between them and jerked as hard as he could*

thumb of one of the buckskin gloves Bert had in a hip
pocket, although how it got there they never knew.

Up to that time the bear had been standing over Bell on
all fours. Now she sat back on her haunches. She hadn't
been able to use her right foreleg because of the smashed
left shoulder, and apparently she had made up her mind
to take a swat at him.

He was still holding on to her jaws and she was trying
now to get rid of his hands. He could see blood running
down his arm, and he had sense enough to know it was
his, not hers. Their faces were only a foot or two apart, she
was still snarling and mumbling, and her eyes were red
blurs with little black centers. Bert could taste the briny-sour
flavor of fright and his feet wanted to run, but she must

have been sitting on them. At least he found he couldn't move.

He glanced toward Dave again, and it seemed the rifle was pointed straight at his head. "For God's sake don't shoot me!" he screamed.

He saw the bear's right front leg go back the way a boxer cocks his arm, and he knew what was coming. Then Dave's second shot rang out. He fired just as she swung her leg up, holding his crosshairs on the base of her hump. But she turned enough that the bullet went into her armpit instead and blew up in her lungs and heart.

She didn't move or shiver, but a change came over her. She still had the foreleg cocked, but her eyes began to fade and glaze and Bert knew she was dying at last. He let go of that gaping mouth, struggled out from under her and staggered to his feet. Dave ran in, held the muzzle of his rifle at the butt of her ear and hammered a third shot into her head. She fell over very slowly, with her leg still raised as if to deliver one final blow.

Bert looked down at his hands. The left one was fairly gushing blood and the right was dripping from deep punctures. Dave ripped the front from his shirt, made a bandage for the left arm and tightened it to slow the bleeding. Then he looked at Bert's side.

Bell was wearing a heavy wool shirt over a T-shirt and wool underwear. The bear had torn a big patch out of all three. She had bitten through the leather gloves in his hip pocket, too. His side felt numb, and there were a lot of puncture holes there and one long gash, from her teeth, but it wasn't bleeding much, and he could walk.

"Let's get out of here while we can," he urged Dave.

They had a mile to go to the horses, much of it through down timber, all rough traveling. Bert was a mighty tired hunter before he finished that hike, and his left hand was still bleeding badly.

Dave led Bert's horse to a down log, helped him up, and tied the reins together so he could hold them in his right hand. Not until then did the wrangler say what was in his mind. "I'll bet you thought you were dead," he murmured in his soft Texas drawl.

"Yes, and I wasn't sure whether it was you or the bear that was going to be to blame," Bert told him.

Dave was a redhead, and when Bert looked down at him from the saddle, his face, against his flaming hair, was exactly the color of new snow.

"I don't suppose mine looked much better, either," Bert admitted later.

They had between two and three miles to ride to camp. By the time they got there Bell was completely exhausted and he knew what was coming. Shock was certain under the circumstances.

Jess and Martin had heard Dave's three shots, and figured that Bell and Rhinehart had killed the bear and would skin it and bring the pelt in. Martin's knee was still bothering him, so they went back to their horses and rode to camp. They got in just ahead of Dave and Bert.

Jess got out his medical kit and in less time than it takes to tell it they were soaking the injured man's hands and doctoring his side. They got a hot fire going in his tent and he crawled into his bag just as shock and relief set in together. For the next hour he shook like a willow in a gale.

Jess was all for sending a man to telephone for a helicopter to take him out, but Bert bucked. "You'll ride a good horse to death getting out to the phone," he warned. "Give me an hour. I don't think there's too much wrong with me. But if I don't come out of these shakes then you can send for your helicopter."

The outfitter agreed, somewhat reluctantly. By the end of the hour Bell was in fair shape, and they decided to wait for morning and see what happened.

The guides went out that afternoon to skin the bear. They told Bert that they followed his blood trail back to her from where the horses had been tied. He left a better trail than she had the night before, they said.

By supper time he was feeling well enough to put away his share of another of Gene Wolford's masterpieces, a meal that included T-bone steak, a baked potato and sour-cream dressing for the salad. But everybody kept talking about the bear and he didn't even want to think about her. Finally he growled, "Dammit, shut up and let me enjoy this supper."

He didn't sleep much that night, because of the pain in his side and back and hands, but he managed a good breakfast the next morning, knowing he'd need all the strength he could muster for the long ride out.

Martin made a sling for his left arm, and they saddled his horse and helped him up. The hunt was finished, the elk and the two grizzly pelts were in camp. The rest of the party would follow him as soon as the pack string was ready. If he got into trouble he would climb off his horse and wait for them.

Ridgy, his gelding, acted as if he knew he had to take things easy. He picked his way over and around rocks as carefully as if he were packing eggs, and Bert was telling him what a hell of a good horse he was. Then he shook his head, the way a horse will now and then on the trail.

But when he shook his head he shook all over, and the result was pure murder. Bert felt as if every rib on his left side were broken (it wouldn't have surprised him to learn they were), and he let out a scream of agony that could have been heard a mile.

"Then I cussed that jughead with every name I could think of," he told me. "But he didn't have the slightest idea what all the fuss was about, and he went right on shaking his head as often as he felt like it."

That was a long lonesome ride, worst of all over the

Eagle Creek Divide, where Bell couldn't help worrying about what the altitude might do to him. But he made it all right, and when he rode within sight of the Eagle Creek Meadows they had never looked so wonderful to him. In that clear fall day they were a golden saucer fringed with thick green timber, and all of a sudden he realized how grateful he was to be seeing that spot again.

The rest of the party never did overtake him. He had a lot of pain, and waves of nausea began to wash over him as the afternoon wore on. But nine hours after he rode away from camp he pushed Ridgy across the Shoshone River and they plodded the last mile to Holm Lodge.

By that time Bert Bell needed medical help more urgently than he had thought. He didn't want to scare the daylights out of his wife Joan, but he did call her and ask her to have a doctor standing by, telling her only that he had cut his thumb pretty badly.

He got his horse loaded in the back of his truck and started the 40-mile drive to Cody. The road along the Shoshone is crooked, and his hands were so swollen and stiff that he had a hard time with the steering wheel. That was a very long 40 miles. But two doctors, J. A. Gautsch and A. M. McGuire, were waiting for him, and at 6 o'clock that evening he was in the hospital, fairly comfortable and extremely grateful.

The doctors left his wounds unbandaged to give them a chance to drain. By a miracle Bert had no broken bones and no internal injuries. He came along fast and was able to leave the hospital at the end of three days.

Today he is as good as new, although his hands are pretty well scarred up and his left side from the ribs down to the hip bone is spotted with purple welts as if somebody had peppered him with buckshot.

"It was a very lucky thing for me that our young horse wrangler kept his head and his nerve when the bear jumped me," he summed things up months afterwards. "I told him so the best way I knew how, and I also said a few words of thanks to the Man Upstairs."

But he'll never stretch either his luck or his faith that far again. He gave the old Enfield to Dave and told him to wrap it over a stump. Next he bought a .30/06 Winchester Model 70 and scoped it to suit him. He figured then that he was ready for any bear that might come along. But if no other ever comes along, that will be all right with him, too.

Old
Shuguli

The two buffalo bulls, the crippled one and his pal, had stopped and were looking back. Don Rundgren and Robin Hart and Alice Landreth rounded a thorn clump and there they were, heads high, tattered black ears drooping sullenly under the wicked curve of their horns, staring truculently, hardly more than 50 yards ahead.

Then Alice saw a calf elephant a few steps off to one side of the buffaloes, looking uncertainly their way, and next she also saw the calf's mother on the other side. The cow elephant was looking straight at the hunters, and Alice realized they had a pretty sticky combination on their hands.

They had been on safari about a week, in southern Tanzania, formerly Tanganyika, and she had kept one eye on the ground every time she put a foot down, watching for snakes. Maybe that came from living in Texas, or maybe it's just natural for a gal when she knows she's in snake country. Anyway, Alice forgot all about it now. With two buffaloes, one of them crippled, and a cow elephant and her

calf almost in their laps, their hands were too full to think
about anything else.

It was a hot, dry October day, and they had hunted hard
until lunch time without finding even a track big enough to
interest them. They came back to camp, dusty and tired, took
a rest, and late in the afternoon drove out in the Land
Rover, following a narrow, rutted dirt road that had been
gouged out for a few miles through very thick bush, by a
native crew working entirely by hand and using the most
primitive of tools. That road-building crew was about as
interesting as anything Alice saw in Africa.

A couple of miles from camp the two buffaloes galloped
across in front of the car, put on speed and disappeared.
Alice hopped out, grabbed her rifle and went racing up a
steep slope with Don and Robin close behind. When she
got to the top of the ridge the two bulls had stopped and
were standing 100 yards off.

The shot should have been easy, but she was winded from
running 200 yards uphill and she muffed it. She hit the bigger
bull and saw her 500-grain solid spank dust up from his
black hide, but too far back, and she realized she had a gut-
shot buffalo to deal with. The two ran, the wounded one
lagged but his buddy waited for him, and the hunters took
after them.

Alice's husband George had crippled a buffalo on a hunt
three years earlier, in 1961, and it came for him in very
thick brush. He killed it at eight feet with the last shell in his
rifle, and ever since she had had an awful lot of respect for
the big black tanks. But now these two had run between the
cow elephant and her calf, entirely by accident, and she knew
there was far greater danger from the elephant than from
the buffaloes.

The cow resented them and resented the humans, and she
was showing it. Her huge ears came forward and her tail
stiffened out like a curved, stubby cane. She lifted her trunk
and Alice expected her to scream, but she didn't. In fact, for
a few seconds none of the actors in the tight little drama

made a sound. Then the unwounded buffalo took the hint and ran, and the other one started to snort and paw the ground.

"You take care of him," Don Rundgren said quietly. "I'll watch the elephant!"

George Landreth had always talked to his wife when she was shooting at major game, coaching her to keep her steady. She had told Don that, and he was good about doing the same thing.

Her rifle was a .458 bolt-action Browning, carrying three shells in the magazine and one in the chamber. That's quite a lot of gun for a slender woman who stands only five feet eight, but she never felt the recoil when she shot at game.

She got in a good shoulder shot but the buffalo didn't go down. "Wallop him in the spine," Don urged, and she did. That one took care of it. He dropped and stayed, and when Alice looked around the elephant and her calf were pounding off in a cloud of dust.

All of a sudden the elephants and the second buff were gone and the girl from Texas had a fine trophy on the ground. But all of a sudden, too, her knees started to feel rubbery and she realized the whole fracas had scared the dickens out of her.

Her bull just missed the record book. His horns measured 35 inches in length, with a spread an eighth of an inch short of 39. He was as good a trophy as a woman, on safari by herself 10,000 miles from her home and husband and youngsters, could ask to take.

Alice Landreth was a Texas housewife, living in the oil city of Midland, and the mother of four girls and a boy, 10 to 16 at that time.

"Never mind how old I am, but George is 38 and that will give you the general idea," she told me.

When they were married, early in 1949, she was a music major in college with vague dreams of becoming a concert artist, and didn't know the stock of a gun from the muzzle. But George was one of three brothers who grew up in quail and duck country at Joplin, Missouri, under the guidance of a father who started all three of them hunting when they were hardly taller than their .22 rifles.

His boyhood habits stuck. Hunting has played a very important part in his life, and today the trophy room in their home holds big-game mounts from all over North America and from Africa and Asia as well.

Not all the mounts in that trophy room are George's, either. Alice can claim a respectable share of them, including four rams that add up to a grand slam in North American sheep, a polar bear and an Alaskan brown, both in the record-book class, and a few others.

George still had eight months to go at the University of Oklahoma when they were married, and his young wife realized even before he graduated that she had a rival. He loved hunting almost as much as he loved her. First it was ducks, quail, geese and other small stuff. Then he got deer fever, and after that it was elk. Alice was getting more and more tired of being left at home, and finally she decided if she couldn't beat him she'd join him. In 1952 she announced that she wanted a rifle and a shotgun for Christmas. She was going to take up hunting in self-defense.

One obstacle hindered her progress. They had five children in six years, and she wasn't exactly free to go hunting whenever the mood overtook her. But she managed to sandwich in a few good trips, for ducks and deer and elk. At first they didn't produce much, but in 1955 she broke the ice with a pronghorn antelope, and followed that a year later with a good elk and a black bear. At that point she counted herself a full-fledged member of the fraternity, and the bug had bitten her as hard as it had George. The two of them have hunted every chance they've had since, usually together, but by themselves a few times when one or the other couldn't go along.

That was the case with the African trip. In September of 1964, right after George and Alice got home from a sheep hunt in British Columbia (she took a record-book Stone ram, a caribou, a moose, two goats and a grizzly) a good friend of theirs, R. B. Cowden, died of a heart attack. He was a quiet, unassuming Midland sportsman who had hunted in Canada, Alaska, Mexico, Africa and India. A few days after his death the Landreths learned that he had intended to leave in less than three weeks for a safari into the great Selous Reserve in Tanzania.

The Reserve had been opened to hunting only a year earlier, after being closed for 40 years. The authorities had issued five elephant permits for 1964, limiting the kill to bulls with more than 60 pounds of ivory to a side, and Cowden had held one of those coveted permits. A member of the family offered it to George.

That was one of the toughest decisions he ever had to make. The opportunity was just too good to pass up, but his work as a petroleum engineer was such at the moment that he could not possibly get away. He thought it over for quite a long time, shook his head—and then suddenly looked at his wife with a familiar gleam in his eye.

She knew what was coming, and the idea of going off on an African safari by herself hit her like a wave.

"I won't go alone," she blurted before he could say a word.

"Who would you want to take along?" George asked with a grin, and she knew she was hooked.

She called one of her closest friends, Dr. Phyllis Huffman, a Midland pediatrician of about her own age and a keen amateur photographer, and asked her if she'd like to go to Africa for a hunt with her cameras. Dr Huffman accepted on the spot, and in turn she phoned a college classmate in New York. Dr. Wilhelmina Haake, also a pediatrician. Within an hour the plans were made and Alice had accepted the offer of the Cowden elephant permit. She didn't have an elephant gun, so she borrowed the .458 Browning from a friend in Midland.

They left in early October and flew to Dar-es-Salaam in Tanzania via London, Copenhagen, Vienna, Cairo and

Nairobi, sightseeing on the way. From Dar-es-Salaam a
small Cessna ferried them to a landing strip in the 5,000-
square-mile Selous Reserve, a few miles from their camp
site.

Outfitted by Tanzania Wildlife, Ltd., their two white
hunters were much younger than Alice had expected. Robin
Hart was only 19, Don Rundgren 23, and because he had
been in the bush three months without a haircut he looked
even younger. The three women had a sneaking suspicion
that they had been palmed off on the young hunters because
they were a trio of females by themselves. Alice could
imagine the outfitters talking it over among themselves and
saying, "Now here's this woman, coming out to hunt elephants. None of the old hands wants her; we'll give her to
young Rundgren."

Actually they couldn't have done better. Don and Robin
proved thoroughly competent, and both were crack shots.
The women saw Robin pick off geese and grouse for the
table with head shots from an iron-sighted .22 at 60 yards.
And as the son of Eric Rundgren, one of the top white
hunters of East Africa, Don had had the best of training
from early boyhood. He was to guide Alice, Robin would
handle Phyllis and Billie.

The latter two could stay only a week, long enough to
make sure that Alice was in good hands and could make out
safely on her own for the rest of the safari. They all took
things fairly easy that week, but before it ended she had
shot one of Africa's most prized trophies, a greater kudu
whose right horn measured 55⅜ inches in length, a head
that went into Rowland Ward's East African kudu record
list in 18th place.

They spotted him standing in a thicket 75 yards off the
road, but when Don drove on, stopped the hunting car, and
Alice climbed out for the stalk he spooked and ran.

Don's ace tracker, Nyanje, picked up the track and they
went after him. He stopped once, but melted into the brush
before Alice could shoot. The kudu is not called the gray

ghost of the forest for nothing. They trailed him a mile and when he stopped the second time he was up on an anthill, silhouetted against the sky, proud and regal looking, the most beautiful thing Alice had ever seen.

"To me the kudu is a magnificent animal, right up with any of Africa's big five," she said afterward. She had never hunted anything she wanted more.

Then Don, looking through his binoculars, said softly, "Better take him; he's got a record head," and the whole deal got even bigger.

The bull was 150 yards away and Alice was carrying a rifle she was not familiar with, a battered Model 70 Winchester .30/06. Her own .30/06, a Weatherby, had suffered damage in shipping and she had borrowed this loaner from the outfitters.

There was nothing around for a rest, but Don put his back to her and said quietly, "Lay it across my shoulder."

The shot hit square in the shoulder and the kudu died in its tracks.

"All right, Alice Landreth," she said to herself after the excitement had quieted down, "if you don't kill another thing, this safari will still be a big success." She really meant it, too. She had never been more willing to rest on her laurels than she was right then.

Phyllis and Billie were having a fine camera safari, filming wildebeest, wart hogs, baboons, and a long list of birds and flowers. They left for home at the end of the week. Alice killed the buffalo, Robin left, and she and Don went on hunting by themselves, with their safari boys. She took a record-book impala, watched a cheetah try to run down a small antelope, and they had a lively encounter with a rhino that met them on the road and came for the Land Rover on sight. She didn't have a rhino license, and she half hoped she'd have to shoot him in self defense, for he had a good horn. But Don outmaneuvered him, and he was left snorting and looking for something else to charge, his little piglike tail standing straight up.

One morning they went to pay a social call on Melva Nicholson, the wife of Bryan Nicholson, chief game ranger of the Selous. She was camped at Luwegu Junction, a few miles from their camp, with her 5-year-old son Philip and four native game scouts. Her husband was off on a foot safari, scouting the Reserve.

Alice and Don got back to their camp to find things in a high state of excitement. Nyanje had found a buffalo calf killed by lions during the night, and the tracks around the kill pointed to a real trophy.

They had heard lions roaring every night, across the Luwegu River, but Alice had had no chance at one and didn't really expect to have. Don had had a pet lioness as a boy, had a lot of respect and affection for the big cats, and was very reluctant to bait them. That meant if she took one it would have to be done by tracking, so Nyanje's news was very welcome.

They hurried out to the kill and took the track. Nyanje and Don agreed that two lions were involved, likely a female and a big male.

Following that track, through thick stuff where frequently they had to bend down and peek ahead to see what they were getting into, was the most exciting thing Alice had ever done on a hunt. They stayed on it for three hours, and it was hard work as well as exciting, too, for the day was steaming hot, with not a breath of air stirring, and enough of the bush had thorns to make tough going.

Nyanje was in the lead, Alice was following him and Don was close behind her when they finally overtook the lions. They came to a dense thicket and the tracker stooped and peered under. He was eyeing head-on a lioness and a big maned male at 25 yards.

Nyanje grunted out something in startled Swahili, but both Don and Alice missed his point. She thought he was telling her to bend down and take a look. She was pretty jumpy, but she started to do it, and then the lion hunt blew up in their faces.

The lioness came crashing straight at them. It wasn't a charge. She wanted out of the thicket and that happened to be the handiest route. She tore past about six feet away, making as much noise as a runaway moose. Then the male went out the other way, and he sounded like two moose. Even cats can create a lot of commotion if one of them weighs something like 500 pounds.

Nyanje couldn't pick up the track, and that was the last chance Alice had at a lion, although later she did come face to face with a lioness and two cubs at 20 feet.

They went down to a dry river bed and dug a pit, let it fill, and she sat down and refreshed herself in the cool water.

The trophy she hoped for most on this hunt was a big elephant, of course. When she reached Dar-es-Salaam, at the start of the safari, John Glenn of the outfitting firm mentioned that game scouts in the Selous Reserve had seen a bull at Shuguli Falls, where the Kilombero and Luwegu Rivers come together and join the Rufiji, with ivory that would go 150 pounds to the side. Alice didn't take that rumor very seriously, but she did ask Glenn whether she could hunt there. His answer was that it was outside the block for which her permit called, and that only one man, Bryan Nicholson, could give her permission to switch blocks.

Later she questioned Don Rundgren about that legendary bull. He had heard the stories, but neither he nor Alice believed them. However, in a case of that kind you naturally want to go and look.

They hunted all of her area that was accessible and some that wasn't. The bed of the Luwegu wasn't entirely dry that year, and they got the Land Rover stuck in wet sand time after time. They saw plenty of elephants, cows and calves in groups of eight to 12, and quite a number of bulls, mostly two or three together. But they saw nothing with good ivory.

The Selous Reserve was a tsetse fly area. The flies ate the hunters alive much of the time. That meant that cattle could not survive there. Consequently no natives lived in the

Reserve, and there was not much ivory poaching. It had been closed to legal hunting for 40 years.

But Don had told Alice at the outset, "Don't get the idea that there's a big elephant behind every bush, by any means. The authorities gave out five permits for this year. If there were more bulls with good ivory they'd allow more permits.

"Nicholson has his headaches. He's willing to see the game harvested but doesn't want it overdone, and he's reluctant to have too many hunters flock in. A lot of people think that because it's been closed there's big ivory running all over the place. That's just not so. If there's an elephant in here with 100 pounds to the side, I'd like to see him."

"So would I," Alice agreed fervently.

Bryan Nicholson finally got back and joined his wife at their camp, and she sent them an invitation to visit her for lunch. They accepted, and all the while they talked she sensed that Nicholson was quietly sizing her up, trying to decide what made a woman tick who would come halfway around the world on safari by herself, feeling her out for her attitudes toward hunting and sportsmanship and wild-life protection.

Finally she brought the conversation around to the big bull at Shuguli Falls. "Know anything about him?" she asked.

Bryan smiled. "An old acquaintance," he replied.

"You really mean there is such an elephant?"

He nodded. "Right enough. I've known him a long time."

Alice waited a minute, screwed up her courage and took the plunge. "Would you give me permission to change areas and hunt where he is?" she asked anxiously.

"Yes," Bryan said. It was as simple as that.

"I don't think anybody has ever paid me a greater compliment in my whole life, and I realized it was quite a feather in Don Rundgren's cap, too," Alice said afterward.

They broke camp that same afternoon and arranged to pull out at dusk, since Don wanted to reach the new location by daylight. It would be an all-night drive over a rough road, and Nicholson warned them they would find trees uprooted by elephants blocking the road in places.

To save Alice the hard night trip in the hunting car, the Nicholsons invited her to stay with them that night, and Bryan offered to drive her up the next day, when camp was established.

They left shortly after breakfast, and stopped a few times to leave the car and look over groups of elephants they saw from the road. They got to the camp just before dusk, to be greeted by a very dejected white hunter. Driving the last three or four miles to the new location at daylight that morning, Don had found a huge elephant track crossing the road, followed it, and walked up on the bull they had been talking about.

"It was Old Shuguli, for sure," he told Alice. "I've never seen anything like him. And you back at Nicholson's, 90 miles away! I'd give odds we never lay eyes on him again."

He was really sick about it, and he didn't feel any worse than she did. Finally he tried to soften the blow a little. "There's one thing wrong with him," he said. "He has a broken tusk. The right one. Almost half of it gone, I should say. But he's still the best elephant left in Africa."

Nobody slept in their camp that night. They were away at daybreak, driving out a few miles in the Land Rover, then leaving it to walk to the waterhole where Don had seen the bull.

His tracks were there, in the drying mud, and they were enough to take any hunter's breath away. When Don laid a steel tape across one of them, it measured 28 inches. That's easy to say but hard to imagine. Alice could scarcely believe that an animal walked the earth that would leave such a footprint.

The tracks showed there were two other elephants with him, smaller but still big enough to be worth following.

"Askari bulls," Don said. "That's Swahili for soldier.

They're along to guard and look after him. Nobody knows
why they do it, but it's a common occurrence when an old
bull goes off by himself."

They had three trackers along, Nyanje and Ngutha and
Esa. The area was heavily wooded and the trackers moved
off on the track at a fast walk. The day was not too hot,
perfect for what they had to do, and Alice kept up without
any trouble.

After a few miles the track led into dry grassy country
and became harder to follow. The three trackers fanned out,
and she and Don lagged behind to give them as much time
as they needed. They had been on the track about four hours
when Ngutha came back at a run.

"Tembo, bwana," he panted out, and went on in excited
Swahili.

"He's found the big one," Don said. "Come on!"

They covered a quarter mile, half running, and all of a
sudden Alice saw the three elephants in a patch of thick
woods 60 yards ahead. They seemed to materialize out of
nowhere. One second she saw nothing, the next she was
staring at the huge gray hulks. Her heart skipped a beat,
and then came up in her throat.

The bulls were breaking branches off trees, feeding, and
almost in the first instant she saw that one had a broken
tusk—and that the other tusk all but reached the ground.
That bull was bigger than any living thing she had ever laid
eyes on, and right then he looked beautiful, too.

The askaris were on either side of him, but the one to the
left was moving off, as if he sensed something wrong. He
took a few slow, deliberate steps, trunk swaying, giant ears
flapping back and forth, and uncovered the left side of the
bull she wanted.

She was carrying the .458 Browning with solid loads, and
Don was backing her with a Model 70 Winchester in the
same caliber. He and she had discussed a brain shot if she
got a chance at an elephant, and she would have preferred

it, believing it more foolproof than any other. But because of the way the big fellow was standing, quartering away, there was no chance for it now. She heard Don say quietly, "Take him in the heart," and a question flashed through her mind. In that vast bulk where was the heart?

She heard the .458 go off, but didn't feel it kick. Her 500-grain hit behind the shoulder and the bull wheeled away and ran, with the askaris keeping pace on either side.

Alice ran after him, as hard as she had ever run in her life. She knew she mustn't take her eyes off him, lest one of the others should cross over and she down the wrong elephant with her next shot.

"I'd like to have been a bird in a tree, watching that foot chase," she told me. "Either of the guard bulls could have turned back and tossed me and I wouldn't have known what was happening until he picked me off the ground. I had eyes for only one thing in the world, Old Shuguli."

As she ran she remembered to shove another load into the magazine of the Browning in case she needed it. At the end of 50 yards the big bull slowed and she drove another shot into him in the same area. That wheeled him around, rump toward her, and she made a split-second decision. If she could shoot him in the slope of his huge back, above the tail, she would break his spine and he'd have to go down.

She placed the shot exactly right and he collapsed and fell dead. She learned later that she had made two perfect heart shots and smashed his spine about four feet up from the tail.

There he was, the elephant she had dreamed about before she left home; more, much more, than she had dared to hope for. It was half an hour before she and Don and the safari boys got quieted down enough to realize just what she had killed. They took pictures galore, and no more elated woman hunter ever posed. Then the trackers went about getting the tusks out.

Back at camp a few hours later, she and Don tried to rig a scales to weigh them. The balances he had brought along

Alice ran after the elephant as hard as she had ever run in her life

could handle up to 100 pounds. He hadn't expected ivory heavier than that. They took care of the broken tusk nicely. It tallied 91 pounds. But when it came to weighing the unbroken one, they hooked on a water can to bring them up to 130 but that wasn't enough. They figured the good tusk, measuring almost 22 inches in circumference and nine feet in length, weighed green not less than 140. It was worn off and polished white on the bottom side at the tip, where it had rubbed on the ground as the bull walked.

Shuguli was an old elephant, far past the prime of a long

life, with abcessed teeth and an ulcer on one shoulder. How he came by the broken tusk they never knew, but Shuguli Falls, in the vicinity of wihch he had lived for many years, is a long, fairly shallow stretch of white water, split into chutes and channels and looking more like a stream in the Canadian bush than an African river. It was Alice's belief that not too long before she killed him, this aging bull lost his footing on the slippery rocks there and fell, breaking off more than a third of his right tusk.

The broken tusk went into the Rowland Ward record list

at 91 pounds, was 6 feet 1¼ inches long and 19½ in circumference. The good one scored 141 pounds and measured
20⅜ inches around and 8 feet 11¾ inches in length. Alice
Landreth had taken the 33rd best elephant of all time, and
of the first 32 fewer than half were hunter killed. Hers was
among the top 10 in that category.

"And to me, Old Shuguli will always be the greatest
elephant that ever lived," she says now.

Bear
That Broke
a Jinx

Bob Munger held up the bottle of wine and squinted at it against the light.

"It says on the label that this stuff should be served at room temperature," he chuckled. "How we gonna get it out of the bottle?"

It was a good question. "Room temperature" in the tent was so low that the wine had congealed into slushy ice. In the end they heated it in a pan of water until it poured, and it went good with fried seal liver.

The party of three hunters was after polar bears the hard way, camped on the ice 40 miles off Point Barrow and hunting with snow machines. The tents were pitched on shore ice which, unlike the polar pack that drifts endlessly the year around, is anchored on the beach and doesn't break up until the spring thaw, usually around the end of May. The men had made camp the middle of April, setting up the tents 10 or 15 miles from the outer edge of the anchored ice. They would be safe, and reasonably comfortable, for the six weeks they were allowing themselves for the hunt.

The ice under the tents was five to seven feet thick, and just behind the camp a pressure ridge was piled 30 feet high. It formed a good windbreak and provided salt-free ice that could be melted for a water supply. Also, since seals make their spring dens under drifted snow along those jumbled ridges and the polar bears hunt them there, the hunters hoped this hog's-back might be the means of luring a bear right into camp.

They got their wish on that score, but unfortunately the bear arrived on the scene before they did, tore up the tents and left. The guides had put up two of the tents the day before the party flew out to the camp, and some time in the intervening 24 hours a big bear came along—with the usual results. The men found one tent down and both ripped and torn. They made repairs, cussing their luck that they hadn't been on hand. They didn't see their visitor again, either, in spite of everything they could do to entice him back.

The three hunters were Munger, Fred Bear and Cliff Robertson.

Robertson was known to just about every movie and TV fan in the country. He was the Hollywood actor picked by the late John F. Kennedy to play the role of Kennedy in a film on the PT boats of World War II. The picture was withheld from distribution after the President was assassinated. An enthusiastic hunter, Cliff wanted a white-bear rug the worst way, and hoped it would be wall-to-wall size.

Munger was a sporting goods and hardware dealer from Charlotte, Michigan, a hunting partner of Bear's for many years. He had taken a very good polar bear in 1960 and did not want another. He was along this time to help cover the hunt with a camera.

The hunt was really Fred's. It was his third try at taking a polar bear, and for him it would have to be done with a bow or it wouldn't count. Head of the Bear Archery Company at Grayling, Michigan, at that time (he has since retired), it had been more than 30 years since he had hunted any other way, and he was known internationally as one of the foremost bowhunters in the world.

His first two attempts at an ice bear had wound up as fairly close shaves. Now the white bear of the north stood as the only major trophy game on the North American continent, and one of the few dangerous animals on earth, that was not on his list of arrow kills.

He had taken deer, elk, moose, sheep, mountain goat, caribou, jaguar, mountain lion, black bear, grizzlies, Alaska browns, an Indian tiger, an African elephant, buffalo, leopard and lion, all with a bow. But up to now the white bear had proven to much for him.

He had had good shots on both of the earlier hunts, at close range, but the instant an arrow sliced into the bear, it had charged and had to be killed with a rifle.

It happened the first time in April of 1960. On the ice off Point Barrow Fred and George Thiele stalked a bear to within 17 yards. Its rump was toward them, and the guide urged Bear to plunk in an arrow and then kill the animal when it turned to fight the arrow. Fred figured George knew what he was talking about, so he followed the advice. He got a good hit but the bear came for them like white lightning, and George downed him at nine paces with two shots from a Winchester .300 Magnum.

The second time was in the spring of 1962, again off Point Barrow, with Thiele as the pilot and guide once more. They got to within 25 yards of that bear and the same thing happened. George killed that one with a 180-grain in the head at 10 steps.

Both times Fred had been left with a filled license but could not claim the trophy, since the pelts had bullet holes as well as arrow holes in them.

One of these days, he was sure, he'd collect a polar bear that he could count. And when that happened, he would consider that he had killed with a bow the most dangerous animal a hunter can tangle with on this continent. Now, in the spring of 1966, he was back on the ice once more with a 65-pound-pull Kodiak hunting bow, ready to try again, and hoping to prove the truth of the old saw, "Three times and out."

To him the white bear was one of the greatest trophies on earth, found far out on the inaccessible ice, hard to get to, not much afraid of man, likely to fight at the drop of a hat, and big and tough enough to give a good account of himself. Fred had concluded that hunting this magnificent animal with snowmobiles, without the help of aircraft, would be the last word.

In addition to getting a bear, he hoped to make a motion picture for use on a national TV show, and also wanted a movie for his own film library. A sizable crew of New York cameramen was along to take care of the filming.

Munger and Bear flew from Chicago to Fairbanks on April 13, met the others there; and the party went on to Point Barrow by charter plane the next day.

Barrow had changed fast since Fred saw it last in 1962. Motor sleds had ousted dog teams, and motor bikes were replacing bicycles. Natural gas had come in, and dial phones were common. But some things were the same. A skinny hamburger still cost 90 cents and a can of Coke 40 cents. The Eskimos, too, were the same: a whale had been reported offshore, and they were readying the same whaling gear they had always used.

The Top of the World Hotel was crowded with guides and bear hunters. Ninety-three bears had been taken up to that time, all with planes, and a number of wolves with snow machines.

The hunters were delayed two days at Barrow by a 30-knot wind and swirling snow that cut visibility to zero. The weather cleared on Saturday, April 16, and they flew by bush plane to Bud Helmericks' headquarters in the Colville River Delta, 160 miles to the east. Bud and his 21-year-old son Jim would be the pilots and guides. Bud has been in that business for years and Jim was following in his dad's footsteps.

The first sight of their home from the air reminded Fred of a lonely lighthouse set in a vast and empty expanse of white. The sea ice ran as far north as he could see, and to the south the arctic prairie sloped up for 50 miles to the foothills of the Brooks Range. But for all its isolation, the place had every modern convenience. A diesel generating plant churned day and night, and a radio set sputtered, keeping a link with the outside world.

The party flew out onto the ice Sunday morning, repaired the bear mischief and got the rest of the tents up. They had two big pop models and two of the prairie schooner type, 8 x 12 with plenty of headroom. For greater warmth they were all doubled, by setting two exactly alike, one inside the other. Pitched on hard snow that had been leveled off, they were floored with pieces of plywood and banked with snow around the bottom.

The cook tent was heated with a stove fed from a small tank of bottled gas; two sleeping tents had catalytic heaaters that used white gasoline; and a third sleeping tent was warmed by an oil burner. The heaters didn't do the job, however, and things wound up with seven men sleeping in the tent that had the oil burner. For want of room, most of the gear and cameras were stored under a tarp outside.

The plans for the hunt hit a snag right at the outset. Fred didn't want to use a plane for spotting bears if he could help it, and so had decided to try baiting them in. The problem was to find seals for bait.

In the shore ice, where there are no open leads, the seals hide their winter breathing holes under deep snow that piles up in drifts along the pressure ridges. When it's time for the young to be born, the female scratches out a den under a drift beside her breathing hole, and there the little seal is hidden—unless a bear smells it out first—until it's old enough to follow the mother under the ice. The men couldn't locate seals in those retreats, and until the weather turned warmer and open water started to appear, they wouldn't have much luck hunting them.

As a substitute, they soaked a bag of fish in seal oil and towed it behind a snowmobile to make a drag trail. In the next few days seven bears passed within a half a mile of camp, and they saw the tracks of other a few miles away, but none followed the bait trail.

The wind kept the ice scoured free of snow, too, so the bears could not be tracked. The hunters would find a track where snow had drifted at the foot of a ridge, but as soon as the bear turned out across the open ice they lost him.

The weather stayed rough, with snow, gale winds and temperatures down to 20 below for days on end. The men built windbreaks of snow blocks around the camp and huddled in the tents trying to keep warm. But when they complained about the cold Bud Helmericks laughed at them. In early March he had had three straight days of 65 below at his place on the Colville. "This is a heat wave," he kidded.

Toward the end of April Cliff Robertson left for home. He had hunted hard but failed to kill a bear. Shortly before he left, however, he did take a big bearded seal of the kind the Eskimos call Ugrug, a somewhat rare trophy. A week later the camera crew took off for New York. Munger, Jim Helmericks, Simon Ned, and Indian guide from the interior village of Allakaket, and Fred were left on the ice by themselves. They would hunt until Fred killed a bear or the spring breakup forced them ashore, and Bud Helmericks would fly back and forth from his headquarters and bring out supplies.

The first chore was to move camp to a new site. They had cut a hole through seven feet of ice for fishing, and although they caught nothing so much water came up through the hole that they were flooded out at the old location.

The weather turned warmer now that May had come, and

seal hunting picked up. The seals were beginning to sun themselves on the ice beside their breathing holes, and although most of them were in the open and hard to stalk, it was easy to kill what were needed for bait. It was not work for the bow, however, since it was almost impossible to approach them within bow range, and in the second place, unless they were killed instantly—it took a shot in the head, even with a rifle—they'd flop into their holes and sink like stones.

The first one, a big Ugrug, was killed by creeping up behind a block of ice and drilling him through the head with Bob's .244 Remington, but not many could be approached that easily.

Fred and Bob hit on another method that worked very well, however, and also provided some interesting and suspenseful hunting. Bud brought out a small hand sled, and they fashioned a screen at the front of it, made from a piece of plywood covered with white cloth, with a peephole to watch through. They lay flat on their bellies on the sled and propelled it along with their hands. A seal sunning itself snoozes for a minute or so, then lifts its head for a quick look over the ice in all directions. Generations of polar bears have taught them to take that precaution. By pushing the sled ahead while a seal was napping and waiting motionless when it raised its head, the hunters could get within about 150 yards. With the scope-sighted, flat-shooting .244 that was close enough. It called for a lot of patience. Some of the stalks took more than an hour. But it was fun, and it produced.

The party made every effort now to bring a bear in with bait. They dragged skinned seal carcasses behind the snowmobiles to lay scent trails in 10 and 12-mile circles all around camp, dropping chunks of blubber at intervals to keep a bear interested. They also set up a catalytic heater on an oil drum outside the tents and cooked seal blubber on it 24 hours a day, sure that the aroma would get results. Bob and

Fred found they could pick up the smell of seal oil half a
mile downwind from the bubbling pot. Comparing Nanook's
nose with theirs, they concluded that any bear that passed
within 10 to 15 miles could hardly fail to tune in.

They put out seal carcasses for bait only 80 yards from
the tents, lashing them to ice toggles, and built a blind of
snow blocks nearby to shoot from. Next they rigged a device
that Fred had used in hunting black bears. They ran a wire
from the bait to a stake inside their tent and hung a bundle
of tin cans on it. Any bear that tugged at one of the frozen
seals would be sure to touch off that alarm. And no matter
when the bear came, day or night, Fred would have plenty of
light for shooting. The time of continuous daylight was
only a few days away now. The sun sliced down in the northwest about 11 o'clock, came up in the northeast a couple of
hours later, and a bright glow lighted the northern sky all
night.

Before they were through they had six seal carcasses in
the bait area, anchored so they could not be dragged off.
Weighing from 80 to 150 pounds apiece, they made quite
an imposing cache of meat.

"You'll get an easy shot," Bob predicted. "Any bear that
comes in here will wind up too stuffed to walk away." But no
bear came in.

They hunted hard with the snow sleds, too, fanning out
from camp to prowl the ice for tracks. But with the onset
of the arctic spring they were plagued with wretched
weather: fog, freezing rain, blinding snowstorms and, worst
of all, the dreaded white-outs.

It's hard to imagine what a white-out is like until you have
gone through one. The horizon is lost and it's impossible to
distinguish a snow drift three feet high from a depression
three feet deep, even close up. Level ice or hummocks, everything looks alike, or rather it all looks like nothing. Your
next step may fetch up against a block of ice or pitch you
on your face in a drift. Men on foot stumble through a

white-out like alcoholics, and flyers dread it above all. Between white-outs and the fogs and snowstorms, Fred and Bob went 10 days without a day of hunting weather, and in the end all the baiting failed to turn the trick.

They knew from tracks and other sign that about the time they set up camp eight bears had passed within half a mile. But after that, despite the lure of fresh seal meat, scent trails and the blubber pot, not a bear came within five miles. The only game they attracted were white foxes that found a bag of fish near camp.

They would probably have done better had they camped farther out, nearer to open water. But Fred still warns any hunter wanting to try that to hire an Eskimo guide familiar with those limitless ice fields. Along the edge of the pack, there is always danger of being blown adrift on a floe.

The men went north of camp one morning to make a seal drag and found the tracks of a good bear that had hit one of their earlier trails. But he had followed it the wrong way and left it where they had turned the snow sled around. When that happened twice they gave up. On the morning of May 11, almost four weeks after they arrived on the ice, they took to the air in two light planes in the hope of finding what they had come for. Bob flew with Jim Helmericks, Fred with Bud.

It was a clear, beautiful spring day. They flew north toward the open leads that were showing up now at the edge of the pack ice, and 15 minutes after leaving camp they spotted a bear walking along the side of a pressure ridge. He was the first one they had seen in 25 days.

He was quite a distance away and had not noticed the planes. The last thing Fred wanted was to disturb or anger him from the air. It was his belief that his first two polar bears turned on him so swiftly and furiously in part because aircraft had flown too close in looking them over, putting them in a bad temper. He didn't want that to happen this time.

"He's hunting seals," Fred told Helmericks, "and he'll follow that ridge for miles, until he finds one. Let's give him a wide berth, land a long way ahead, and try to waylay him."

They were about seven miles from the bear when they set the two planes down on smooth ice, and he had taken no notice of them at all. They hiked back two miles in his direction and found an ideal place for an ambush. Fred crouched behind a pile of ice where he would be out of sight, but high enough for shooting whichever side of the pressure ridge the bear appeared on. Jim, Bud and Bob took cover 20 yards back of Fred, with the cameras and two rifles. A back-up rifle is a precaution that has to be taken when you're bow-hunting an animal as quick-tempered as the ice bear.

This one was nowhere in sight now, but if he stayed on his course, as Fred hoped he would, he was bound to come meet them. The hunters waited an hour and a half, cramped and cold, before they saw him coming half a mile away. He showed up dark against the sunlit snow, shuffling along, taking his time, investigating every crack and ice pile he came to, intent on a seal dinner. Everything was going exactly as Fred wanted it to.

Then, when the bear was 400 yards away, he swerved and angled off through rough ice, and Fred could see that he was going to pass beyond bow range. Fred hated to leave the spot he had picked, but his trophy was about to slip through his fingers and there was only one chance of getting a shot. Fred waited until the bear went out of sight behind upturned ice, then ran for a new hiding place. He made it without the bear catching sight of him, and when he looked around his three companions were in position behind him once more, well hidden. The bear reappeared very quickly, coming straight for the men at a rolling walk.

He padded ahead, his long snaky head swinging from side to side to let his nose take in everything within range, pausing now and then to look around, the undisputed king of those silent white wastes. He had prowled them all his life, in the sun of the arctic summer and the dark of the long night, served well by his keen nose and eyes, his tireless legs and the thick pelt that shielded him from the bitter cold of both water and wind. Save for the chance of an infrequent encounter with a pack of killer whales, he had only man to fear, and in all likelihood he had never encountered a man. Certainly so far as he knew now there was no man within miles of him.

Fred watched him cut the distance to 300 yards, 200, then 100. "I could actually feel my blood pressure going up," he recalled afterward. Waiting for any major game to walk into your lap in that fashion is one of the most pulse-quickening things a hunter can do. And in the past, two bears of this same kind had turned on Fred Bear like infuriated cats. He couldn't quite put them out of his mind as he watched this one come on.

Sixty yards—50—then finally he was within good bow range and still coming. Fred's razorhead arrow was on the string, his bow up, and he was starting his draw when the wind shifted ever so little and betrayed him.

The bear jerked to a halt, facing the hunter at an angle, looking his way. The animal's nose went into the air and his black muzzle wrinkled as he sniffed, not certain what he had smelled. From his earlier encounters, Fred was sure one of two things would happen in the next second or two. Either the bear would wheel and run or he would come full tilt. A charge would almost surely mean another bear killed with a rifle, and that was the last thing Fred wanted. He didn't wait any longer.

He raised up behind the ice block and drove an arrow. It looked good all the way and he heard it hit with a resounding smack. Instantly a red blotch started to spread near the bear's shoulder.

He went down in loose snow, recoiling from the hit and snapping at the arrow. For an instant he lay on his side, fighting the thing that had hurt him. Then he rolled to his

he raised up behind the ice block and drove an arrow

feet. Fred's first two white bears had charged like thunder-bolts. This one ran like a rabbit. Probably he never knew the man was there. He bolted for the pressure ridge, crossed it, and fell dead in his tracks 100 yards beyond. Fred had made a lung shot and done a swift and perfect job.

The bear was a handsome trophy, a big thick-furred boar with 10 gallons of seal oil in his belly. The bowhunter had broken his jinx at last, and killed the bear he had coveted so long. He hadn't done it quite the way he had hoped, but the trophy had been taken in fair chase, after a long and patient stalk, with the nearest aircraft two miles away and the bear not knowing it existed. And there were no bullet holes in that wonderful white pelt. The gap in Fred Bear's trophy list was finally filled.

How It
Feels to Die

THE elk hunt had been a good
one, in spite of the fact that no trophies had been taken.
The time was September of 1953, and the party was camped
in northwestern Wyoming, in the high country between
Jackson Lake and Two Ocean Pass, about 10 miles south of
Yellowstone.

Ted Adams was outfitter. The three hunters were Dr.
Judd Grindell, a 40-year-old physician and surgeon with a
general practice at Siren in northwestern Wisconsin; Dr.
Lyle French, a well known neurosurgeon from Minneapolis;
and Judd's brother, Jack Grindell, a legal assistant in the
Adjutant General's Department of the Army, with the rank
of captain, then stationed at Camp Carson, Colorado.
None of them had the slightest inkling that Lyle and Jack
were about to see Judd through the most horrible ordeal of
his life.

Elk were plentiful and they saw several fine racks that
would have been easy to take with a rifle, but they were
using bows and that's another matter. Dr. Grindell had

hunted with a bow for 18 years and greatly preferred it to any other method, for its wonderful challenges and the high quality of sportsmanship it calls for. In his book, the hunter who takes a good trophy that way has met his game on even terms, and that's how Judd Grindell liked it best.

"Most bowhunters don't feel too unhappy even when they miss a shot," he explained afterward. "At least they've had the keen delight of stealing to within a few yards or even a few feet of whatever animal they are after. The hunt itself, the love of the outdoors at its best, becomes their goal, rather than the kill."

The three men had had the usual minor frustrations on this hunt. Judd had missed one fairly decent shot at an elk. Jack had used all his arrows one forenoon in a vain attempt to take a big mule deer, then had a fine bull elk walk nonchalantly out in front of him and start grazing while he watched helplessly. "But I had a wonderful morning anyway," he told the others when he got back to camp.

They killed a deer for camp venison, and then were joined by Fred Bear, the well known Michigan bowhunter, and Fred brought along an antelope he had killed east of the mountains on the way out. They were living high on wild meat, which Judd rated the best of all, and enjoying every minute. But time was running out, and on the 20th Jack and Lyle and Judd packed out and headed east for the antelope country around Gillette.

They got to the little town of Recluse, 40 miles north of Gillette, the next afternoon. One of the guides at the elk camp had given them a letter of introduction to a rancher there, Mayne Lester. He invited them to stay overnight at the ranch and start the antelope hunt the next morning, and when he told them what the prospects were he didn't have to twist their arms.

They turned in early and were roused at daylight with a cheery banging on the bedroom door. Half an hour later they sat down to an old-fashioned ranch breakfast, plates heaped with eggs, fried potatoes, toast, coffee, jam and honey.

Their host was too busy to go with them but he gave them detailed information on the lay of the ranch and how to hunt it (it covered 13 square miles, more than 8,000 acres), and they started out. Because it's extremely difficult to get within bow range of antelope in the open country where they are found, the hunters were falling back on rifles for this hunt.

They spent a couple of hours in a 4-section area without seeing game, then crossed the highway and entered a chunk of arid ranch land that covered nine more sections. Lyle saw an antelope and started after it. Jack and Judd walked up a rolling, sage-covered hill about a mile from the road, where they could look across a wide valley, and sat down on a rock outcrop to rest and use their binoculars. They didn't know it, but they were very close to bad trouble.

Within four or five minutes they spotted a pair of ears that they took to be an antelope's, sticking up out of the sage a quarter mile away. They studied the situation and agreed that Jack would try the stalk. By making a big circle he could keep out of sight of the animal and come up behind it, with the wind in his face. He walked away and Judd lay down behind the outcrop to watch through the binoculars.

The animal was so well hidden in the sage that, even though he knew exactly where it was, it disappeared completely whenever it lowered its ears. For a long time nothing happened. Then suddenly it raised its head and looked in the direction from which Jack Grindell was approaching. Judd saw then that it was a doe mule deer rather than an antelope. She got to her feet, listened and looked for a moment, and went rocking off.

The game was up, and Judd stood up to signal his brother. Without the slightest warning something struck him a sharp blow on the back of his right leg just below the knee, and he looked down to see a four-foot prairie rattlesnake, its fangs tangled in the coveralls he was wearing and still imbedded in his flesh, twisting and thrashing to get loose. He reached down, grabbed it behind the head, drew the fangs out, and threw it as far as he could, all in one swift motion.

Up to that minute he had not given rattlers too much thought, although he knew they were present in the area.

"That's the wrong attitude to take anywhere in snake country," he told me long afterward.

He felt no real pain, such as many snakebite victims describe. The strike was like a blow from a branch that has been bent and whips back against your leg, accompanied by two sharp but not very painful pricks, as if he had been jabbed mildly with a pair of hypodermic needles. Actually, that was what had happened. But although the bite did not hurt much, Dr. Grindell knew, even as he pulled the rattler's teeth out of his leg and flung it away, that he had been seriously bitten by a snake that accounts for many cases of terrible suffering and a few human deaths each year.

Dr. French was off somewhere after his antelope, probably two or three miles away by now. Jack was out of sight across the valley, and because of the hard wind that was blowing there was no chance he could hear his brother's shouts. For the moment Judd was entirely on his own.

His first thought was of first aid. As a physician, he knew exactly what needed to be done. (A bad accident with a horse on another elk hunt ten years later forced him into early retirement, and his wife Arline and he live now on the Totogatic Flowage, a beautiful north-country impoundment between Spooner and Superior, Wisconsin.)

He knew what to do but couldn't do it. He realized with a sudden shock that he had no snakebite kit, no hunting knife or other sharp instrument with which to make cuts over the bite, nothing that would serve as an effective tourniquet. His boots were the pull-on kind, without laces, his coveralls

*he reached down, grabbed it behind the head,
drew the fangs out*

were beltless, and because the day was very hot his underwear consisted only of shorts. And he had no way to resort to mouth suction, since the bite was behind his knee where he couldn't reach it.

For an experienced and, he had always believed, a reasonably sensible doctor, he had gotten himself into a sorry predicament. The only first aid he could manage was to lock his hands around the leg and use both thumbs for compression just above the bite.

Jack finally came into sight, half a mile away, and Judd signalled him frantically. But he thought his brother was trying to let him know the location of the animal he had gone after, and he was a long time getting close enough to realize that Judd was pointing to his own bared leg and yelling "Snakebite! Snakebite!" at the top of his voice. Jack ran the rest of the way, so hard that when he got to the scene he was barely able to talk.

Just as he started to run, Judd glanced at the spot where he had thrown the snake, to see what had become of it. It was no longer there. Next he saw it only a few feet away, crawling slowly but steadily straight at him. He could hardly believe his eyes. He knew the rattler was not coming back to attack him. In all likelihood it had a hole under the small outcrop from which it had struck, and was bent on getting back into that retreat. Later he learned that that is typical snake behavior.

The outcrop formed a flat shelf a foot or two above the ground. Apparently the snake had been lying there and had stayed motionless and silent, without rattling, while Jack and Judd walked up, sat down only a few feet away, and even when Judd lay behind the rock to watch what he thought was an antelope. He must have been within a foot or two of it at that time, but it did nothing to reveal its presence and because of its natural camouflage among the rocks and dry grass, he failed to see it. It was only when he got to his feet that it finally lashed out. Had it been lying on the ground instead of on the rock shelf, it would have hit his boot and probably done him no harm.

Whatever its intentions were now, however, he wanted nothing more to do with it. He brought his rifle up and blew it almost in half, and then resumed the tight hand-lock above the bite. Right after that Jack panted up.

But when Judd asked him for his hunting knife he looked blank. He wasn't carrying one, either. The doctor knew that cutting was essential, to drain the wound and get rid of part of the venom, but they still had no way to do it. The two brothers had hunted together since Judd was 13, and had cleaned plenty of game in the field. That was the first time they could remember that either of them had been without a knife.

Jack was wearing laced boots, however, They could at least make a tourniquet. They tied one of the boot thongs in place, tightening it just enough to impede the circulation of lymph, and Jack fired three slow-spaced shots to let Lyle know that they were in trouble. He repeated that signal two or three times and then, as soon as he recovered his breath, he hurried off to find their partner and bring him back. Judd was by himself once more.

He lay there on the ground and faced the fact that he might die. He remembers thinking, "Well, what better place, with the sun and wind in your face?" He even saw a certain element of justice in it. They were hunting wild things, and a wild thing had struck him down. "That's only fair," he reminded himself.

He had felt no pain from the bite itself, but now he became aware that his scalp, lips, tongue and hands were getting numb, and speech was becoming difficult. That meant the venom was spreading through his body. Next he looked off into distance and everything he saw was doubled, as when you look through the range finder of an unfocused camera. Only by the greatest effort could he make the two images coincide. In a few more minutes even that became impossible, and his vision faded gradually into a series of crazily unrelated and momentary images.

His ordeal was beginning, and although he had never treated a case of snakebite he knew enough about it to realize that what was coming would be one of the most terrible experiences a human being can endure.

"It's matched in my opinion only by the agony of severe and extensive burns," he says today.

Once the general symptoms appeared they progressed with frightening swiftness. The numbness and tingling and weakness grew worse. He remembered that he must loosen the tourniquet for 20 or 30 seconds at regular intervals, but the third time he did that he realized that after each loosening he was experiencing an increasing wave of weakness and a strange sensation of floating. It was as if invisible hands were pushing him sideways. He knew it all resulted from the release of more venom into the general circulation.

There is some question in medical circles as to the benefits of first-aid procedures in snakebite, especially the use of a tourniquet, and a few doctors have suggested that it might be better to omit both cutting and constriction. But Judd Grindell is sure that that boot lace of Jack's saved his life in the first 90 minutes after he was bitten, and he strongly advises the victim of any such mishap to take first-aid measures at once if possible.

Next he became aware of nausea and a deep pain in the abdomen, which was relieved by a session of terrific vomiting. For two or three minutes he felt a little better, but then the floating-away sensation returned and this time it was accompanied by a roaring, rushing sound in his ears. He knew what that meant, too. His blood pressure was falling below shock levels and into the critical survival range. He was going into shock.

Then he must have a fast, thready pulse, he reminded himself, and he mustered strength to try to check it. His hands waved weakly and without much co-ordination, but finally settled in the right position. He could feel nothing. His fingers were too numb to detect a pulse beat.

That bit of activity had called for tremendous effort and somehow the tourniquet had slipped loose. He could expect a real jolt now. He tightened and tied the lace again, and just in time. The roaring and illusion of floating came once more, much louder and faster, and he realized his chances of survival were growing very slim.

In his years as a doctor he had seen a lot of life begin and a lot of life end. He delivered some 4,000 babies before he retired from practice, and he had spent almost four years overseas as an Army doctor in World War II.

But now for the first time he knew firsthand how it feels to die. Fragments and scraps of thought went through his mind, as they apparently do in the closing minutes of life:

> *This must be what it's like—just peaceful float-ing away and the most delicious tiredness—what of Arline and the three girls—fine wife, wonderful kids—they need you—too tired, can't—you're a quitter, you can try.*

He fought back then, in brief flashes of crystal-clear and lightning-fast thinking, resisting the feel of drifting off, refusing to be pushed into the oblivion that seemed to be waiting for him.

Then belly pain racked him once more and he vomited again. He noticed that his mind cleared briefly each time that happened. The effort of the retching was raising his blood pressure for a minute or so, and his brain was getting more oxygen. He decided to try breathing deeply, but he kept vomiting, and the drawing in of deep breaths deliber-ately became too much of an effort. Then he heard foot-steps, and Dr. French was bending over him.

French had a knife. "Turn a little," he said gently. But nothing happened, and Judd realized that he was hesitant about making the needed cuts through the fang punctures. Sick as Judd was, it struck him as odd that such a small thing should give pause to a surgeon who was used to the most intricate brain surgery. Later, when the whole thing was over with, he asked Lyle about that moment of reluctance.

"That was the first time in my life I had ever cut into flesh while the patient was conscious," Dr. French told him with a smile, "and I confess I didn't like the idea."

But at last Judd felt severe pain in his leg, grinding and burning. He could measure the length of each cut, and feel the knife rip out. He asked Lyle if the incisions were bleeding.

"Yes, good flow," was the reply.

> *Then the furious roaring again, even faster now— pain in abdomen worse—whole leg numb and heavy —trying to see Lyle's face—no use—balanced on a tightrope—going to fall off—vomit and vomit and vomit.*

And then, on the top of everything else, he suffered the misery and embarrassment of diarrhea.

He was hardly aware that Jack had left, to make a fast hike down to the car and race back to the ranch to summon a doctor from Gillette. Judd lost track of time, but finally heard voices all around. Jack's and Lyle's and a stranger's, and then a girl's, and he understood dimly that the doctor from Gillette had arrived and had brought a nurse along.

He heard someone mention Antivenin, and the doctor said, "I'll put part above the bite where the leg is swelling, and the rest higher up." Then to his nurse, "Mix up that other vial right away."

Judd felt pain as the needle went in near the wound, but none from the rest of the shots, and did not even know when the second vial was injected.

The Antivenin took effect far more quickly than the venom itself had, and with equally dramatic results.

> *More vicious vomiting—the taste of bile—bitter—*
> *can't see—the roaring and floating back again*
> *—somebody's opening my eyes with fingers—re-*
> *member to breathe—pain in belly more and more*
> *severe—more diarrhea—wish I could see Jack—*
> *touching him in a blinding, dazzling cloud—can't*
> *hold arm up—floating away faster and faster—this*
> *is curtains.*

If the phrase more dead than alive is ever justified, it would have applied to Judd Grindell at that point.

Then in the midst of it all there was a sudden lurch, the dizzying sense of motion was gone, the roaring in his ears subsided, and he came back to where he was, lying on the ground in the sagebrush. He could hear better, and the interval before he vomited again was longer. He heard the young doctor (it was many hours before Judd learned his name, Dr. R. V. Plehn) ask about blood in the vomit, and when somebody answered no Dr. Plehn said quietly, "He may have a chance then."

Next they made ready to start for the hospital, and sur-denly Judd was sure he could endure the trip, just as he had been sure only a short time before that to move him at all meant certain death. But he had to try twice to get out a very weak, "Okay, Jack."

Somehow a car had been driven up on the hillside, and he was laid on the back seat. The 40-mile ride to Campbell County Memorial Hospital in Gillette was fast, but something that to this day he would just as soon forget. Thirst began, not ordinary thirst but a burning, cottony clogging of mouth and throat. Lyle French gave him water from a canteen, but Judd was unable to swallow. His chest cramped so he could hardly breathe and he asked to have all the car windows opened. The rush of wind on his face gave him some relief, but he remembers vomiting two or three times, and feeling dirty and ashamed. His mind seemed clearer, but he still saw everything outside the car window only as a gray fog.

He heard Lyle's voice again, "Nearly there, Judd. Hang tough!" Then the car stopped, there were more voices, and someone said, "Bring the bed right out to the car." Judd felt himself between cool, soft sheets, being rolled down a hospital corridor. He was aware of an increasing and intense craving for sweetened fluids, reflecting dehydration and lowered blood sugar level from the vomiting and diarrhea.

"If I were ever to treat a snakebite of this type in the future, where those symptoms had been present, I'd take special care to supply additional sugar and fluids," he says. "I tried to tell one of the nurses walking beside me how terribly I wanted a cold sweet drink, but I could no longer speak."

Next he was aware of new pain developing in his lower abdomen, sharp and intense, as if he were being pulled apart. He sensed that another doctor had come into the room—he proved to be an older associate of Dr. Plehn—and Judd heard him exclaim, "My god, look at that swelling!"

Grindell's eyes were pried open again and he tried to let them know that he could hear what they said, but it was no use. The torture in his belly grew and the whole abdominal wall turned rigid as a board. Every breath became a fight against pain and knotted muscles, and for the second time he knew what it is like to die. But he was too tired and had suffered too much to care. Dying would bring relief. At last, five hours after the snake struck him, he passed out.

It was six hours before he regained consciousness. In the meantime Jack had rustled up the additional Antivenin that saved his life. A third vial was available at the hospital and was injected at once. There was no more in Gillette, but Jack located two vials in Billings, Montana, and the Montana State Highway Patrol rushed them south. Jack met the patrol car and brought them the rest of the way, and Judd got them at once. Without them, he is sure he would have died in that venom-induced coma.

He returned to the world of awareness to hear his doctors discussing "the optimum level for amputation." Should they take his leg off below the knee or above, and how far? He tried to let them know that he was against the whole idea, but it was half an hour before he could open his eyes, roll his head and move an arm enough to alert a nurse to the fact that he was conscious. An hour after that he had his first look at the bitten leg.

"There is no adequate way to describe the consequences of such a snakebite as I had received," Dr. Grindell says now. The whole leg looked more like an elephant's than a man's, both in size and color. It was slate gray, with patches of pink, and he no longer had either a foot or ankle. Swelling had engulfed everything, clear to the base of his toes.

He has been asked since whether the severity of his experience might have been due to the fact that one of the snake's fangs penetrated a vein, introducing venom directly into the blood. Bites of that kind have unusually grave and dangerous consequences, for obvious reasons. But he does not think that happened in his case. It was about 20 minutes after he was bitten before he felt the first effects of the spreading poison. If a vein had been punctured the general symptoms would have appeared almost at once.

Instead, Judd believes he got an abnormally large dose of venom in comparison with the size of the snake, probably almost the entire contents of its poison sacs, as a result of it hanging on and struggling to free itself.

"I'm sure that before I got his half-inch-long fangs out of my leg he must have pumped in far more than he would have delivered with one lightning stroke, and I think that accounted for what happened to me," Grindell told me years afterward.

He was not going to part with that leg if it could be

avoided. As he pointed out to Jack and Lyle, he thought
he might have quite a few years left after he got over this
thing, and he contemplated spending some of his time at the
same kind of activity that had gotten him into this fix. For
that an artificial leg would hardly do.

They did some judicious pin-sticking in the swollen member and learned that fairly normal sensation was still scattered over most of it, and the amputation was postponed.
In the end it proved unnecessary. In fact, in view of the
severity of swelling and general symptoms, and the very
close call Judd had had, the final outcome was a most fortunate one. The rattler did him no permanent damage at all.

He left the hospital at the end of 10 days, and headed
home to Wisconsin. The arrangements for the drive were a
bit strange. Judd was settled comfortably on pillows laid
across the back seat, with a bulky and highly unusual looking leg protruding out of a rear window. He rode all the
way from Gillette to Siren that way, too.

But right then he was the most thankful antelope hunter
in the whole United States. He still is.